Joe L. Frost • Pei-San Brown • John A. Sutterby • Candra D. Thornton

# THE DEVELOPMENTAL BENEFITS OF
# Playgrounds

Corporate Sponsor:
Tom Norquist
GameTime, a PlayCore Company

Contributors:
Jim Therrell
Debora Wisneski

Association for Childhood Education International
17904 Georgia Ave., Ste. 215, Olney, MD 20832 • www.acei.org

*Cover Design:* Becker Design Group, Inc. (www.beckerdesigngroup.com)
*Cover Photo:* Craig Harrold Photography (www.craigharroldphotography.com)

*Photo Credits:*
    p. 72 and 74 - John Sutterby and Jim Therrell
    p. 104 and 105 - Pei-San Brown
    p. 138 - Pei-San Brown and Candra Thornton
    p. 181 - Pei-San Brown and Debora Wisneski
    p. 192-194 - Pei-San Brown
    p. 207 - John Sutterby and Candra Thornton
    p. 216 - Danna Keyburn
    p. 217 - Laura Reyna


Anne W. Bauer, ACEI Editor/Production Editor
Bruce Herzig, ACEI Editor

*Library of Congress Cataloging-in-Publication Data*
The developmental benefits of playgrounds / by Joe L. Frost ... [et al.] ; Tom
Norquist, corporate contributor/sponsor, and Jim Therrell and Debora Wisneski,
contributors.
      p. cm.
   Includes bibliographical references.
   ISBN 0-87173-164-9 (pbk.)
1. Playgrounds. 2. Child development. I. Frost, Joe L. II. Association for Childhood
Education International.

   GV423.D48 2004
   790'.06'8—dc22

                                                              2004011204

# TABLE OF
# Contents

# Foreword

I am very pleased to write a foreword for this timely and revealing book. Internet and literature searches indicate that this publication is the most current and comprehensive compilation of research focusing on the developmental benefits of play and play environments.

The research in this book demonstrates that play is incredibly important to the development of children's social, emotional, cognitive, and physical development as well as to their creativity and imagination. Moreover, play is essential to brain development and is related to the development of intelligence and certain academic and reasoning abilities. Conversely, a growing body of research shows that a lack of free, spontaneous play can be harmful to the developing child.

Play is accompanied by heightened feeling states. The fondest memories of childhood are frequently those from times when children were able to play freely in their neighborhoods, on the farm, at the military base, and in other "safe" places. Such memories bring a smile to one's face, a warm and loving feeling within one's soul, and a longing for those wonderful "free" years of play. Those of us who as children enjoyed the freedom and spontaneity of such play and the wonder of such places are now witnessing their gradual disappearance.

We who create playgrounds have come to believe that many of the rapid technological gains that astound us are directly related to their inventors' creative and intellectual development through play. While that is not the premise of this book, the scholars who continually coach all of us at GameTime® have convinced us of the intellectual, social, emotional, and physical benefits of free play. I have come to believe that there is a positive correlation between this generation's inventions and their inventors' ability to play freely while they were growing up.

It seems unfortunate that so many adults in this quick-paced life seem to take children's play for granted. Why do politicians and educators appear to forget that free, unstructured play can have a profound impact on a child's education, social interaction skills, and overall intelligence level? In this era of "leaving no child behind," why are elementary schools eliminating recess? Why does little Johnny (who is labeled ADD/ADHD) say to his teacher that he can't handle school anymore now that his normal recess periods have been eliminated? When I went to elementary school, my favorite time, and that of my friends, was recess and "PE." We enjoyed our teachers and the classroom activities, but we also wanted and needed unstructured time to simply play. Recess and free play were for experimenting, testing the rules, gaining valuable social skills, and releasing the pent-up energy that accumulated as we sat and tried to concentrate on our studies. A lifetime of playing and helping create play opportunities has led me to believe that play is to childhood as blood is to the heart. One doesn't work without the other.

Some scholars believe it is unfortunate that over the past 20 years the play equipment industry has been almost exclusively focused on safety. Our society seems trapped in the belief that if someone is hurt, someone must pay! How things have changed. When I grew up in the 1960s, my parents disciplined me for breaking my collarbone while playing with my younger brother. As playground designers and builders, we have participated in the development of "safety standards" that focus on reducing the possibility of an injury. This safety emphasis has eliminated developmental equipment that can be "safely configured." For example, at the time of this writing, most playground safety guidelines do not recommend the use of upper body equipment for preschoolers. This and certain other recommendations seem to be based upon injuries to preschool children playing on equipment for school-age children, improperly designed equipment, and inappropriate surfacing. Recent data indicate that these types of injuries have not decreased since the introduction of national safety standards. Research presented in this book concludes that properly designed and installed overhead apparatus is beneficial for older preschool children.

A major key to safer, yet more challenging, equipment is to promote research into both developmental and safety factors and build the results into the design of the equipment, and to attempt to provide younger children with access to equipment that matches their needs and abilities. So the question becomes, are we better off promoting properly designed upper body equipment for preschoolers or should we remain with the status quo and deny preschoolers upper body equipment and the resulting development? We hope that public dissemination of the research in this book will help promote research and experimentation through novel approaches to playground design. Common safety guidelines, standards, and regulations may also be refined to encourage thoughtful consideration of alternate routes to playground equipment design and function.

Finally, news reports and professional articles are published almost every day about the growing epidemic of child and adult obesity in America. With obesity comes the onslaught of Type 2 diabetes and other diseases that can financially strain our health care system. What is happening to America's children? The research in this book shows that free play is an excellent means of caloric burn and may even increase our children's metabolic rate, fitness, and overall health.

"Why don't you go outside and play" is becoming an expression of the past. Parents no longer feel it is safe to let their children play outside. The healthy risk-taking in natural and created environments we took for granted during our youth is now increasingly considered to be hazardous to a child's health. Television and computer play and other sedentary activities are rapidly replacing spontaneous outdoor play. Fewer communities are created to encourage walking and playing in safe places. Trails and linking paths are absent as minivans and sport utility vehicles transport children and adults to stores, schools, and places for sports and entertainment. Major challenges presented in this book are to preserve and create natural, yet challenging, places for children to play, and to preserve recess and other daily times for children's free, spontaneous play.

GameTime, a PlayCore Company, sponsored independent research into the values of free play in the child's development throughout the past decade. We have been honored to work with Dr. Joe Frost, Professor Emeritus of the University of Texas, and his many fantastic doctoral candidates and students. Their work has led to this compilation of profound independent research and documentation about why it is critical that children have opportunities to play freely in enriching environments. I am certain that the readers will find this book one of the most interesting, complete, and fulfilling exposés on play and child development. Good reading!

Tom Norquist
Senior Vice President
GameTime, a PlayCore Company
www.gametime.com

# Introduction

The University of Texas play and play environments research project started in 1974 with the construction of a community-built playground in Lockhart, Texas, followed by a second at Redeemer Lutheran School in Austin, Texas. This endeavor led to the development of university graduate and undergraduate courses on children's play and play environments and identification of research sites for dissertation and sponsored research. While several private and public schools graciously volunteered their children and playgrounds for research, over the years Redeemer School, the first research site, continued to cooperate with the University of Texas to the present time and was the site for the recent research reported in this book.

The first book featuring early research from the University of Texas play and play environments research project, *When Children Play* (Frost & Sunderlin, 1985), also was published by the Association for Childhood Education International (ACEI). This book contained 47 papers from the 1983 International Conference of Play and Play Environments held at the University of Texas in Austin. This conference, sponsored by 14 professional organizations, was attended by more than 500 professionals from 12 countries, and featured 120 presentations. In 1996, ACEI published *Playground Injuries and Litigation* (Frost & Sweeney), perhaps the most detailed case studies of playground injuries available. The studies were based on 190 detailed analyses of children's injuries gleaned from extensive litigation-related data, including answers to interrogatories; responses to requests for production; depositions; personal interviews; police reports; hospital records; design, installation, supervision, and maintenance records; and on-site inspection of injury sites.

Now in 2004, ACEI is publishing the present volume, *The Developmental Benefits of Playgrounds*, and thus extending the knowledge base about appropriate playground materials, equipment, and use patterns. The initial chapter focuses on the importance of play, with special attention to contemporary research by neuroscientists that reveals, through the aid of high-tech brain imaging techniques, concrete support for the centuries-old contention of noted philosophers and other academicians that play is critical to children's healthy development. This conclusion, seemingly obvious, has yet to be adopted by many who influence children's opportunities and environments for play. Later chapters identify developmental sequences for children's motor behaviors during their play on several types of playground equipment. Chapter 1 sets the stage for placing these sequences in developmental context by reviewing patterns and stages of play behaviors across the age spans: infant, toddler, preschool, and school age. A primary focus throughout the book is considering individual levels of physical, social, and cognitive development, rather than chronological age, when making decisions about children's play and playgrounds. Although not discussed in this book, play also carries profound therapeutic benefits for all children, especially those who are traumatized, abused, and/or stressed.

During the last decade of the 20th century, disturbing concerns emerged about the health and fitness of American children, and a growing number of studies are addressing these issues. The contemporary decline in children's physical fitness and the rapidly growing incidence of childhood obesity and related diseases are prompting a new look at the role of active outdoor play in enhancing children's development, fitness, and health. The growing proportion of time spent in sedentary activity compared to active play, the substitution of indoor technology play for outdoor play, the overemphasis on high-stakes testing, and the deletion of recess and physical education in many schools are among the factors discussed in Chapter 2 that are depriving children of free, outdoor, spontaneous play.

A major emphasis of the present book is on the functions and developmental benefits of playground equipment, focusing on heights (Chapter 3), overhead apparatus (Chapter 4), climbers (Chapter 5), and swings (Chapter 6). Manufactured playground equipment in the United States initially evolved as society's antidote for children playing in the hazardous streets, alleys, and vacant lots of major cities. Country children, having few such perceived problems, continued for many decades to enjoy playing in the wild spaces of the countryside. The early play equipment, featuring extreme heights, massive rotating mechanisms, hard surfaces, and little maintenance, quickly resulted in a growing pattern of injuries to children. Eventually, the U.S. Consumer Product Safety Commission (CPSC, 1997) published two handbooks on public playground safety; later, the American Society for Testing and Materials (ASTM, 1993) published a playground safety standard. The two documents are very similar in their recommendations.

As the CPSC and ASTM recommendations were implemented, an increase in lawsuits also contributed to growing standardization of playground equipment. CPSC playground safety guidelines essentially became the "national standard of care" in playground injury litigation, meaning that cases were won or lost based on compliance or non-compliance with CPSC guidelines. Several states passed the guidelines into law. Despite these actions, the National Electronic Injury Surveillance System reported a growing incidence of injuries on playgrounds, increasing from about 117,000 in the early 1970s to well over 200,000 by the turn of the 21st century (Frost et al., 2005, p. 343). Several probable reasons for this increase are the growing decline of children's physical fitness in the United States; childhood obesity; reduced opportunities to engage in extensive, active outdoor play; and growing numbers of preschool and kindergarten enrolled in public schools where the play equipment is suitable only for school-age children. As playground equipment became increasingly standardized, limited room remained for creativity by designers, manufacturers, and consumers. Consider the following:

> In September 2003, the State of Texas adopted new regulations for child care facilities, homes and agencies to be enforced by the Department of Protective and Regulatory Services. These regulations identified eleven types of playground equipment that "children ages two through five years must not be allowed to use . . . at or away from the child care center." (p. 136)

The restricted equipment includes:

- Chain or cable walks
- Freestanding arch climbers
- Freestanding climbing pieces with flexible parts
- Fulcrum seesaws
- Log rolls
- Spiral slides with more than one turn
- Overhead rings
- Parallel bars
- Swinging gates
- Track rides
- Vertical slide poles.

The research reviewed in this book and the original research reported herein indicates that most 3- to 5-year-old children need much of this equipment. Based on this information, the writers believe that creative designers familiar with the research and knowledgeable about the development of preschool children can develop more challenging equipment designs appropriate for preschoolers' abilities and useful for their development. Unfortunately, existing guidelines, standards, codes, and admonitions, coupled with threat of litigation, presently restrict such design. For example, throughout our research over several years we have observed, on a consistent basis, children 3 through 5 years of age learning to use and using specially designed overhead apparatus featuring low heights, protective surfacing, and soft take-off platforms; as well as vertical slide poles four to five inches in diameter attached to low decks and protected by 12 inches of loose surfacing. Indeed, preschool children commonly "hug" the support posts of overhead equipment to dismount or slide to the ground, thus mimicking their actions on vertical sliding poles. The major differences between this equipment and that for older children, where many preschool children are injured, are lower heights and soft take-off and landing surfaces.

The most critical factor in preventing serious injuries to preschool children is installing equipment at low heights and *maintaining* surfacing per ASTM specifications. Several national surveys and our own studies of serious injuries resulting in litigation show that few playground sponsors maintain loose surfacing in proper condition and at proper depths. Large numbers of injuries to preschool children continue to result from their using equipment designed for older children (featuring excessive heights and hard fall surfaces). We believe, although we cannot provide concrete evidence, that properly installed and maintained loose surfacing, especially loose, manufactured wood and rubber chips, are more effective than manufactured mats for preventing fractures in falls.

Given our observations and research over the past quarter century, we believe that many creative designs would be appropriate and valuable for most preschool-age children. For example, we propose chain or cable walks suspended four to six inches above resilient surfacing with support bars to grasp with the hands for balance; low arch climbers made of molded plastic to prevent stepping through and impacting steel rungs; low, freestanding climbing events with flexible climbing components to help absorb shock; parallel bars placed at low heights, some angled and attached to decks, for creative hanging and sliding (not as gymnasts would use them); and overhead apparatus, as seen in this book, installed at low heights and protected by resilient surfacing. All overhead apparatus needs soft, elevated take-off platforms.

*We propose that* manufactured *playground equipment be subjected to observational studies by groups skilled in research and child development before making it widely available for play by the nation's children. We do not advocate violation of national or state playground safety guidelines, standards, or codes. As new knowledge emerges from research, safety standards should be modified to encourage the development and use of creative, developmentally sound play equipment and materials. Research involving children on playgrounds should be carefully approved and monitored by qualified research committees.*

Fixed, heavy duty, manufactured playground equipment is only one important component of developmentally sound play environments. Consequently, we extended the content of this publication to address qualities of comprehensive play environments. Chapter 7 focuses on sand and water play, an indispensable element for young children's development. Sand and water are universally available and inexpensive. They are flexible, porous, compelling to touch and manipulate, and offer unlimited opportunities to construct, create, and imagine. The messiness attributed to both indoor and outdoor use is a small inconvenience indeed compared to the benefits derived.

The final chapter complements the preceding chapters by focusing on recommendations for comprehensive playgrounds designed to enhance all forms and levels of children's development. The recommended elements include gardens, special or private places among vegetation, vegetable gardens, butterfly gardens, stimulus shelters, and natural, wild places. A number of previous studies, reported in *When Children Play* (Frost & Sunderlin, 1985), conclude that loose parts (portable materials), such as blocks and construction materials, tricycles, sand and water play materials, and organized games areas are equally or perhaps more valuable than fixed equipment for promoting broad developmental goals. Making playgrounds developmentally sound means providing ever-growing challenges and variation to match children's developing skills.

Adult supervisors need to be trained observers who understand how to guide children when needed and who are wise enough to then stand back and let children play. While we take precautions to provide safe, challenging, stimulating playgrounds, we understand that risk is inherent in play, and indeed is essential for learning through play. Supervision may be improved by taking cues from the playleadership and playwork programs common on many European adventure playgrounds. All playgrounds should provide for a wide range of abilities and disabilities. We caution readers that no two play environments are identical; different manufacturers design individual playground equipment types in a variety of forms, and there are differences in available space, portable materials, natural elements, and age groups served. Consequently, *care should be exercised in generalizing conclusions from studies on one playground to other playgrounds.*

*The content of this book is intended for instructional purposes and should not be used for legal advice.*

## References

American Society for Testing and Materials. (1993). *Standard consumer safety performance specification for playground equipment for public use.* Philadelphia: Author.

Consumer Product Safety Commission. (1997). *Handbook for public playground equipment.* Washington, DC: Author.

Frost, J. L., & Sunderlin, S. (Eds.). (1985). *When children play. Proceedings of the International Conference on Play and Play Environments.* Olney, MD: Association for Childhood Education International.

Frost, J. L., & Sweeney, T. B. (1996). *Cause and prevention of playground injuries and litigation: Case studies.* Olney, MD: Association for Childhood Education International.

Frost, J. L., Wortham, S. C., & Reifel, S. (2005). *Play and child development* (2nd ed.). Columbus, OH: Merrill Prentice Hall.

# Acknowledgments

The sponsor of the recent research reported herein was GameTime, a PlayCore Company, one of America's oldest and largest playground equipment manufacturers. The writers express appreciation to the GameTime staff who traveled to Austin, Texas, to join the teams of volunteer workers to periodically remove outmoded playground equipment, install new equipment, and redesign the playgrounds. Throughout the process, the research teams were granted full discretion in developing research methods and in conducting the studies. The major studies reported herein were reviewed and approved by University of Texas human subjects committees to ensure ethical standards were followed.

We extend our sincere gratitude to GameTime, sponsor of the major studies reported in this book, especially to Bob Farnsworth (CEO), Tom Norquist (Senior Vice-President), Brian Johnson (Vice-President), and Hollis Gentry (Product Manager) for their personal interest and assistance in every phase of the research. We are especially grateful for their willingness to take the risks associated with leaving the design and conduct of the research to the researchers, and we compliment them for their willingness to modify equipment when the research pointed to such need. We share their concern to "listen closely to children," to "make children's dreams a reality," and their belief that "every child is unique."

We are very grateful to the Redeemer School and Church administrators, faculty, staff, parents, and children, all who worked cooperatively to tirelessly modify their outdoor play environments to accommodate new generations of materials and equipment and eventually to add the natural spaces and gardens, leading to their certification as a Classroom Habitat by the National Wildlife Federation in March 2004. While we cannot identify and recognize the hundreds of adults and children contributing to this work over the years, we wish to acknowledge a few of those who made special, enduring contributions: Norman Stuemke, first principal of Redeemer School, now Emeritus; Louis Pabor, Senior Pastor Emeritus; David Schroeder, Senior Pastor; Glen Kieschnick, Principal; O. T. Greer, leader of numerous renovation and maintenance teams; John Saegert, tireless worker and contributor of many beautiful plants and trees; and Danna Keyburn, teacher, skillful gardener, and chief creator of Redeemer's gardens and nature spots.

During the three decades of continuing research at Redeemer, several national and international playground manufacturing companies contributed materials, equipment, and/or support for graduate students. These included Educational Systems, Inc., Creative Playground Corporation, KidStruction, Big Toys, Kompan, Grounds for Play, Iron Mountain Forge, Little Tikes, and GameTime. We are grateful for their support and compliment them for the playground improvements they made in response to the conclusions and recommendations of our research.

We extend appreciation to Gerald Odland, Executive Director of ACEI, for his support of our work, and to Anne Watson Bauer, ACEI Editor/Director of Publications, for her congenial manner and skillful editorial work throughout the publication process. ACEI, one of America's oldest and most respected professional organizations, continues to influence education and child development through its emphasis on the diverse contributions of spontaneous, creative play to the healthy development of children.

We express appreciation to our many professional colleagues and friends who work skillfully and tirelessly on behalf of children and in support of play with the U.S. Consumer Product Safety Commission, the American Society for Testing and Materials, the International Playground Equipment Manufacturer's Association, the National Program for Playground Safety, and the Consumer Federation of America. We admire and respect their many contributions to improving children's play and playgrounds and trust that the material in this book will assist their work in making playgrounds safer, yet more appropriate for children's physical, cognitive, social, and emotional development.

Research during the 1970s, '80s, and '90s by University of Texas graduate students, not named herein, preceded and contributed to the success of the research reported here. Ph.D. dissertations, books, reports, and professional articles resulting from the University of Texas project, along with hundreds of out-of-print, rare, and contemporary books, are being deposited in a special library collection on play and play environments housed at the University of the Incarnate Word (UIW) in San Antonio, Texas, and will be accessible on site and by Web site in 2005. A special thanks to the International Playground Manufacturer's Association, which serves as a sponsor of this collection, to Mary Ruth Moore, Professor of Education at UIW, for her administrative role in making this collection possible, and to Mendell Morgan, Dean of Library Services at UIW, for his expert assistance in organizing and housing the collection.

Finally, the authors extend personal thanks and appreciation to Jim Therrell and Debora Wisneski, Ph.D. candidates at the University of Texas, for their contributions to portions of the research reported here.

# CHAPTER 1
# Child Development, Play, and Playgrounds

*Indeed, the conclusion seems admissible, in summing up the biological significance of play, that perhaps the very existence of youth is due in part to the necessity for play.*

—Karl Groos, 1898, p. xx

Beginning in the early 1900s and continuing throughout the 20th century, with the exception of the world war years, U.S. manufacturers designed and distributed to the nation's parks and schools a wide variety of playground equipment. This activity was spurred by the "playground movement" emanating from concern about the health and welfare of children playing in the streets and vacant lots of large cities. Two parallel trends can be identified during this early period: a broad-based child development perspective in kindergartens and child development centers, and a movement focused on physical development in city parks and public schools. The child development movement initially followed the philosophies and practices of Friedrich Froebel, the originator of the kindergarten (children's garden), and John Dewey, the eminent American educator/philosopher. The resulting playgrounds for preschool children featured a wide range of natural play materials, equipment, and gardens. The emphasis on development was further stimulated and confirmed by the work of American child development research centers during the first quarter of the 20th century. The post-world war years saw a flurry of activity by designers of differing backgrounds with the creation of manufactured rockets, animals, and other features intended to encourage imagination, reflect real life, and provide opportunities for physical exercise. During the latter period of the 20th century, creative designers used a wider range of materials, including plastics, aluminum, wood, and recycled products, to create monolithic play structures intended to link play activities and events within confined spaces.

At the turn of the 20th century, major northeastern cities, city parks, and public schools looked to manufacturers for heavy-duty steel playground equipment to replace the limited outdoor gymnasia (indoor-type gymnastic equipment transported out of doors) that had been initiated in American playgrounds in 1887. In 1907, the Playground Association of America (PAA) was formed; their journal, *The Playground*, coupled with books about playgrounds by a number of renowned educators and parks and recreation specialists, added additional force to the development of such playgrounds across the country. PAA became the Playground and Recreation Association of America in 1910, and was re-named the National Recreation Association (NRA) in 1930. Finally, the NRA merged with other associations in 1966 to form the National

Recreation and Park Association (NRPA), which exists today. With these mergers, the emphasis increasingly became placed on recreation rather than spontaneous play and playgrounds. In recent years, NRPA has increased their emphasis on play and playgrounds, more specifically on playground safety and commercial equipment. Thus, the early manufactured playground equipment efforts established patterns that, to some degree, endure to the present time in city parks and public schools.

In 1981, the Consumer Product Safety Commission (CPSC) published national playground safety guidelines and the American Society for Testing and Materials (ASTM) published national playground safety standards in 1993. The influence of these guidelines and standards, as well as the growing number of injury lawsuits, led to the standardization of equipment and, in many cases, the closing of playgrounds. Although the CPSC and ASTM guidelines and standards were intended to apply to manufactured products, continuing modification, complexity, and overzealous application led to their affecting virtually every aspect of playgrounds, including adult supervision and natural areas. For example, a court judgment in a 2004 lawsuit compensated a child who tripped over a *stump* in a schoolyard *forest area*. Lack of restraints in our legal system continues to increase liability risks associated with playgrounds and, indeed, with virtually all places where children play.

A major missing element in this playground history, especially with respect to present city park and public school playgrounds, is the lack of emphasis on the broad developmental needs of children. We revisit this emphasis throughout the book. The works of major ancient philosophers such as Plato, Aristotle, and Quintilian, as well as those of more recent scholars such as Comenius, Pestallozi, Luther, Locke, and Froebel, extol the virtues of play for not only its contribution to physical development, but also its help in the overall development of the child (e.g., intellect, learning, behavior, artistic expression, serenity, and happiness). These great educators and philosophers spoke of the value of free, unrestrained, spontaneous play, in favor of over-regimented or controlled play, except as related to work/play activities where direct instruction may be needed, such as gardening and woodworking. Research throughout recent decades has confirmed the tenet that play is essential for healthy, comprehensive human development, and that it is an indispensable element in the educative process.

Playgrounds are among the most important environments for children outside the home. While most forms of play are essential for healthy development, spontaneous free play, the kind that occurs on playgrounds, is the most beneficial type of play (Morgan, 2003). Free play is defined by play scholars as an activity that contains five key dispositional factors: free play is voluntary, allowing players to enter or leave play at will; free play is spontaneous in that the play can be changed by the players; free play involves a pretend element and is different from everyday experience; free play is engaging as players are involved in the activity, separated from all surrounding activities; and free play is fun, pleasurable, and enjoyed by the players (Ackerman, 1999; Frost, Wortham, & Reifel, 2001; Johnson, Christie, & Yawkey, 1999; Sawyer, 1997; Sutton-Smith, 1997, 1999).

Outdoor free play allows children to do what their bodies need to do—move. Young children's development depends upon movement; it is "unnatural [for children] not to run, jump, and play" (Thompson, 2000, p. 189). In fact, movement "is one of the best indicators of overall well-being in the first year of life" (Santos, Gabbard, & Goncalves, 2001, p. 143). Gallahue (1993) says this about movement:

*Movement is at the very center of young children's lives. It is an important facet of all aspects of their development. . . . To deny children the opportunity to reap the many benefits of regular, vigorous physical activity is to deny them the opportunity to experience the joy of efficient movement, the health effects of movement, and a lifetime as confident, competent movers.* (p. 24)

Education literature is rich with empirical research and academic theory supporting the relationship between play and learning (e.g., Bodrova & Leong, 2003; Fromberg, 2001; Leppo, Davis, & Crim, 2000), and the notion that play is a highly appropriate vehicle for the development of social, emotional, physical, and cognitive competence (e.g., Sandberg & Samuelsson, 2003). Developmental theory holds that the predominant way young children acquire information (i.e., learn) is through play: "Researchers have discovered that play is related to greater creativity and imagination and even to higher reading levels and IQ scores. Based on the research evidence, a new equation is in order: PLAY = LEARNING" (Hirsh-Pasek & Golinkoff, 2003, p. 208, capitals in original).

Studies of young children's cognitive development support the play/learning relationship, citing such very specific learning outcomes as creativity and divergent thinking (Holmes & Geiger, 2002; Sutton-Smith, 1997), language development (Clawson, 2002), and memory (Jensen, 2000) (see Isenberg & Quisenberry, 2002, p. 4 for additional studies). Play is "a primary factor in the development of intelligence, personality, competencies, sense of self and social awareness" (Van Hoorne, Nourot, Scales, & Alward, 2003, p. iii). Other developmental benefits are identified throughout Smilansky and Shefatya's hallmark work, *Facilitating Play: A Medium for Promoting Cognitive, Socio-emotional and Academic Development in Young Children* (1990), including verbalization, vocabulary, language comprehension, attention span, imagination, concentration, impulse control, curiosity, problem-solving strategies, cooperation, empathy, and group participation. In addition, a meta-analysis of studies on the relationship between physical activity and cognition identified a statistically significant positive relationship between physical activity and cognitive functioning (Sibley & Etnier, 2003). These researchers further report that "the results support the possibility that participation in physical activity *causes* improvements in cognitive performance" (p. 251, emphasis in original).

**Neuroscience and Play**

According to Lichtman (2001), neurologists worldwide are studying whether the relationship between the human brain and learning capabilities is biological or social (see also Isenberg & Quisenberry, 2002). Collectively, findings support the notion that a connection exists between play, learning, and overall development. Neurological data indicate that this link is indeed biological, and is the result of electrochemical synapses working within sensory cells inside the brain (see McCabe, 1999, for an extensive list of over 80 brain studies pertaining to ways in which physical movement facilitates cognitive functioning).

The human brain contains billions of neurons, most of which are present solely for the purpose of cognitive, language, social, emotional, and physical development (Jambor, 2000; Wolfe & Brandt, 1998). Neurons contain two prongs: axons and dendrites; axons send electrochemical signals to other neurons and the dendrites of those neurons receive the signals. At the point where the axon of one neuron connects with the dendrite of another neuron, a synapse is formed (Bailey, Bruer, Symons, & Lichtman, 2001; Hirsh-Pasek & Golinkoff, 2003). From birth to 3 years, the quantity of synapses in the brain rapidly increases. By age 3, the brain has about 1,000 trillion synapses, twice the number in an adult's brain (Frost, 1998; Lichtman, 2001). The electrical signals generated from synapses between the neurons and sensory cells work toward cognitive, physical, etc., development. Sensory data are interpreted, compared with previously acquired information, and then enacted as responses (see chapter 2 of Hirsh-Pasek and Golinkoff, 2003, for a thorough and non-technical explanation of brain functioning).

The presence of previously acquired information is critical in the synaptic relationship between sensory cells and neurons; utilization of prior knowledge ensures the perpetuation of development. Because the highest number of synapses is present during the early childhood years, acquiring information during that period of time is of paramount importance. In fact, the risk is that if some experiences are not had early, the brain may be ill prepared to respond to similar experiences later in life (Brown, 1995a; Christie, 2001; Frost, 1998; Isenberg & Quisenberry, 2002; Ladd, Birch, & Buhs, 1999; Lichtman, 2001). Sally Jenkinson, author of *The Genius of Play* (2001), concurs: "Success in social play, skill in the use of good interventions, good interactions, and flexibility all develop social competence and prepare the child not only for integration into school but also for life itself" (p. 18).

A prime example of the experience/neurology relationship is found in Stuart Brown's study (1995a, 2000) on the relationship between adult social deviance and childhood play. Brown investigated the backgrounds of 26 convicted murderers and found that over 90 percent of them either did not play as young children or that they played in abnormal ways (e.g., violent, aggressive). Brown's data support the notion that both quantity and quality of social play experiences in childhood correlate with later adult social interaction skills.

Acquiring social skills via play during early childhood is essential. Jenkinson (2001) elaborates: "Success in social play, skill in the use of good interventions, good interactions, and flexibility all develop social competence and prepare the child not only for integration into school but also for life itself" (p. 18).

In addition to the long-term effects of social play experiences, Hirsh-Pasek and Golinkoff (2003) and Perry (2003) describe the growing body of evidence reporting neurological connections between cognitive competence and high-quality pretend play. According to these authors, if children lack opportunities to pretend, their long-term capacities related to critical thinking, problem solving, and social functioning, as well as to academic areas such as literacy, mathematics, and science, may be diminished. These complex and multidimensional skills involving many areas of the brain thrive in those milieus rich in high-quality pretend play (Bergen, 2002). This contention recently was studied from a cognition theory perspective. The study's conclusion concurred with the developmental theory argument that a specific neurological component is connected with children's pretense experiences (Bergen, 2002). Pretend play engages all components of the brain, thus triggering further development of synaptic connections (Bergen & Coscia, 2001).

Jenkinson (2001) considers the role of imagination in pretend play to be a means for children to live simultaneously in two worlds. She argues that failure to provide children with frequent opportunities for imagination and pretend play "stunts [their] inner growth, and brings about a kind of soul poverty" (p. 63). Research shows that children deprived of play experiences are prone to depression and hostility (Azar, 2002) and that they may become victims of fear, rage, and obsessive worry (Brown, 1995b). Frost (1998) captures the dire need for play when he says, "During the first years of life it is playful activity, not direct instruction, seclusion, deprivation, or abuse that makes a positive difference in brain development and subsequent human functioning" (p. 8).

## Outdoor Play and Playgrounds

The playful activities Frost described as being vital for appropriate development are largely experienced during outdoor free play. Despite the volume of research on the relationship between outdoor free play and healthy development, outdoor play remains grossly misunderstood. Two common misconceptions are that 1) outdoor play is a time for children to expend excess energy, and that 2) playgrounds are merely places for children to developing gross motor skills. Analyzed evidence overwhelmingly suggests that the benefits of outdoor play are much more extensive. For example, Taylor (2004) explains that when playing outside, children are able to participate in their community, to socialize, and to explore the world around them. Perry (2001) points out that although children's outdoor play behaviors may seem random, one can find purposefully chosen, self-generated, and recurring actions and themes embedded within it. Outdoor play is also children's opportunity to be free from the confined spaces of schools and homes:

*Not only is there typically more space out-of-doors, there is less in that space to bump into, break, or lose parts of. One's body is no longer under need of tight control—its capabilities to shout, sing, leap, roll, stretch, and fling are unleashed. Outdoor voices are suddenly acceptable. One is more carefree.* (Rivkin, 1995, p. 11)

Research into the impact of milieu on children's free play suggests that appropriate and stimulating play spaces require thoughtful consideration of those who use them (Frost, 1997; Hartle, 1996; Taylor, 2004). When designing playgrounds, it is essential to "consider design on the basis of types of play activities (e.g., What will this offer the child?), rather than simply on types of equipment (e.g., How many swings and slides do we want?)" (Morgan, 2003, p. 51). In other words, when considering outdoor play environments, the most important thing on which to focus is that playgrounds are for children; thus, they should be planned with specific objectives for children's development in mind. Activities and equipment that provide opportunities for children to "make decisions, try ideas, work, and play with others without fear of harm or destruction" are essential (Taylor, 2004, p. 100).

Obviously, children's play needs change over the passage of time. The gradual increase in their capability to do more and more complex cognitive and physical tasks also means an increase in their play complexity. Currently, architects, child development specialists, and playground equipment manufacturers are devoting a great deal of time collaborating on ways to design more stimulating and more creative outdoor play environments (Rivkin, 1995). The purpose of this chapter is to work toward that end. It should be noted that, unless otherwise specified, the research presented here is based exclusively on children raised in Western cultures.

## Nature of Young Children's Play

*Infants.* Historically, early childhood theorists have not agreed upon the temporal aspects of the emergence of play. Piaget, Vygotsky, and Elkonin, three education theorists who focused on play as a social and cognitive action, consistently viewed the activities of infants as either non-play or as mere imitation of play (Bodrova & Leong, 1996). Others, such as Frost et al. (2001), argue that play emerges early in the postnatal period. The debate over when play begins is largely due to the ambiguity of play's definition and, subsequently, what activities may be considered as play (see Sutton-Smith, 1997; Thornton & Sutterby, 2003).

Jean Piaget relayed his theory of infant play by describing the physical manifestations of play behaviors. He judged the play of infants as rudimentary, declaring it to be only practice or functional movement, not true play like pretend play/fantasy or games with rules, which are much more complex. Instead, infants focus on the actions of their own bodies; as they mature, they become more interested in their environment and the materials around them. It is at this point that "real" play is said to begin (Piaget, 1962). Similarly, Vygotsky narrowed his definition of play to include only imaginary situations based on unrealizable desires; however, such ideas do not appear until children are capable of representational thought (Berk, 1994; Vygotsky, 1962). Vygotsky's student Elkonin also focused his research on children's play. Like Vygotsky, he felt that play emerges only when children are able to attach language to their actions (Bodrova & Leong, 1996). Within the theoretical model articulated by these three men—Piaget, Vygotsky, and Elkonin—play is considered to follow cognition.

An alternative perspective argues that play emerges very early in life: "Infants are able to engage in physical play shortly after birth. Very young infants use their senses for play" (Frost et al., 2001, p. 6). By approximately 4 months of age, infants incorporate mouthing, sucking, banging, and grasping in their play. By approximately 12 months, infants generally are capable of playing with two objects at the same time (Hughes, 1999). As opposed to the "play follows cognition" model described above, this theoretical framework believes play to be inter-connected with physical and cognitive development. The experiences infants have during play are believed to perpetuate and foster both learning and mastery of motor abilities.

Findings from Santos, Gabbard, and Goncalves's (2001) study of motor development during the ages of birth to 12 months support this thesis. In an attempt to determine whether physical skill acquisition is the result of experience or is due to biological hardwiring, researchers cross-culturally compared the physical development of Brazilian and American babies during their first year of life. Data revealed that during the 3- to 5-month age span, Brazilian infants were less skilled in independent sitting and in hand-eye coordination (e.g., grasping) than their American counterparts. Santos et al. (2001) concluded that the differences in skill level were solely the result of environmental factors. Many Brazilian mothers believe that placing infants in standing or sitting positions damages the spine and legs; subsequently, they are reluctant to place infants on floor surfaces during the first 6 months of life. Instead, infants are generally held and carried throughout the day. This, according to the researchers, limits the infants' opportunities to develop rudimentary motor skills, thereby causing lower ability levels in comparison to

American babies, who are raised with frequent opportunities for independent movement. Poor motor control was determined to be directly related to a lack of practice, rather than biology (see also Thomas, 2000).

Play environments are the ideal place for infants to engage in motor skill practice. Unfortunately, infant playgrounds are the most overlooked play environments (Frost, 1992, 1997). Very young children are avid explorers; thus, their outdoor play environments must allow for and promote interests in investigation and exploration (Wardle, 1997) such as sensory-, exploratory-, and action-oriented playground devices (e.g., equipment that has varying levels and means of entry and exit, bells or pulleys to make sounds, dynamic components such as steering wheels to manipulate, and slides or climbers to promote action). In addition, play yards should include access to sand and water play, swings, and equipment that develops gross motor skills, such as inclines and steps. When offered rich exploratory and motor opportunities, infants' abilities expand quickly as their motor skills are mastered (Wardle, 1997).

*Toddlers (18-36 months).* Children between the ages of 2 and 3 years (i.e., "toddlers") understand the world in very physical ways. As infants mature into toddlers, their curiosity about the environment intensifies, their ability to move within the environment grows, their play with objects increases in duration, and their capability to participate in symbolic play begins. Beginning around 24 months, toddlers have the cognitive complexity necessary to use one thing in deliberate pretense for something else. Piaget explains this period of development as the stage in which children exit the sensorimotor stage and enter the preoperational stage. In the preoperational stage of development, children increasingly are interested in incorporating symbolic or pretend aspects of objects into their play. Pretend/symbolic play emerges when infants begin to use objects in a representational manner, transforming the meaning of the object from what it is into something it is not. With infants, object play is very physical (e.g., mouthing and handling) and all actions are based upon the function and/or physical manipulation of objects. Toddlers' object play, on the other hand, is more connected with imagination. Play becomes enriched with ideas to use sticks as boats, sand piles as cakes, and brooms as horses. "Instead of relying on actual objects as they are, they now have the power to transform them and to serve their own purposes. This is creative thinking at its best" (Hirsh-Pasek & Golinkoff, 2003, p. 227).

Furthermore, toddlers begin to include other actors such as (peers, caregivers) and/or inanimate objects (like dolls and stuffed animals) in their symbolic play. However, although toddlers may be able to interact socially with peers and caregivers, their play remains largely solitary with simple actions directed toward themselves until the age of approximately 36 months (Johnson, Christie, & Yawkey, 1999).

In addition to cognitive and social skill development, motor skills rapidly develop during the toddler years. By age 2, children have achieved full mobility and are able to climb and run with impressive ability (Frost et al., 2001). They have overcome their battles with gravity and are able to move about and handle objects with fair ease. Three sets of motor skills are beginning to emerge during toddlerhood: locomotor, small motor, and stability. Locomotor movements include walking, running, jumping, hopping, and climbing; small motor movements include object manipulation like throwing, catching, kicking, and hitting; and finally, stability movements involve bending, stretching, and balancing while walking. Mastery of these movements depends upon physical development, experience, and practice gained through play (Johnson et al., 1999). Appropriate play environments for toddlers accommodate these physical development needs while simultaneously perpetuating growth. According to Frost (1992), outdoor environments should "allow a wide range of movement, stimulate the senses, offer novelty, variety, and challenge, and be safe and comfortable" (p. 259).

With toddlers' special developmental growth patterns in mind, play environments should be designed to facilitate a wide range of movement; engage children's multiple senses; offer novelty, variety, and challenge; and be safe for exploration. Specifically, toddler outdoor play environments should provide a variety of textures (e.g., sand, water, rocks, wood, metals, shrubs, etc.); loose parts (e.g., wheeled toys, buckets, scoops, balls, etc.); dramatic play props (e.g., dress-up clothing, hats, dolls, etc.); and challenge (e.g., things to jump over, balance beams, ramps, stairs, etc.) (Caesar, 1998; Stephenson, 2002; Thornton, 2003).

*Preschoolers (3-5 years).* The preschool years, roughly from 3 to 5 years of age, are times of accelerated maturity in all developmental domains. More than ever, play reveals how well children are developing (Sawyers, 1994). Cognitive progress is highly noticeable in their play, particularly their fantasy and imaginative play (Hughes, 1999). Preschoolers' maturing imaginations supplant the functional, repetitive, practice play of toddlerhood with constructive and multifaceted symbolic play. By age 4, constructive play, manipulating objects by drawing, painting, cutting, woodworking, and block building—activities regarded as constructive play—becomes the most prevalent form of play (Hughes, 1999). Four-year-olds are more organized and goal-oriented than 3-year-olds in their constructions; nevertheless, actual planning and placing emphasis on precision or reality does not typically emerge for approximately another year.

Maturing preschoolers engage in complex actions on the physical world (Gowen, 1995), and this is reflected in their symbolic play. As discussed earlier, symbolic play first emerges during infancy as cognitive abilities to use objects in representational manners develops. Toddlers' object representation is more connected with imagination and deliberate pretense. Now, within the preschool years, imaginative object play develops into imaginative role-play. Children within this age range continue to use objects in a representational manner, but are now more capable of imagining the role identities behind their pretend play. As a result, play has greater coherence, enjoyment, and meaning. Furthermore, as they advance linguistically, cognitively, and socially, the themes for roles become more diverse and their play becomes more planned, diversified, and persistent (Jenkinson, 2001; Johnson et al., 1999).

While preschoolers continue to play alone or alongside others as they did as toddlers, they now begin to interact directly with a friend or a small group with varying levels of intensity and complexity (Hirsh-Pasek & Golinkoff, 2003). Learning to play with other children rather than next to them motivates preschoolers to seek more opportunities for such social play. Role-playing that was previously solitary play becomes sociodramatic play as playmates are added. Sociodramatic play is a much more challenging level of pretend play in that it requires "sophisticated social skills" (Perry, 2001, p. 10). Outdoor play environments need to contain elements that inspire sociodramatic play so that children have maximum opportunity to develop these important social skills (Calabrese, 2003). Such play helps children learn turn-taking; sharing; idea and fantasy development; negotiation and listening skills; as well as respect for one another's feelings, thoughts, ideas, and physical space. It also provides an essential sense of belonging. Without social play, preschool children become prone to antisocial behaviors and feelings of alienation (Brown, 1995a).

Regarding preschoolers' physically developing bodies, they are in what Gallahue (1993) classifies as the Fundamental Movement Phase. Movement development in this phase includes activities such as walking, running, jumping, galloping, skipping, throwing, catching, kicking, striking, dynamic balancing, static balancing, and axial movements. Gallahue (1993) emphasizes that "opportunities for practice, encouragement, and instruction are crucial to the development of mature patterns of fundamental movement" (p. 39). Hence, children should be provided with a range of physical challenges so that regardless of individual abilities, all children have opportunities to exercise and extend their own physical skills. Free play on challenging equipment is the best way to provide such opportunities for preschool-age children. Frost (1992) observes that "motor skills are developed naturally during free play on playgrounds" and that "abundant equipment to promote various motor functions is essential for both playgrounds and physical education settings" (p. 47). Play that fosters development within this age group is necessary for producing healthy, well-balanced children as they transition from preschool to elementary school.

*School-age (6-8 years).* The last three years of what is generally considered to be "early childhood" are the school-age years. Within this time of life, children's cognitive and social behaviors undergo dramatic changes. Piaget explains these changes as being the result of a shift in thinking. Specifically, children's thinking shifts from the preoperational stage to the concrete operations stage. During the preoperational stage (generally ages 18 months to 6 years), children's cognitive development is largely centered on their ability to use symbols. During the concrete operations stage of development, those symbols are put to use as children become more logical thinkers (Bee & Boyd, 2004) and participate in games-with-rules (Hughes, 1999; Van Hoorne et al., 2003).

Games-with-rules (GwR) is a category of play characterized by logic, order, and rule-based government. It is a level of play in which, because externally imposed rules must be followed, children must be able to curb their personal ego needs (Wardle, 2003) and control their behaviors (Smilansky & Shefatya, 1990). Games may be physical, such as tag, football, marbles, and jacks, or they may be intellectual, such as chess, board games, and video games. However, "the greater the complexity . . . the stronger the indication that they will also develop higher levels of social competence, and interpersonal (i.e., knowing and communicating with others) and intrapersonal (i.e., self-knowledge and management) skills" (Jenkinson, 2001, p. 22). Although 1st-grade children participate in GwR on a regular basis, rules are relatively simple since complete understanding of game rules, strategy, and planning does not emerge until 2nd or 3rd grade (i.e., 7 or 8 years old) (Johnson et al., 1999; Piaget, 1962).

One element that must be present in order for a playground to support GwR play is space. School-age children are cognitively, physically, socially, and emotionally able to participate in team sports or other rule-driven outdoor activities like tetherball and Red-Rover. Pellegrini, Kato, Blatchford, and Baines (2002) conducted a longitudinal study of 1st-grade students' playground games and found that games are of utmost importance in development during the school-age years. On average, school-age children are developing increased flexibility, balance, agility, and strength and are thus physically capable of challenging tasks like jumping rope and riding two-wheeled bicycles. They are developing increased flexibility, balance, agility, and strength in their play. When provided opportunities to play in safe spaces, they are able to refine these skills and tone the muscles that will be needed later for sports and other outdoor events (e.g., rock climbing and skateboarding). Unfortunately, most school-age children do not have as many opportunities for free play as their younger counterparts. "Providing school-age children with play breaks maximizes their attention to school tasks that involve thinking. . . . Eliminating opportunities for play at schools is 'misguided and may actually do harm'" (Hirsh-Pasek & Golinkoff, 2003, p. 214, quoting Pellegrini).

Although school-age children's cognitive transition from preoperational thought to formal operations is reflected in all facets of their lives, perhaps the most visible manifestation is in their social behavior. Pellegrini et al. (2002) also found a significant gender difference in playground games. Boys were observed playing more frequently than girls, and playing a wider variety of games than girls; in addition, boys' games were predominantly physical, whereas girls' games were mostly verbal. Gender segregation is a hallmark trait of play behaviors with this age group. Bee and Boyd (2004) say that with regard to social relationships, "Gender segregation becomes virtually complete by age 6 or 7" (p. 457). Along similar lines, in her book *Gender Play* (1993), Thorne presents vignettes that indicate girls' play behavior is distinctly and predominantly social. She explains that girls tend to pair with each other in best friend dyads; because each girl generally participates in multiple pairs at the same time, complicated social networks are created.

A cognitive attribute of school-age children, particularly the late 6- and 7-year-olds, is that they attend less to surface properties and instead focus more on the internal realities of objects. For example, they can explain that a group of five blocks maintains its quantity as long as no blocks are added or taken away; they are able to conserve the construct of quantity even when the spatial and surface display is changed. Younger children respond that there are more blocks when the original five are spread out and fewer when they are tightly bunched together. This same method of reasoning also may parallel the way school-age children consider playground equipment. Whereas toddler and preschool-age children are imaginatively inspired by the visual presentation of a playground, school-age children look instead at the equipment components. Providing events that are both physically challenging and socially inviting, in addition to visually stimulating, should be of utmost priority when playgrounds for elementary school children are constructed (Frost, Shin, & Jacobs, 1998).

## Conclusion

Collectively, the above review and the chapters to follow argue that time, opportunity, materials, and equipment for children's free and creative play, unfettered by overzealous or over-cautious adults, is essential for children's healthy development from infancy to middle-childhood. It is also an argument for the re-examination of America's playgrounds, although not to revert back in time to the concrete and steel jungles of the early 20th century or to continue the downward slide toward sameness. Rather, we must consider carefully the nature of outdoor environments for children's play, using the views of eminent philosophers of the past and the ground-breaking research of the last decade.

A central factor contributing to the growing disappearance of children's spontaneous outdoor play and to the standardization of playgrounds is the prevailing view, even among many professional groups, that free, wild, spontaneous play is frivolous, inconsequential, and irrelevant in the educational program of schools. A second mitigating factor against outdoor free play is the prevailing focus, particularly in community parks and public school playgrounds, on chronological age and physical development to the neglect of developmental skills and social, intellectual, and emotional development. We also tend to overlook the natural therapeutic qualities of play, the role of play in passing on culture through traditional games, and the eminently invaluable bonding and learning qualities of children's play in nature with natural materials.

Long-held and extensively supported truisms in human development are that no two individuals are the same in any developmental dimension, and that each individual is unique, with each having different needs and abilities. As we reconsider current trends in children's play and playgrounds, we must direct time and energy to ensuring that children of all ages have opportunities to play and learn together; to providing time and materials for children to engage in many forms of traditional and contemporary play; to engaging children in the ongoing development and care of their playgrounds; to helping adults understand the value of play and creative playgrounds; to looking to existing research as well as engaging in new studies on children's play and playgrounds; and, finally, to resolving the ill-conceived notions of substituting high-stakes testing, indoor sedentary play, physical education classes, and organized sports for recess and free play.

## References

Ackerman, D. (1999). *Deep play*. New York: Random House.

American Society for Testing and Materials. (1993). *Standard consumer safety performance specification for playground equipment for public use*. Philadelphia: Author.

Azar, B. (2002, March). It's more than fun and games. *Monitor on Psychology*, 50-51.

Bailey, D. B., Jr., Bruer, J. T., Symons, F. J., & Lichtman, J. W. (Eds.). (2001). *Critical thinking about critical periods*. Baltimore: Paul H. Brookes.

Bee, H., & Boyd, D. (2004). *The developing child*. Boston, MA: Allyn & Bacon.

Bergen, D. (2002). The role of pretend play in children's cognitive development. *Early Childhood Research and Practice, 4*(1), 17-26.

Bergen, D., & Coscia, J. (2001). *Brain research and childhood education: Implications for educators*. Olney, MD: Association for Childhood Education International.

Berk, L. E. (1994). Vygotsky's theory: The importance of make-believe play. *Young Children, 50*(1), 28-32.

Bodrova, E., & Leong, D. (1996). *Tools of the mind: The Vygotskian approach to early childhood education*. Englewood Cliffs, NJ: Prentice-Hall.

Bodrova, E., & Leong, D. (2003). The importance of being playful. *Educational Leadership, 60*(7), 50-54.

Brown, S. (1995a). Through the lens of play. *ReVision, 17*(4), 4-13.

Brown, S. (1995b). Concepts of childhood and play. *ReVision, 17*(4), 35-43.

Brown, S. (2000). *Institute for play*. Retrieved from www.instituteforplay.com/13stuart_brown.htm

Caesar, B. (1998). Safe playgrounds for infants and toddlers. *Parks and Recreation, 33*(4), 70-74.

Calabrese, N. (2003). Developing quality sociodramatic play for young children. *Education, 123*(3), 606-611.

Christie, J. (2001). Play as a learning medium. In S. Reifel (Ed.), *Theory in context and out*, Vol. 3 (pp.

358-365). Westport, CT: Ablex.

Clawson, M. (2002). Play of language: Minority children in an early childhood setting. In J. L. Roopnarine (Vol. Ed.), *Conceptual, social-cognitive, and contextual issues in the fields of play: Vol. 4* (pp. 93-116). Westport, CT: Ablex.

Consumer Product Safety Commission. (1981). *Handbook for public playground equipment.* Washington, DC: Author.

Fromberg, D. (2001). *Play and meaning in early childhood education.* Boston: Allyn & Bacon.

Frost, J. L. (1992). *Play and playscapes.* New York: Delmar Publishers.

Frost, J. L. (1997). Child development and playgrounds. *Park & Recreation, 32*(4), 54-60.

Frost, J. L. (1998, June). *Neuroscience, play, and child development.* Paper presented at the Meeting of IPA/ USA Triennial National Conference, Longmont, CO.

Frost, J. L., Shin, D., & Jacobs, P. J. (1998). Physical environments and children's play. In O. N. Saracho & B. Spodek (Eds.), *Multiple perspectives on play in early childhood education.* Albany, NY: State University of New York Press.

Frost, J. L., Wortham, S., & Reifel, S. (2001). *Play and child development.* Upper Saddle River, NJ: Merrill/ Prentice Hall.

Gallahue, D. L. (1993). Motor development and movement skill acquisition in early childhood education. In B. Spodek (Ed.), *Handbook of research on the education of young children* (pp. 24-41). New York: Macmillan.

Gowen, J. (1995). The early development of symbolic play. *Young Children, 50*(3), 75-81.

Groos, K. (1898). The play of animals. New York: D. Appleton.

Hartle, L. (1996). Effects of additional materials on preschool children's outdoor play behaviors. *Journal of Research in Childhood Education, 11*(1), 68-81.

Hirsh-Pasek, K., & Golinkoff, R. M. (2003). *Einstein never used flash cards: How our children really learn and why they need to play more and memorize less.* New York: Rodale.

Holmes, R., & Geiger, C. (2002). The relationship between creativity and cognitive abilities in preschoolers. In J. L. Roopnarine (Vol. Ed.), *Conceptual, social-cognitive, and contextual issues in the fields of play* (pp. 127-148). Westport, CT: Ablex.

Hughes, F. (1999). *Children, play, and development.* Needham Heights, MA: Allyn & Bacon.

Isenberg, J. P., & Quisenberry, N. (2002). Play: Essential for all children. A position paper of the Association for Childhood Education International. *Childhood Education, 79,* 33-39.

Jambor, T. (2000). Informal, real-life play: Building children's brain connections. *Dimensions of Early Childhood, 28*(4), 4-8.

Jenkinson, S. (2001). *The genius of play.* Gloucestershire, UK: Hawthorn Press.

Jensen, E. (2000). Moving with the brain in mind. *Educational Leadership, 58*(3), 34-37.

Johnson, J. E., Christie, J. F., & Yawkey, T. D. (1999). *Play and early childhood development* (2nd ed.). New York: Teachers College Press.

Ladd, G. W., Birch, S. H., & Buhs, E. S. (1999). Children's social and scholastic lives in kindergarten: Related spheres of influence? *Child Development, 70,* 910-929.

Lichtman, J. W. (2001). Developmental neurobiology overview: Synapses, circuits, and plasticity. In D. B. Bailey, Jr., J. T. Bruer, F. J. Symons, & J. W. Lichtman (Eds.), *Critical thinking about critical periods* (pp. 27-42). Baltimore: Paul H. Brookes.

Leppo, M. L., Davis, D., & Crim, B. (2000). The basics of exercising the mind and body. *Childhood Education, 76,* 142-147.

Morgan, J. (2003). To help children with disabilities, design by types of activities, not types of equipment. *Parks & Recreation, 38*(4), 50-54.

Pellegrini, A. D., Kato, K., Blatchford, P., & Baines, E. (2002). A short-term longitudinal study of children's playground games across the first year of school: Implications for social competence and adjustment to school. *American Educational Research Journal, 39*(4), 991-1015.

Perry, J. P. (2003). Making sense of outdoor pretend play. *Young Children, 58*(3), 26-30.

Piaget, J. (1962). *Play, dreams and imitation in childhood.* New York: W. W. Norton.

Rivkin, M. (1995). *The great outdoors: Restoring children's right to play outdoors.* Washington, DC: National Association for the Education of Young Children.

Sandberg, A., & Samuelsson, I. (2003). Preschool teachers' play experiences then and now. *Early Childhood Research & Practice, 5*(1),

Santos, D., Gabbard, C., & Goncalves, V. M. (2001). Motor development during the first year: A comparative study. *The Journal of Genetic Psychology, 162*(2), 143-153.

Sawyer, K. (1997). *Pretend play as improvisation: Conversation in the preschool classroom.* Mahwah, NJ: Lawrence Erlbaum.

Sawyers, J. (1994). The preschool playground: Developing skills through outdoor play. *Journal of Physical Education, Recreation, and Dance, 65*(6), 31-33.

Sibley, B. A., & Etnier, J. L. (2003). The relationship between physical activity and cognition in children: A meta-analysis. *Pediatric Exercise Science, 15*, 243-256.

Smilansky, S., & Shefatya, L. (1990). *Facilitating play: A medium for promoting cognitive, socio-emotional, and academic development in young children.* Gaithersburg, MD: Psychological and Educational Publications.

Stephenson, A. (2002). What George taught me about toddlers and water. *Young Children, 57*(3), 10-14.

Sutton-Smith, B. (1997). *The ambiguity of play.* Cambridge, MA: Harvard University Press.

Sutton-Smith, B. (1999). Evolving a consilience of play definitions: Playfully. In S. Reifel (Ed.), *Play and culture studies, 2* (pp. 239-256). Stamford, CT: Ablex.

Taylor, B. J. (2004). *A child goes forth: A curriculum guide for preschool children* (10th ed.). Upper Saddle River, NJ: Merrill/Prentice Hall.

Thomas, J. R. (2000). Children's control, learning, and performance of motor skills. *Research Quarterly for Exercise & Sport, 71*(1), 1-10.

Thompson, T. (2000). P.E. and the "normal" American child. *Clearing House, 73*(4), 189-190.

Thorne, B. (1993). *Gender play: Girls and boys in school.* New Brunswick, NJ: Rutgers University Press.

Thornton, C. D. (2003). Outdoor play for toddlers. *Today's Playground, 3*(7), 12-15, 18.

Thornton, C. D., & Sutterby, J. A. (2003). What is play? *Today's Playground, 3*(4), 8-9, 36.

Van Hoorne, J., Nourot, P., Scales, B., & Alward, K. (2003). *Play at the center of the curriculum* (3rd ed). New York: Merrill.

Vygotsky, L. (1962). *Thought and language.* Cambridge, MA: MIT Press.

Wardle, F. (2003). *Introduction to early childhood education: A multidimensional approach to child-centered care and learning.* Boston: Allyn & Bacon.

Wardle, F. (1997, Winter). Playgrounds: Questions to consider when selecting equipment. *Dimensions of Early Childhood Education*, 9-15.

Wolfe, P., & Brandt, R. (1998). What do we know from brain research? *Educational Leadership, 56*(3), 8-13.

# CHAPTER 2
# Obesity and Changing Lifestyles of Children: Diet and Physical Activity

*Obesity itself has become a life-long disease, not a cosmetic issue, nor a moral judgment—and it is becoming a dangerous epidemic.*
—Robert H. Eckel, M.D.,
Vice Chairman of the AHA's Nutrition Committee (1998)

Concern about the long-term consequences of poor diet, lack of physical activity, declining fitness levels, and obesity and obesity-related diseases among children led the authors to include this chapter. Our research over the past several years, much of which is presented in the chapters to follow, placed us in close proximity to hundreds of children, allowing us to see firsthand the effects of obesity on children's play behaviors and physical abilities. We trust that inclusion of this chapter will help parents, teachers, and others concerned with children's play and playgrounds understand the importance of free, spontaneous play; physical education; and time for play both at school and out-of-school. Recess is a critically important dimension of every school day and must remain honored and alive. We now know that the case for play and recess extends well beyond developmental benefits to include critical health benefits and, indeed, mortality. More than 300,000 Americans die from diseases associated with obesity each year, now rivaling smoking as the leading cause of preventable deaths in the United States.

Increasingly, childhood obesity is a key topic of discussion for health organizations and the media (American Academy of Family Physicians [AAFP], 2004; American College of Sports Medicine [ACSM], 1995; American Heart Association [AHA], 2000b; American Obesity Association [AOA], 2002; BBC Online, 2000; Centers for Disease Control and Prevention [CDC], 2002; Irvine, 2002; *Obesity*, 2002; Reuters via Yahoo, 2004). Health care experts, educators, and other people working with children have noticed, and research is revealing, an alarming upward spiral of childhood obesity.

Obesity results from a combination of too many calories and too little exercise, leading to weight gain over time. This chapter examines the causes of obesity, the long-term health consequences, and possible solutions for the obesity epidemic. Programs to decrease levels of obesity and improve children's physical activity typically focus on two areas of children's lifestyles: dietary intake and physical activity. The solutions to this obesity epidemic are complex and will require focused efforts by parents, schools, government, and business to ensure that obesity in children is prevented and they have the opportunity to grow up healthy and active.

## REVIEW OF LITERATURE

### Gaining Weight

When energy intake exceeds energy output, we gain weight (AOA, 2002; Moran, 1999b). When children consistently consume more calories than they burn off, the calories result in extra weight; if this trend continues over an extended period of time, children can become overweight or obese. Unlike adults, children consume calories through their natural growth. This natural growth complicates weight control measures for children, since severely curtailing their caloric intake can lead to stunting of growth (Sutterby & Frost, 2002).

To put this in numbers, one pound of weight gain is equivalent to 3,500 calories (AOA, 2002; Moran, 1999b). If a child consumes as little as 35 extra calories per day (calories not expended through physical activity or through natural growth), after only 100 days that child may gain one pound over what they would gain through natural growth. If a child consumes only 100 extra calories per day, that child may gain 10 pounds in a year over their normal growth. One hundred calories could come from as little as a small bag of potato chips or half a can of a non-diet soft drink. For both adults and children, excess weight gain is typically a slow, long-term process.

### Definitions of Obesity and Overweight

A measure called the Body Mass Index (BMI) is commonly used to identify the level of overweight or obesity in people of all ages. BMI is calculated by dividing body weight in kilograms by height in meters squared ($kg/m^2$) (CDC, 2002; Moran, 1999b; Wagner & Heyward, 1999). The American Academy of Family Physicians (AAFP) defines obesity as having a BMI equal to or greater than the 85th percentile with respect to age and gender (Moran, 1999a; Moran, 1999b). The Centers for Disease Control and Prevention (CDC) avoids using the term "obese" in reference to children and adolescents; it refers to people at or above the 85th percentile of BMI as "at risk overweight," and people at or above the 95th percentile of BMI as "severe risk overweight." The American Obesity Association (AOA) identifies people at or above the 85th percentile of BMI as "overweight" and people at or above the 95th percentile as "obese" (AOA, 2002). For adults, a BMI of 25 corresponds to the 85th percentile and a BMI of 30 corresponds to the 95th percentile (AOA, 2002). The American College of Sports Medicine (1995) states that obesity-related health risks begin to increase significantly when a person's BMI reaches 25 to 30.

BMI is not a perfect measure of being overweight in that it differs in people due to factors such as gender, amount of muscle mass, and body structure. The advantage of BMI as a measure is that it can be assessed quickly without the use of high-cost equipment. Other quick and simple methods of assessing body composition include skin fold tests and anthropometrical measures of size and proportion of body segments (Wagner & Heyward, 1999).

Issues of weight are slightly different for children than for adults. Because children's body mass distribution is not the same as an adult's, the 95th percentile changes as children get older. The 95th percentile for children at age 6 corresponds to a BMI of 18.6, while the 95th percentile for children at age 10 corresponds to a BMI of 22.2. Figure 1 is a chart published by the CDC that demonstrates how BMI changes for children as they get older.

# Figure 1: BMI Changes With Age

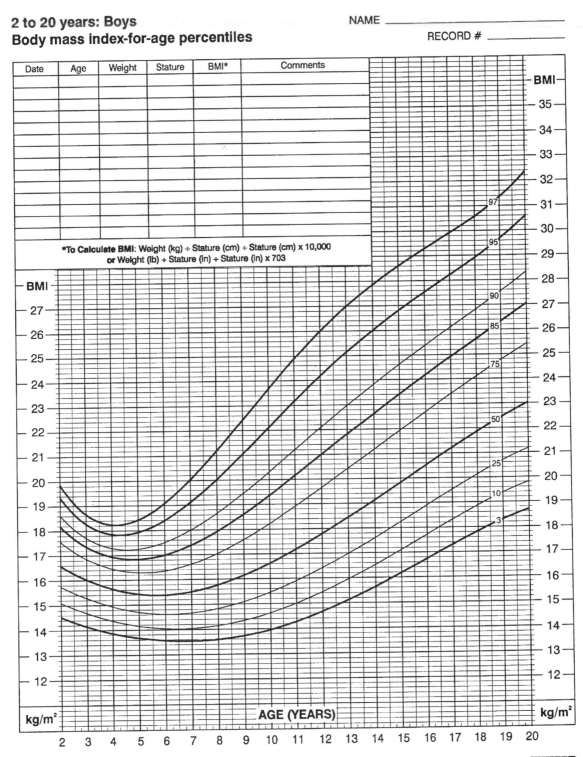

**2 to 20 years: Boys**
**Body mass index-for-age percentiles**

NAME _____

RECORD # _____

| Date | Age | Weight | Stature | BMI* | Comments |
|------|-----|--------|---------|------|----------|

*To Calculate BMI: Weight (kg) ÷ Stature (cm) ÷ Stature (cm) x 10,000
or Weight (lb) ÷ Stature (in) ÷ Stature (in) x 703

AGE (YEARS)

Published May 30, 2000 (modified 10/16/00).
SOURCE: Developed by the National Center for Health Statistics in collaboration with
the National Center for Chronic Disease Prevention and Health Promotion (2000).
http://www.cdc.gov/growthcharts

SAFER·HEALTHIER·PEOPLE™

33

## Physical Health and Obesity

Pediatricians and other doctors are most immediately concerned with the effects of obesity on children's short- and long-term physical health. Numerous health organizations, such as the American Academy of Family Physicians (AAFP), American Heart Association (AHA), American Obesity Association (AOA), American Academy of Pediatrics (AAP), and the American College of Sports Medicine (ACSM), provide much useful information about the health issues associated with childhood obesity and the associated health trends in younger and younger populations.

The AAFP suggests that doctors screen obese children for cardiac risk factors, orthopedic problems, and skin disorders (Moran, 1999b). Cardiac risk factors include high levels of "bad" cholesterol and low levels of "good" cholesterol, high blood pressure, smoking, diabetes mellitus, lack of physical activity, and a family history of early heart disease (AHA, 2000a; Moran, 1999b; Robinson & Killen, 1995). Orthopedic problems include arthritis, tibial torsion, bowed legs, slipped capital femoral epiphysis, and weight stress in the legs (Moran, 1999b). Skin disorders, especially when deep skin folds are present, can include heat rash, intertrigo, monolial dermatitis, and acanthosis nigricans, which may be a marker for Type 2 diabetes (Moran, 1999b).

Type 2 diabetes, formerly known as "adult-onset diabetes" and more commonly seen in adults over the age of 40, is being increasingly diagnosed in younger populations due to obesity (BBC Online, 2000), including children as young as 5 years of age (Stoneham, 2001). Type 2 diabetes has been linked to increased health risks for the eyes, heart, kidneys, and nervous system (Bowser, 2001; Stoneham, 2001). AAP (2000) has identified a sharp increase in children diagnosed with Type 2 diabetes, from 4 percent in 1990 to 20 percent in 2000; 85 percent of these children are obese. Diabetes is reported to be the seventh leading cause of death in the United States (AAP, 2000). Obesity is the most controllable risk factor for type 2 diabetes, and researchers have found that 30 minutes of physical activity daily and a 5 to 7 percent reduction in body weight reduces the risk of developing Type 2 diabetes by almost 60 percent (Stoneham, 2001).

Other diseases that have a high correlation with obesity, including heart disease, cancer, joint disease, menstrual irregularities, hormonal complications, insulin resistance, gallstones, gout, and increased possibility of stroke also are affecting younger populations (AHA, 2000a; AOA, 2002; BBC Online, 2000; Children with Diabetes, 2000; Robinson & Killen, 1995). In addition, cardiopulmonary health is threatened by obesity, as heart and lungs are put under enormous stress to supply oxygen to all the cells in the body (AHA, 2000a; Bowser, 2001). According to the Centers for Disease Control, there also has been a fivefold increase in the diagnosis of sleep apnea connected to childhood obesity over the past 20 years (Irvine, 2002).

## Obesity Persists

*Prevention is the best hope for decreasing the prevalence of [obesity]. . . . Obesity tends to "track" throughout life, meaning that its presence at any age will increase the risk of persistence at subsequent ages. . . . Evaluation of obesity in childhood is important . . . it offers the best hope for preventing disease progression with its associated morbidities into adulthood.* (Moran, 1999b, p. 861)

Doctors are concerned with treating and preventing obesity in childhood because obese and overweight children are more likely to become obese and overweight adults (Moran, 1999b). AAFP (1999) reports that children with at least one obese parent also are more likely to be obese adults; as children advance in age, their chances of remaining overweight increase tremendously. For instance, children who are obese at 6 years of age have a 50 percent chance of remaining obese into adulthood, and between 70 percent and 80 percent of obese adolescents will be obese as adults (Moran, 1999b). The American Academy of Pediatrics reports that children who are heavy at 5 years of age are more than twice as likely to become obese adults than children who were not heavy at 5 years of age (AAP, 1998).

## Psychological Health and Obesity

Children's psychological health can be severely affected by being obese. Overweight children often endure ridicule, torment, and prejudice from other children, as well as adults (Loewy, 1998). AAFP encourages doctors to screen for psychiatric as well as physical risks associated with obesity. Psychiatric issues include depression, low self-esteem, negative self-image, and possible withdrawal from peers (Moran, 1999b).

Prejudice against obese and overweight children can start as early as the preschool years. Preschool children given a choice of playing with thin dolls or fat dolls chose the thin dolls (Dyrenforth, Freeman, & Wooley, 1978; Rothblum, 1992). Children choose to play with disabled or disfigured children over children who were considered obese (Richardson, Boodman, Hastorf, & Dornbush, 1961; Rothblum, 1993). Children as young as elementary school view obese and overweight classmates as lazy, sloppy, dirty, stupid, ugly, less likely to have friends, less liked by parents, less likely to do well at school, less satisfied with their appearance, and more likely to be teased (Hill & Silver, 1995; Levine, 1987; Moran, 1999b; Rothblum, 1992; Staffieri, 1967). As adolescents, overweight individuals are more likely to suffer from low self-esteem (Braet, Mervielde, & Vandereycken, 1997; French, Story, & Perry, 1995), especially because of the great importance placed on physical appearance during this age (Wadden & Stunkard, 1987).

Even adults are not immune to prejudice against overweight children. Obese children are viewed consistently by adults as being less attractive, less energetic, less socially outgoing, less intelligent, and having less leadership ability, lower levels of self-esteem, and more personal problems than children of average weight (Quinn, 1987; Shroer, 1985). Consequently, obese children are more likely to be the targets of conscious and unconscious stereotypes, which can result in direct or indirect prejudicial treatment from almost everyone who interacts with these children. For instance, one study found that obese children were not as likely as their average weight counterparts to be accepted into prestigious colleges even though the two groups did not differ significantly in academic performance during high school (Canning & Mayer, 1966). Another researcher found that obese and overweight girls were less likely to receive financial support from their parents for their college educations, regardless of family income, size, and ethnicity (Crandall, 1991, 1995).

Over the long term, therefore, obesity can be a determinant of low socioeconomic status, especially for obese women, who, on average, complete fewer years of school, are less likely to be married, and have lower than average household incomes (Gortmaker, Must, Perrin, Sobol, & Dietz, 1993). Clearly, children's weight can affect their lives significantly on many different levels in addition to their immediate physical health (Bowser, 2001).

## CAUSES AND CURES OF OBESITY

American educators, physicians, and politicians have been aware of the increasing threat of obesity (Sutterby & Frost, 2002). The identified causes of and solutions for obesity in children typically focus on children's diet and physical activity. A number of studies have focused on interventions attempted to alter either children's diets or children's levels of physical activity. The effects of lifestyle changes in diet and physical activity combined have been documented in a large number of research articles.

### Increased Food Intake

*No one wakes up to discover his/her BMI has reached the 95th percentile; obesity presumably represents an outcome of prolonged poor habits.* (Gable & Lutz, 2000, p. 298)

According to the American Academy of Family Physicians, "only a small percentage of childhood obesity is associated with a hormonal or genetic defect, with the remainder being idiopathic in nature" (Moran, 1999b, p. 863). Idiopathic obesity refers to obesity of unknown or uncertain cause. Obesity found to be idiopathic may be combated with lifestyle modification.

Dramatic lifestyle changes over the past 40 years have been cited as the main reason for the drastic increase in childhood obesity (Irvine, 2002; *Obesity*, 2002). Diet is one area that has changed greatly: convenience foods such as prepackaged meals and fast food are high in sugar, saturated fat, and calories, and are being increasingly consumed by children, especially during sedentary activities such as watching television and playing with video games (Bar-Or, 2000; Irvine, 2002; Robinson, 1999). Additionally, television advertising during children's programming consists mainly of food commercials, thus compounding and strengthening the relationship between television watching and the consumption of high sugar, high calorie, and high fat foods (Bar-Or, 2000). Eat all you can hold buffets and larger servings have become increasingly popular as people become increasingly over-weight.

Television viewing also is implicated in the increase in dietary fat consumption. Children who eat meals while watching television tend to eat more high-calorie foods like pizza, snack foods, and sodas than children in families that separate meals and television viewing (Coon, Goldberg, Rogers, & Tucker, 2001; Robinson & Killen, 1995). Research concludes that decreases in the amount of television watching by 3rd- and 4th-graders were accompanied by decreases in food consumed in front of the television, as well as decreases in BMI, triceps skin fold thickness, waist circumference, and waist-to-hip ratio (Robinson, 1999).

The problem of obesity is also linked to an alarming paradox. Advertising and the media constantly churn out conflicting messages, offering children super-sized fast foods while marketing clothes on thin models (Irvine, 2002). So while Madison Avenue tempts American appetites with luscious images of convenient foods and large portions, they also help set expectations and standards for appearance with Victoria's Secret and Abercrombie & Fitch models. This paradox places emphasis on both gratification and appearance, and can be confusing to children and others struggling with their weight. Experts concerned with children's health are attempting to refocus the issue on health and find a balance in expectations for children (AAFP, 1999; AHA, 2000a, 2000b; Melcher & Bostwick, 1998).

Getting children to eat more healthfully can be extremely difficult. Parents' ability to control children's diets may be limited in that what children are thought to eat and what they report eating are often different. In a study of parents' and daughters' reports of food consumption, parents reported that their daughters mostly ate home-cooked meals, fruits and vegetables daily, and nutritious after-school snacks. The daughters, however, reported eating many fast food meals, few fruits or vegetables, and primarily chips for after-school snacks. The convenience of fast food items that are prepackaged and more shelf stable led to their inclusion in children's diets even though both parents and children were aware of the low nutritional value of such prepackaged foods (Thompson et al., 2003).

Interventions also are not always successful. Researchers found that an intervention program to reduce children's fat intake at the middle school level, by marketing more healthful food choices from all food sources (including breakfasts, lunches, à la carte menus, and school stores), did not significantly affect children's intake of fat at school in comparison to middle school students who did not receive the intervention (Sallis et al., 2003).

School environment also can be a contributor to dietary behaviors. Students at schools with à la carte programs consumed significantly higher levels of high-fat snacks and calorie-dense beverages and significantly lower levels of fruits and vegetables. At schools with snack vending machines, the majority of snacks available in vending machines are high-fat, low nutrient foods, and students consumed fewer fruits. The vegetable of choice for most teens in this study was fried potatoes, which were available on a daily basis at most schools. Schools looking to reduce students' consumption of high-calorie, high-fat, low-nutrition foods should look for ways to reduce children's access to vending machines, à la carte menus, and fried food items (Kubik, Lytle, Hannan, Perry, & Story, 2003).

Eliminating or changing school food programs can be difficult, as many schools have brought in vending machines and à la carte menus in order to raise additional funds. Cash-strapped schools have turned to food processing companies and soft drink companies to pay for school renovations, stadiums, and other extras. Schools that have signed long-term contracts must keep the vending machines or risk losing or having to return funds generated by those machines (Kubik et al., 2003; Schlosser, 2002).

Although diet is difficult to adjust in children without affecting normal growth, exchanging empty calories like carbonated beverages and sweets for more healthful options can go a long way toward improving children's health. Changing children's dietary lifestyles will require a combination of reducing the amount of advertising for these products during children's television programs and reducing access to these products by taking out vending machines and à la carte menus at schools. Education programs about healthful eating are not sufficient, because these programs are dwarfed by the huge amount of advertising dollars targeting children that promote poor eating choices.

## WEIGHT GAIN AND PHYSICAL ACTIVITY

*Physical activity for children refers to a broad range of structured and unstructured movement including free play, recreation activities, community movement programs, school physical education classes, and routine daily activities like walking, bicycling, playground games, sports, and family chores.* (Ratliffe, 2004, p. 6)

## Statistics and Trends for Physical Activity

Children's participation in television viewing, video game playing, Internet surfing, and other sedentary activities have increased dramatically over the past few decades (Irvine, 2002; *TV linked*, 2002). The increase in such activities seems to be linked to the increase in obesity, as sedentary activities displace moderate and vigorous physical activity and also reduce resting metabolic rates (Robinson, 1999). In fact, MSNBC.com reports that most children are watching television by the age of 2 years, that being overweight as a child is significantly related to the number of hours per day that children spend watching television and videos, and that this significance increases when televisions are located in children's bedrooms (Dennison, Erb, & Jenkins, 2002). Research also indicates that obese children participate in fewer hours of active play and extracurricular activities, and they watch significantly more television (Gable & Lutz, 2000).

According to the National Health Examination Survey Cycles I to III and the National Health and Nutrition Examination Surveys I to III, between a quarter to a third of children in the United States are obese (Gortmaker, Dietz, Sobol, & Wehler, 1987). The CDC (2002) reports that in the years 1999-2000, 15 percent of children and adolescents from 6 to 19 years of age were considered overweight. The AAFP also reports that since the 1960s, obesity has increased by 54 percent in children 6 to 11 years old and 39 percent in children 12 to 17 years old, with severe obesity (BMI at or above the 95th percentile) accounting for most of the increase (Moran, 1999b).

According to the United States Surgeon General (1996):

- Around half of 12- to 21-year-olds participate regularly in vigorous physical activity, and one quarter of people in this age group do not participate in any vigorous physical activity
- Participation in light, moderate, and vigorous physical activity declines as children get older
- Less than one-fifth of all high school students are physically active for at least 20 minutes per day in physical education classes.

Research also indicates that the greatest decrease in physical activity occurs during adolescence (Lowry, Wechsler, Kann, & Collins, 2001).

Obesity is not just an issue for children in the United States. Researchers in both Canada and Europe have reported increasing patterns of childhood inactivity, childhood obesity, and the diseases associated with obesity and inactivity, including diabetes, cancer, and cardiovascular disease (BBC Online, 2000; Canadian Association for Health, Physical Education, Recreation and Dance, 1996).

## Measurement of Physical Activity

Physical activity can be measured using many different methods. Observations and self-report questionnaires are nontechnical methods of estimating physical activity. Accelerometers, pedometers, and heart rate monitors also can be used to measure physical activity (Goran, 1997). The CDC (1997) recommends 60 minutes of moderate to vigorous physical activity daily (MVPA) for children ages 5 to 18. Heart rate is considered to be a good indicator of physical activity in that heart rate typically increases in order to supply the muscles with oxygen during exercise (Eston, Rowlands, & Ingledew, 1997). Moderate to vigorous physical activity corresponds to a heart rate of between 147-149 beats per minute.

## Gender and Physical Activity

Boys and girls differ in the amount of physical activity they engage in on a daily basis and they react differently to different types of interventions to increase physical activity (Pangrazi, Beighle, Vehige, & Vack, 2003; Scruggs, Beveridge, & Watson, 2003). Boys self-report about twice as much vigorous physical activity per week as girls, and boys are also more active, based on Caltrec monitoring (Morgan et al., 2003). Some studies indicate a significant gender by activity interaction effect, as girls are more active than boys during some activities, while boys are more active than girls during other activities. Boys are more active overall than girls during skill drills, game play, recess, and free play (McKenzie, Marshall, Sallis, & Conway, 2000; Sarkin, McKenzie, & Sallis, 1997; Sutterby, Brown, & Thornton, 2004). Girls are as active as boys during fitness activities but less active during free play and game play (Kulinna, Martin, Lai, Kliber, & Reed, 2003; McKenzie et al., 2000).

Girls are disadvantaged in that they have fewer opportunities than boys to play outdoors and participate in sports. In addition, girls report enjoying physical activity less than boys and have lower self-perceptions of their physical competence (Morgan et al., 2003), which may result in less physical activity.

## Schools and Decreased Physical Activity

Schools are directly contributing to the decline in physical activity in children. In response to increased pressure to raise test scores, many schools have decreased or eliminated recess. In the 1950s, children typically had three daily recess periods as well as an hour for lunch. By the 1970s, the lunch period was decreased to 30 minutes. Currently, about 40 percent of schools are eliminating or reducing recess and many school districts have eliminated recess for all elementary schools (Alexander, 1999; Kieff, 2001). Schools are also increasing the amount of homework, which is leading to increased sedentary activity at home (Sallis et al., 1999). In addition, due to budget constraints, less time is devoted to physical education. Active participation in high school physical education classes, defined as exercising for at least 20 minutes during the PE class, decreased among all demographics, from 34 percent in 1991 to 22 percent in 1997, even though high school PE enrollment did not decrease (Lowry et al., 2001).

One important factor contributing to the elimination of recess at many schools is the increasing emphasis on efficiency. "The cult of efficiency extols the values of work and devalues the role of leisure" (Pellegrini & Bjorkland, 1996, p. 6). Time on task is also an important component of the "cult of efficiency," as educators emphasize that more work equals more results (Pellegrini & Bjorkland, 1996).

Many teachers believe that children have many hours to play at home. On the contrary, many children are involved in structured activities like tutoring and homework at home (Kieff, 2001). In addition, a relationship exists between physical activity at school and physical activity at home. Children who are physically active at school tend to be more physically active at home, while children who are sedentary at school tend to remain sedentary once they get home (Dale, Corbin, & Dale, 2000).

Children spend a great deal of time at school and the environment of school can have an effect on the amount of physical activity children engage in while there. Typically, the environment consists of three factors: programs for increasing physical activity, the physical environment of play, and social factors, such as social support.

## Physical Activity and the Environment

*Paraphrasing a line from the movie* Field of Dreams: *If we build it, they will come—and be active.* (Sallis et al., 2001, p. 618)

A number of studies examine the connection between physical activity for children and the environment. One study found that a number of environmental factors are regular correlates to physical activity, including opportunities to be active, lack of barriers, access to facilities, and time outdoors; social factors included support from parents, perceived physical competence, direct help from parents, and social support (Sallis, Prochaska, & Taylor, 2000).

One important aspect contributing the decrease in children's physical activity is how urban planning design has changed. Current urban planning in most cities emphasizes spread-out neighborhoods divided into areas dedicated to housing, apartments, retail, or industry. These areas then are connected by large roads or freeways, necessitating use of automobiles to reach destinations. This change in urban planning is having an effect on children's everyday activity levels (McCann & Ewing, 2003). Adults who live in high walkability areas, defined as mixed-use neighborhoods with short grid-like connected streets with aesthetically pleasing landscaping/views, reported 70 minutes more moderate to vigorous physical activity a week due to increased walking/biking (Saelens, Sallis, Black, & Chen, 2003).

The effect of sprawl is also felt by children. One significant change is in the number of children who walk or ride a bicycle to school. Currently, only about 22 percent of children walk or ride a bicycle to school, while 71 percent of adults report that they either walked or rode a bicycle to school. Schools are either too far away or parents have concerns about traffic or crime and so do not allow their children to walk to school (Surface Transportation Policy Project, 2003).

Finding the time and place for exercise can be a challenge for many children. Latchkey children are often required by their parents to stay indoors while their parents are at work. Sometimes, safety and traffic concerns prevent parents from allowing their children to play outdoors (Stoneham, 2001). In addition, crime rates also have been correlated with lower levels of physical activity in adolescents (Gordan-Larsen, McMurray, & Popkin, 2000).

The environment provided for physical activity at school can have an effect on how active children are. School improvements like tennis courts and supervision led to higher levels of physical activity for middle school students. Conversely, middle school students who did not have facilities and supervision were almost totally inactive during their periods of free activity (Sallis et al., 2001). Children who engaged in play on colorful indoor play environments consisting of climbing tubes and slides were more active than children engaged in play on typical playgrounds; the children in this study averaged heart rates of 158 beats per minute, which is significantly higher than the average heart rates on typical playgrounds (128-138 beats per minute) (Whitehurst, Groo, & Brown, 1996). In another study, researchers painted playground markings of ships, dragons, and snakes on the grass of a playground. The addition of these markings led to increased physical activity, as children were inspired to engage in more active games (Stratton, Marsh, & Moores, 2000).

The addition of playground equipment also can have an effect on how active children are on the playground. In one study (Sutterby, Brown, & Thornton, 2004), children were monitored with heart rate monitors under two different conditions: during free play in an area with playground equipment and during free play in an area without playground equipment. The children without playground equipment had access to a soccer field, a basketball court, and materials for games such as balls, hoops, and jump ropes. The children in the playground equipment condition were significantly more active than the children in the non-playground condition. Higher activity levels occurred across all variables collected, including gender, age, and obesity level, indicating that the presence of the playground equipment encouraged the children to participate in higher levels of physical activity. This finding indicates that while children are interested in loose parts and organized games once they enter elementary school, they are also interested in opportunities to climb, slide, and swing.

## Physical Activity and School Programs

Programs are currently being designed to increase children's physical activities at school (CDC, 1997; Kohl & Hobbs, 1998; McGinnis, Kanner, & DeGraw, 1991). Children during recess often begin with high intensity activity that diminishes over time (McKenzie et al., 1995; Simons-Morton, Taylor, Snider, & Huang, 1993). Heart rates differ depending on the activity engaged in during physical education classes. Fitness activities produced the highest levels of activities in one study, followed by free play, game play, and skill drills (McKenzie et al., 2000).

Scruggs, Beveridge, and Watson (2003) recommended that children engage in structured fitness breaks rather than free play. In a comparison of free play to structured fitness breaks, researchers used heart monitors and pedometers to determine children's activity levels during the two conditions. The fitness breaks were set up as an obstacle course, incorporating activities such as running, dribbling a basketball, and jumping over objects. Children engaged in the fitness breaks had higher levels of physical activity as well as greater intensity of physical activity than during the free play recess periods. Of course, one should consider carefully the type and range of materials and equipment available to the children when making decisions about free play versus structured fitness breaks. Free play offers many developmental advantages other than intensity of physical activity.

A recent study investigated children's physical activity levels during free play and during physical education class. Heart monitors determined children's physical activity levels and observations were taken of the children during their activities. Children were more active during the free play period than during the physical education period, with heart rates averaging 150 beats per minute during free play in comparison to 132 beats per minute during physical education classes. During physical education, the children engaged in activities such as organized games and calisthenics. Although children took time to socialize during the free play period, they were more active overall. This may be due to the time that children spend waiting to participate in the game or awaiting instructions during physical education (Sutterby, Brown, & Thornton, 2004).

In an analysis of heart rates during physical education classes, which consisted of ball games, gymnastics, athletics, and free play, researchers found that average heart rates reached only a mean of 130 beats per minute, which is significantly below the heart rates recommended for moderate to vigorous physical activity. Across activities, the ball games and free play encouraged higher levels of physical activity than the gymnastics lessons. Some of the observations from this study highlight some complications when comparing free play to physical education classes. For example, during the ball games, the children were limited to moving primarily their arms and torsos; teachers limited their movement for safety reasons. The free play condition also was limited to an outdoor basketball court with no playground equipment, which most likely limited both the children's enjoyment of free play and their ability to increase their activity levels (Macfarlane & Kwong, 2003).

Programs that are appropriate for adults are not necessarily appropriate for children (Tomporowski, 2003). Physical education programs are about learning and development as well as physical activity. In response to structured programs, children will attempt to engage in play by altering or modifying the activities suggested by the instructor. They will lose interest in activities that are too structured and therefore offer less than satisfactory responses (Sanders & Graham, 1995). Play and flow-like experiences are often compared, in that play encourages intrinsically motivated physical activity. Flow-like experiences are typically defined as giving the individual a sense of timelessness and total engagement in the activity. Play is considered to be a flow-like experience for children. Key factors to having children engage in play or flow-like experiences requires that the activities be fun, at a level of difficulty that challenges the child (not too difficult, nor too simple), and interesting or modifiable by the child in order to maintain engagement (Mandigo & Thompson, 1998).

## Physical Activity and Socio-cognitive Variables

*The running, jumping, skipping, and laughing of children at recess or after school is joyous, free, and almost contagious in its expression of well being.* (Garvey, 1977)

Teachers may increase physical activity socially through prompting. Teachers who prompted children to be more active helped them maintain higher levels of physical activity. Such efforts also have a multiplier effect, in that children who were active encouraged other children to be more active (McKenzie et al., 1997). Peers and family encourage or discourage physical activity in children through social supports. In addition, affective factors, such as feelings of self-efficacy, also can be important for physical activity. The importance of physical activity is circular; children who are physically active have greater feelings of self-efficacy, while children who have feelings of self-efficacy are more likely to be physically active (Biddle, Sallis, & Cavill, 1998; Fogelholm, Nuutinen, Pasanen, Myohanen, & Saatla, 1999). Parental support for physical activity has been linked to children's feelings of self-efficacy and their interest in physical activity. Intervention programs should increase parents' ability to motivate children to be more physically active (Trost et al., 2003).

A study of the relationship between parental influences and children's attitudes toward physical activity and a healthful diet among African American girls and their parents found that parents encouraged physical activity rather than diet and did so primarily for weight control. In addition, parents and children were concerned with weight for aesthetic reasons. Parents reported fear of asthma, hot weather, and arthritis as deterrents to physical activity.

Girls reported that busy schedules, homework, and television prevented them from being active. Mothers tend to be facilitators and observers of physical activities, while fathers and siblings are more likely to be participants in physical activity (Thompson et al., 2003).

Peers also can have a significant effect on children's desire for physical activity. The chapter on swings in this volume describes observations of children swinging more vigorously while in pairs than while swinging solo, possibly due to a competitive approach to swinging. Children also engage in sports activities for social reasons, such as a desire to belong, achieve social status, and make friends (Allen, 2003).

Children's recess has been shown to have academic as well as physical benefits, as children engage in fewer off-task behaviors when they have recess periods (Jarrett et al., 1998). Studies involving cognition and physical activity have shown short-term cognitive and behavioral benefits:

- Children's computation performance was improved following 50 minutes of vigorous physical activity (Gabbard & Barton, 1979)
- Mathematical computation performance improved by 30-40 minutes of paced walking (MacNaughten & Gabbard, 1993)
- Improved performance on the Woodcock Johnson Test of Concentration following 15 minutes of aerobic exercise (Caterino & Polak, 1999).

According to Tomporowski (2003), the results of these studies should be considered tentative, in that adult prescriptions for physical activity are not appropriate for children. A meta-analysis of the relationship between physical activity and cognition found that the results of experimental studies demonstrate a causal factor between physical activity and higher levels of cognitive functioning. According to Sibley and Etnier (2003), "The results support the possibility that participation in physical activity causes improvements in cognitive performance" (p. 251).

Physical activity is a social activity that can benefit children's sense of self, as well as their social and cognitive development. Prompting from peers, parents, and teachers helps ensure that children stay active when they have the opportunity. The actual activity itself may have benefits for learning as children can return from physical education more ready to focus and with the energy to complete academic tasks. Overall, ignoring the affective benefits of physical activity ignores the important role it plays in healthy development.

## Physical Activity Conclusions

Physical activity is influenced by many factors, and interactions between these factors are often significant. Environment plays an important role in that the facilities for play encourage or discourage physical activity. Schools may be one of the few places for children to engage in physical activity since urban environments offer decreasing opportunities for outdoor physical activity. Access to ball courts and playground equipment encourages children to be physically active, and the interaction effect of parents or teachers or peers prompting children to be active leads to higher levels of physical activity.

Free play and structured fitness activities stimulate vigorous physical activity levels and increased heart rates, yet free play without facilities may not stimulate sufficient activity. Structured physical activities stimulate increasing activity levels, but they may not maintain children's interest long enough. Adults can engage in such physical activities as running or aerobics for long periods. Children prefer activities that are spontaneous and enjoyable, and emphasis on adult-type physical activity may turn children off to physical activity. Finally a third factor, gender, may have an interaction effect; boys prefer free play and are more active during free play while girls appear to be more active during structured fitness activities. A combination of structured fitness along with free play in appropriate facilities appears to be a better mix for school programs.

Finally, many of the activities in physical education classes are not leading to the levels of physical activity needed to achieve desired fitness levels for children. Physical education courses are important for children's development, but they combine education and fitness activities. During these classes, students receive instruction in motion, health, and sports games in addition to opportunities to participate in physical activity and free play. In addition, too many physical education activities require only two or three children to be active at the same time while other children wait in line. Children need extended continuous activity during physical education periods in order to achieve the benefits of high aerobic levels. School programs should include both physical education and free play in order to meet children's developmental needs.

## RECOMMENDATIONS AND STANDARDS

*Exercise is necessary to maintain weight loss and redistribute body fat into muscle. It is, therefore, an essential part of any weight management program.* (Moran, 1999b, p. 866)

Numerous health organizations, such as the American Academy of Family Physicians, American Heart Association, American Obesity Association, and American Academy of Pediatrics, offer guidelines for preventing and correcting childhood obesity and associated health conditions.

In addition to changes in diet, the American Academy of Family Physicians provides the following suggestions for helping to prevent childhood obesity (AAFP, 2004; Moran, 1999a, 1999b):

- Limit television viewing
- Encourage active play
- Establish regular outdoor physical activities
- Set a goal of 20-30 minutes of moderate activity per day in addition to whatever exercise is offered at school.

The AAFP maintains that physical activity is a major component of a successful weight management plan (AAFP, 1999; Moran, 1999b).

The American Heart Association (AHA, 2000a, 2000b) recommends the following:

- Reducing dietary fat
- Becoming more active
- Creating environments that encourage and support physical activity
- Involving adults, especially parents, in efforts to modify obese children's behaviors.

The AHA (2000a) also provides recommendations for children's physical activity:

- Children 5+ years of age should participate daily in at least 30 minutes of moderate physical activity; and at least 3 to 4 times a week, they should participate in at least 30 minutes of vigorous physical activity
- These activities should be enjoyable so that children will want to participate in them for sustained periods of time
- Television watching and other sedentary activities should be replaced by increased physical activity levels
- Children should be encouraged to learn and practice self-management skills, such as setting goals for maintaining active lifestyles
- The main goal should be to achieve and maintain good cardiovascular fitness.

Research has demonstrated that obese children ages 7 to 11 years old who participated in a 4-month-long program during which they engaged in sustained exercise for 40 minutes every day after school experienced significant reduction in body fat even though the children's dietary intake was not altered (Gutin, Riggs, Ferguson, & Owens, 1999). The European Congress on Obesity (ECOG) recommends at least an hour of exercise daily in schools, in addition to extracurricular sports or other physical activity (BBC Online, 2000). Others health experts recommend:

- Establishing healthful eating and exercise patterns (Epstein, 1993)
- Reducing the amount of television watching, as there is a proven relationship between television watching and obesity, as well as television watching and eating (Epstein, 1993; Robinson & Killen, 1995)
- Creating convenient, easy-to-prepare, more healthful food options for time-conscious parents and children (Thompson et al., 2003)
- Limiting children's access to vending machines and à la carte food menus at school in order to reduce their consumption of high-fat, low-nutrition foods (Kubik et al., 2003)
- Achieving a total accumulation of at least 60 minutes daily of moderate intensity activity for children, and at least 30 minutes daily for adolescents and adults (Pangrazi, Corbin, & Welk, 1996)
- Encouraging children to get outdoors; children are more active outdoors than when they are indoors, and getting them outdoors will steer them away from possible sedentary activities such as television watching and video game playing (Bar-Or, 2000)
- Encouraging children to participate in activities that engage the large muscle groups and thus produce large energy expenditures (Bar-Or, 2000).

Doctors, psychologists, therapists, educators, and other experts agree that physical activity should be enjoyable so that children will feel internally motivated to participate in moderate and vigorous physical activity such as sports and outdoor play (AHA, 2000a, 2000b; Bar-Or, 2000; Gould, Feltz, & Weiss, 1985; Government of Canada, 1983; Gutin, Riggs, Ferguson, & Owens, 1999; Loewy, 1998; Mandigo & Thompson, 1998; McCullagh, Matzkanin, Shaw, & Maldanado, 1993; Pierce, 1984). One way of providing children and adolescents with enjoyable opportunities for physical activity is to ensure that they are able to modify and control their own activities to match their needs and abilities (Mandigo & Thompson, 1998). This can be achieved by providing environments that include play equipment that is developmentally appropriate yet challenging for a variety of children on many different levels.

The goal is to support opportunities for children to engage in physical activity in the short term, and to help them form lifelong exercise habits (Gable & Lutz, 2000; Lowry, Wechsler, Kann, & Collins, 2001; Stoneham, 2001; Welk, 1999). Studies show that activity patterns learned at a young age are maintained throughout life (Malina, 1996), and that the physical and psychological benefits of regular exercise persist into adulthood (Hill & Peters, 1998). Making exercise accessible and enjoyable can help achieve both short- and long-term goals.

## SUMMARY

Obesity with children and adolescents is an alarming trend, as obesity has been linked to numerous physical complications and psychological issues, and it is a persistent problem that carries into adulthood. To combat obesity, programs should focus on two areas: improving children's diets and increasing children's physical activity. Improving diets should involve limiting the types of commercials children see as well as improving school lunches and other meals. Children's diets also can improve if parents become better educated about the high-calorie, high-fat foods that are available at fast food restaurants.

Children should have regular opportunities for physical activity at school and at home. These should include different types of activities that engage the body in many different ways, such as climbing and using the upper body. Schools need to play a greater part in creating environments that promote physical activities. School policies need to focus on the importance of physical activity by allowing recess, emphasizing physical education, and de-emphasizing extensive after-school academic activities, such as preparation for standardized testing and homework.

Creating environments that encourage physical activities requires more than simply providing places for children to play. Environments need to be reasonably safe in order to minimize the risks of serious accidents yet also provide motor challenges and reasonable levels of risk. They also must be protected from crime, traffic, and severe hazards (such as deep water and severe vertical fall areas). Play environments should accommodate children of varying physical abilities, thus allowing children with limited physical strength and abilities to engage in play while providing challenging activities for those children with more advanced physical strength and skills. Trained playleaders such as those active in many European countries, particularly Scandinavian countries, are sorely needed on American public playgrounds.

Combating the epidemic of cigarette smoking involved the entire public school system, resulted in laws to limit children's access to tobacco, and placed limitations on advertising tobacco to children. A campaign of like force and intensity is needed to combat childhood obesity. Future generations of children face the prospect of shorter, less productive lives due to poor diets, poor fitness levels, and obesity.

## References

Alexander, K. (1999, November). Playtime is cancelled. *Parents*, 114-118.

Allen, J. (2003). Social motivation in youth sport. *Journal of Sport and Exercise Psychology, 25*, 551-567.

American Academy of Pediatrics. (1998). *Study focuses on predictors of adult obesity.* AAP Press Release, March 2, 1998.

American Academy of Pediatrics. (2000). *Rise in childhood obesity linked to increase in type 2 diabetes.* AAP Press Release, February 23, 2000.

American College of Sports Medicine. (1995). *ACSM's guidelines for exercise testing and prescription* (5th ed.). Media, PA: Williams & Wilkins.

American Heart Association. Press Release: 10 AM ET, 1 June 1998. Available at http://www.americanheart.org/Whats_News/AHA_News_Releases/obesity.html

American Heart Association. (2000a). *Exercise (physical activity) and children.* Retrieved from www.americanheart.org/Heart_and_Stroke_A_Z_Guide/exercisek.html

American Heart Association. (2000b). *Obesity and overweight in children.* Retrieved from www.americanheart.org/Heart_and_Stroke_A_Z_Guide/obesityk.html

American Obesity Association. (2002). Childhood obesity. Retrieved June 11, 2004, from www.obesity.org/subs/childhood/healthrisks.shtml

Bar-Or, O. (2000). Juvenile obesity, physical activity, and lifestyle changes: Cornerstones for prevention and management. *The Physician and Sports Medicine, 28*(11), 51-58.

BBC Online. (2000). *Europe's generation of obese children.* Retrieved from BBC Online, Health, May 24, 2000, http://news.bbc.co.uk/hi/english/health/newsid-762000/762036.stm.

Biddle, S., Sallis, J., & Cavill, N. (1998). Health enhancing physical activity and its association with adult encouragement and social cognitive variables. *Journal of School Health, 66*, 75-78.

Bowser, B. A. (2001). Obese children. PBS Online NewsHour, May 1, 2001. Published online at: www.pbs.org/newshour/bb/health/jan-hune01/obesekids_5-01.html

Braet, C., Mervielde, I., & Vandereycken, W. (1997). Psychological aspects of childhood obesity: A controlled study in a clinical and nonclinical sample. *Journal of Pediatric Psychology, 22*, 59-71.

Canadian Association for Health, Physical Education, Recreation and Dance. (1996). *Time to take off the gloves: Physical inactivity is hazardous to your health.* Ottowa, ON: Author.

Canning, H., & Mayer, J. (1966). Obesity: Its possible effects on college admissions. *New England Journal of Medicine, 275*, 1172-4.

Caterino, M., & Polak, E. (1999). Effects of two types of activity on the performance of second-, third-, and fourth-grade students on a test of concentration. *Perception and Motor Skills, 89*, 245-248.

Centers for Disease Control and Prevention. (1997). Guidelines for school and community programs to promote lifelong physical activity among young people. *MMWR 46*(RR-6)1-36.

Centers for Disease Control and Prevention. (2002). *Fast stats A to Z: Overweight prevalence.* Retrieved June 11, 2004, from www.cdc.gov/nchs/fastats/overwt.htm.

Children with Diabetes. (2000). *Type 2 diabetes. Diabetes 123 and children with diabetes.* Retrieved June 11, 2004, from www.childrenwithdiabetes.com/clinic/type2.htm

Coon, K., Goldberg, J., Rogers, B., & Tucker, K. (2001). Relationships between use of television during meals and children's food consumption patterns. *Pediatrics, E7*, 107.

Crandall, C. S. (1991). Do heavyweight students have more difficulty paying for college? *Personality and Social Psychology Bulletin, 17*, 606-11.

Crandall, C. S. (1995). Do parents discriminate against their heavyweight daughters? *Personality and Social Psychology Bulletin, 21*, 724-35.

Dale, D., Corbin, C., & Dale, K. (2000). Restricting opportunities to be active during school time: Do children compensate by increasing physical activity levels after school? *Research Quarterly for Exercise and Sport, 71*(3), 240-248.

Dennison, B., Erb, T., & Jenkins, P. (2002). Television viewing and television in bedroom associated with overweight risk among low-income preschool children. *Pediatrics, 109*(6), 1028-1035.

Dyrenforth, S. R., Freeman, D., & Wooley, S. (1978). *Self esteem, body type preference, and sociometric ratings of peers in pre-school children.* Unpublished manuscript, Department of Psychiatry, University of Cincinnati College of Medicine.

Eston, R., Rowlands, A., & Ingledew, D. (1997). Validation of the Tritrac-R3D activity monitor during typical children's activities. In N. Armstrong, B. Kirby, & J. Welsman (Eds.), *Children and exercise XIX: Promoting health and well being* (pp. 132-138). London: EFN Spon.

Fogelholm, M., Nuutinen, O., Pasanen, M., Myohanen, E., & Saatla, T. (1999). Parent-child relationship of physical activity patterns and obesity. *Journal of Obesity Related Metabolism Disorders, 23,* 1262-1268.

French, S. A., Story, M., & Perry, C. L. (1995). Self-esteem and obesity in children and adolescents: A literature review. *Obesity Research, 3,* 479-90.

Gabbard, C., & Barton, J. (1979). Effects of physical activity on mathematical computation among young children. *Journal of Psychology, 103,* 287-288.

Gable, S., & Lutz, S. (2000). Household, parent, and child contributions to childhood obesity. *Family Relations, 49*(3), 293-300.

Garvey, C. (1977/1990). *Play.* Cambridge, MA: Harvard University Press.

Goran, M. (1997). Measurement issues related to studies of childhood obesity: Assessment of body composition, body fat distribution, physical activity and food intake. *Pediatrics, 101,* 505-518.

Gordan-Larsen, P., McMurray, R., & Popkin, B. (2000). Determinants of adolescent physical activity and inactivity patterns. *Pediatrics, 105*(6). Online at www.pediatrics.org/cgi/content/full/105/6/e83.

Gortmaker, S. L., Dietz, W. H., Sobol, A. M., & Wehler, C. A. (1987). Increasing pediatric obesity in the United States. *American Journal of Diseases of Children, 141,* 535-540.

Gortmaker, S. L., Must, A., Perrin, J. M., Sobol, A. M., & Dietz, W. H. (1993). Social and economic consequences of overweight in adolescence and young adulthood. *New England Journal of Medicine, 329,* 1008-1012.

Gould, D., Feltz, D., & Weiss, M. (1985). Motives for participating in competitive youth swimming. *International Journal of Sport Psychology, 16,* 126-140.

Government of Canada: Fitness and Amateur Sport. (1983). *Physical activity and the youth of Canada.* Ottawa, ON: Government Press.

Gutin, B., Riggs, S., Ferguson, M., & Owens, S. (1999). Description and process evaluation of a physical training program for obese children. *Research Quarterly for Exercise and Sport, 70*(1), 65-9.

Hill, A. J., & Silver, E. K. (1995). Fat, friendless, and unhealthy; 9-year-old children's perceptions of body shape stereotypes. *International Journal of Obesity, 19,* 423-30.

Hill, J. O., & Peters, J. C. (1998). Environmental contributions to the obesity epidemic. *Science, 280,* 1371-1374.

Irvine, M. (2002). *Experts say weight loss more important than ever for youth.* Associated Press, August 25, 2002.

Jarrett, O. S., Maxwell, D. M., Dickerson, C., Hoge, P., Davies, G., & Yetley, A. (1998). The impact of recess on classroom behavior: Group effects and individual differences. *Journal of Educational Research, 92*(2), 121-126.

Kieff, J. (2001). The silencing of recess bells. *Childhood Education, 77*(5), 319-320.

Kohl, H., & Hobbs, K. (1998). Development of physical activity behaviors among children and adolescents. *Pediatrics, 101*, 549-554.

Kubik, M., Lytle, L., Hannan, P., Perry, C., & Story, M. (2003). The association of the school environment with dietary behaviors of young adolescents. *American Journal of Public Health, 93*(7), 1168-1173.

Kulinna, P., Martin, J., Lai, Q., Kliber, A., & Reed, B. (2003). Student physical activity patterns: Grade, gender and activity influences. *Journal of Teaching in Physical Education, 22*, 298-310.

Levine, M. P. (1987). *How schools can help combat student eating disorders: Anorexia nervosa and bulimia.* Washington, DC: National Education Association of the United States.

Loewy, M. I. (1998). Suggestions for working with fat children in the schools. *Professional School Counseling, 1*(4), 18-22.

Lowry, R., Wechsler, H., Kann, L., & Collins, J. L. (2001). Recent trends in participation in physical education among US high school students. *Journal of School Health, 71*(4), 145-152.

Macfarlane, D., & Kwong, W. (2003). Children's heart rates and enjoyment levels during PE classes in Hong Kong primary schools. *Pediatric Exercise Science, 15*, 179-190.

MacNaughten, D., & Gabbard, C. (1993). Physical exertion and the immediate mental performance of sixth-grade children. *Perception and Motor Skills, 77*, 1159.

Malina, R. M. (1996). Tracking of physical activity and physical fitness across the lifespan. *Research Quarterly for Exercise and Sport, 67*(3), 48-57.

Mandigo, J. L., & Thompson, L. P. (1998). Go with their flow: How flow theory can help practitioners to intrinsically motivate children to be physically active. *Physical Educator, 55(3)*, 145-159.

McCann, B., & Ewing, R. (2003). *Measuring the health effects of sprawl.* Washington, DC: Smart Growth America.

McCullagh, P., Matzkanin, K. T., Shaw, S. D., & Maldanado, M. (1993). Motivation for participation in physical activity: A comparison of parent-child perceived competencies and participation motives. *Pediatric Exercise Science, 5*, 224-33.

McGinnis, J., Kanner, L., & DeGraw, C. (1991). Physical education's role in achieving national health objectives. *Research Quarterly of Exercise and Sport, 62*, 138-142.

McKenzie, T., Feldman, S., Woods, H., Romero, S., Dahlstrom, V., Stone, C., Strikmiller, P., Williston, J., & Harsha, D. (1995). Children's activity levels and lesson context during third grade physical education. *Research Quarterly for Exercise and Sport, 66*, 184-193.

McKenzie, T., Sallis, J., Elder, J., Berry, C., Hoy, P., Nader, M., Zive, M., & Broyles, S. (1997). Physical activity levels and prompts in young children at recess: A two year study in a bi-ethnic sample. *Research Quarterly for Exercise and Sport, 68*, 195-202.

McKenzie, T., Marshall, S., Sallis, J., & Conway, T. (2000). Student activity level, lesson context, and teacher behavior during middle school physical education. *Research Quarterly for Exercise and Sport, 71*, 249-259.

Melcher, J., & Bostwick, G. J., Jr. (1998). The obese client: Myths, facts, assessment, and intervention. *Health & Social Work, 23*(3), 195-202.

Moran, R. (1999a). Helping your child keep a healthy weight. *American Family Physician, 59*(4), 871.

Moran, R. (1999b). Evaluation and treatment of childhood obesity. *American Family Physician, 59*(4), 861-868.

Morgan, C., McKenzie, T., Sallis, J., Broyles, S., Zive, M., & Nader, P. (2003). Personal, social, and environmental correlates of physical activity in a bi-ethnic sample of adolescents. *Pediatric Exercise*

*Science, 15,* 288-301.

*Obesity may be beginning earlier.* (2002). MSNBC.com Health. Retrieved June 17, 2002, from www.msnbc.com/news/768467.asp?0dm=H16NH

Pangrazi, R., Beighle, A., Vehige, T., & Vack, C. (2003). The impact of promoting lifestyle activity for youth (PLAY) on children's physical activity. *Journal of School Health, 73*(8), 317-321.

Pangrazi, R. P., Corbin, C. B., & Welk, G. J. (1996). Physical activity for children and youth. *Journal of Physical Education, Recreation & Dance, 67*(4), 38-43.

Pellegrini, A., & Bjorkland, D. (1996). The place of recess in school: Issues in the role of recess in children's education and development. *Journal of Research in Childhood Education, 11*(1), 5-13.

Pierce, W. J. (1984, November). *Socialization and stress factors of youth sports participants.* Paper presented at the Olympic Scientific Congress, Eugene, OR.

Quinn, B. H. (1987). Attitudinal ratings of educators toward normal weight, overweight, and obese teenage girls. Doctoral dissertation, Texas Woman's University. *Dissertation Abstracts International, 48*/10-B, 3156-B.

Ratliffe, T. (2004). Introduction to children's fitness: Developing lifetime physical activity. *Teaching Elementary Physical Education, 15*(1), 6.

Reuters via Yahoo. (2004). *TV, eating out makes kids fat, studies agree.* Retrieved February 25, 2004, from http//Yahoo.com.health

Richardson, S. A., Boodman, N., Hastorf, A. H., & Dornbush, S. M. (1961). Cultural uniformity in reaction to physical disabilities. *Sociological Review, 26,* 241-247.

Robinson, T. N. (1999). Reducing children's television viewing to prevent obesity: A randomized controlled trial. *Journal of the American Medical Association, 282*(16), 1561-7.

Robinson, T. N., & Killen, J. D. (1995). Ethnic and gender differences in the relationships between television viewing and obesity, physical activity, and dietary fat intake. *Journal of Health Education-March/April 1995 Supplement, 26*(2), 91-98.

Rothblum, E. D. (1992). *The stigma of women's weight: Social and economic realities. Feminism & Psychology, 2.* Newbury Park, CA: Sage Publications.

Rothblum, E. D. (1993). I'll die for the revolution but don't ask me not to diet: Feminism and the continuing stigmatization of women's weight. In P. Fallon, M. Katzman, & S. Wooley (Eds.), *Feminist perspectives on eating disorders* (pp. 53-76). New York: Guildford Press.

Saelens, B., Sallis, J., Black, J., & Chen, D. (2003). Neighborhood-based differences in physical activity: An environment scale evaluation. *American Journal of Public Health, 93*(9), 1552-1558.

Sallis, J., Conway, T., Prochaska, J., McKenzie, T., Marshall, S., & Brown, M. (2001). The association of school environments with youth physical activity. *American Journal of Public Health, 91*(4), 618-620.

Sallis, J., McKenzie, T., Conway, T., Elder, J., Prochaska, J., Brown, M., Zive, M., Marshall, S., & Alcaraz, J. (2003). Environmental interventions for eating and physical activity: A randomized controlled trial in middle schools. *American Journal of Preventive Medicine, 24*(3), 209-217.

Sallis, J., McKenzie, T., Kolody, B., Lewis, M., Marshall, S., & Rosengard, P. (1999). Effects of health-related physical education on academic achievement: Project Spark. *Research Quarterly for Exercise and Sport, 70*(2), 127-134.

Sallis, J., Prochaska, J., & Taylor, W. (2000). A review of correlates of physical activity of children and adolescents. *Medical Science Sports Exercise, 32,* 965-975.

Sanders, S., & Graham, G. (1995). Kindergarten children's initial experiences in physical education: The relentless persistence of play clashes with the zone of acceptable responses. *Journal of Teaching in Physical Education, 14,* 372-383.

Sarkin, J., McKenzie, T., & Sallis, J. (1997). Gender differences in physical activity during fifth-grade physical education and recess periods. *Journal of Teaching in Physical Education, 17*, 99-106.

Schlosser, E. (2002). *Fast food nation: The dark side of the all-American meal.* New York: HarperCollins.

Scruggs, P., Beveridge, S., & Watson, D. (2003). Increasing children's school time physical activity using structured fitness breaks. *Pediatric Exercise Science, 15*, 156-169.

Shroer, N. A. (1985). Perceptions of in-service teachers and pre-service teachers toward obese and normal weight children. Doctoral dissertation, Texas A&M University. *Dissertation Abstracts International, 47/01-B*, 434-B.

Sibley, B., & Etnier, J. (2003). The relationship between physical activity and cognition in children: A meta-analysis. *Pediatric Exercise Science, 15*, 243-256.

Simons-Morton, B., Taylor, W., Snider, S., & Huang, I. (1993). The physical activity of fifth grade students during physical education class. *American Journal of Public Health, 83*, 262-264.

Staffieri, J. R. (1967). A study of social stereotype of body image in children. *Journal of Personal and Social Psychology, 7*, 101-104.

Stoneham, L. (2001). Diabetes on a rampage: Texas physicians mount a prevention effort. *Texas Medicine, 97*(11), 43-48.

Stratton, G., Marsh, I., & Moores, J. (2000). Promoting children's physical activity in primary school: An intervention study using playground markings. *Ergonomics, 43*(10), 1538-1546.

Surface Transportation Policy Project. (2003). *American attitudes toward walking and creating better walking communities.* Retrieved April 2003, from www.transact.org/report.asp?id=205. Accessed January 11, 2004.

Sutterby, J., Brown, P., & Thornton, C. (2004, April). *Physical activity levels during free play and physical education.* Paper presented at the annual conference of the American Educational Research Association, San Diego, CA.

Sutterby, J., & Frost, J. (2002). Making playgrounds fit for children and making children fit on playgrounds. *Young Children, 57*, 36-41.

Thompson, V., Baranowski, T., Cullen, K., Rittenberry, L., Baranowski, J., Taylor, W., & Nicklas, T. (2003). Influences on diet and physical activity among middle-class African American 8- to 10-year-old girls at risk of becoming obese. *Journal of Nutrition Education and Behavior, 35*, 115-123.

Tomporowski, P. (2003). Cognitive and behavioral responses to acute exercise in youths: A review. *Pediatric Exercise Science, 15*, 348-349.

Trost, S., Sallis, J., Pate, R., Freedson, P., Taylor, W., & Dowda, M. (2003). Evaluating a model of parental influence on youth physical activity. *American Journal of Preventive Medicine, 25*(4), 277-282.

*TV linked to obesity in very young.* (2002). MSNBC.com Health. Retrieved June 3, 2002, from www.msnbc.com/news/760878.asp

U.S. Surgeon General. (1996). *Physical activity and health.* Washington, DC: U.S. Department of Health and Human Services.

Wadden, T. A., & Stunkard, A. J. (1987). Psychopathology and obesity. *Annals of the New York Academy of Sciences, 499*, 55-65.

Wagner, D. R., & Heyward, V. H. (1999). Techniques of body composition assessment: A review of laboratory and field methods. *Research Quarterly for Exercise and Sports, 70*(2), 135-49.

Welk, G. J. (1999). Promoting physical activity in children: Parental influences. *ERIC Digest.* Washington, DC: ERIC.

Whitehurst, M., Groo, D., & Brown, L. (1996). Prepubescent heart rate response to indoor play. *Pediatric Exercise Science, 8*, 245-250.

# CHAPTER 3
# The Relevance of Height for Child Development and Playground Safety

*It's a matter of physics. The higher the fall and harder the surface, the worse the injury.* (Henzy, 2001, p. 1)

The overall purposes of the study in this chapter were to review existing research, survey professional opinion, and collect original data responsive to the following major questions associated with playground equipment heights: Does height of playground equipment contribute to play value and child development value? Does increasing the height of playground equipment increase the risk of injury in falls? Should maximum potential fall heights from playground equipment (not equipment heights) be established? These study questions were answered by reviewing research and opinion in professional literature, interviewing professionals in child safety, and conducting observations of children playing on playground equipment representing some of the tallest in the industry.

The research topics reviewed are: 1) scope of playground fall injuries, 2) professional opinion on children's propensities to climb and the value of height for child development, 3) children's fear of heights, 4) history of height as a hazard, 5) national guidelines and standards on heights and surfacing, 6) playground equipment height research, 7) relationships between height and injuries, and 8) height data from national surveys of playgrounds. In addition, two original studies were conducted. In the first study, researchers interviewed prominent playground safety specialists; in the second study, researchers observed children playing on play equipment more than 8 feet tall.

Following collection and analysis of data, conclusions and recommendations were derived. Special efforts were made to ensure that conclusions were derived directly from the data, avoiding investigator opinion unless so labeled. On issues with mixed data or responses, the investigators drew conclusions based on the overriding weight of evidence.

## Scope of Playground Fall Injuries

Falls are the second leading cause of unintentional injury and the most common cause of injuries resulting in hospital admissions for trauma (Baker, O'Neill, Ginsburg, & Li, 1992). National Electronic Injury Surveillance System (NEISS) data for 1999 (205,850 cases) show that falls, primarily to the surface below playground equipment, accounted for approximately 79 percent of the injuries on public playgrounds and 81 percent of injuries on home playgrounds (Tinsworth & McDonald, 2001, p. iii). All of the hospitalized injuries (3 percent) resulted from falls (Tinsworth & McDonald, 2001, p. iii).

Small NEISS sample sizes for severe head injuries in 1999 precluded drawing firm conclusions about the relative severity of fall injuries onto protective versus non-protective surfaces, as well as the contribution of fall heights. However, one-half (53 percent) of injuries involving playground equipment involved climbers and 67 percent of the falls from climbers were from heights greater than 48 inches. NEISS data for 1988 showed that "serious head injuries, such as fractures and concussions, were reported to have occurred from distances of about four and one-half feet or higher" (Tinsworth & Kramer, 1990, p. 8).

The distribution of public playground equipment injuries across age groups is 37 percent under age 6, 40 percent between ages 6 and 8, and 23 percent over age 8. These age-group data lead to a concern that the very young suffer the most injuries and are at greater risk than older children when falling from heights, particularly from slides, which are the most frequently implicated equipment for injury to children under age 6 (Consumer Federation of America [CFA], 1992, p. 4). Head injuries are involved in about three-fourths of the fall-related deaths associated with playground equipment. Several experts in child injury litigation agree that falls from overhead apparatus are the leading cause of broken limbs for young children, due primarily to excessive heights of equipment and hard surfacing in fall zones (personal conversations). "Protective surfacing under and around all play equipment is the most critical safety measure on playgrounds" (CFA, 1992, p. 13). For additional review of data on heights and injuries, see Thompson and Hudson (2001).

## Children's Propensities To Climb and Value of Height

For decades, professionals have researched, theorized, and speculated about children's motives for engaging in various forms of play. The resulting explanations are multifaceted and include physiological, psychological, sociological, and biological factors. The best explanations appear to lie in an integration of these factors. Ellis (1973) proposed that the most satisfying explanation involves a composite of play as arousal seeking, play as learning, and play as development. Play is a process of exploration, investigation, and manipulation; the broader the range of experiences, the better for development. Therefore, adults should proscribe only experiences that are damaging to the child, for "there clearly are limits on the degree to which any toy or playground (equipment) can satisfy the requirements for play" (Ellis, 1973, p. 136).

Particularly for young children, physical and developmental maturity and immaturity must be considered as significant factors in injury prevention. Perceptual-motor discrimination, depth and distance judgment, response to form and shape, neuromuscular maturation, mobility, strength, agility, coordination, and refinement of fine and gross motor skills all contribute to the ability to climb, avoid obstacles, steer wheeled vehicles, throw balls, and manipulate toys and play equipment (Marotz, 2001).

Preventing injuries is not merely a matter of making play environments safe for children, but also a matter of making children safe for playgrounds. Children vary in their development of climbing, running, balancing skills; coordination and strength; and judgment and reasoning (Frost & Henniger, 1979). While some children are models of fitness, a rapidly growing number are exhibiting marked fitness and health deficits. These deficits result from loss of free play, recess, and physical education, as well as an increase in sedentary activity such as television viewing, computer activity, pay-for-play entertainment, and consumption of junk food. In addition to a decline in fitness, serious health deficits among younger and younger children are found, including obesity, diabetes, osteoporosis, stress and anxiety, and heart disease (Dietz, 1999; Epstein, 2000; Frost & Jacobs, 1995; Gabbard, 2000; Perry, 2001; Therrell, 2001).

Readdick and Park (1998) contend that the one play activity most likely to be feared and punished by parents, discouraged by teachers, and overlooked by researchers and writers is climbing. Why do children climb? The observations of those who observe children carefully lead to a range of conclusions. Children climb trees, fences, furniture, or playground equipment because "they're there" (Readdick & Park, 1998, p. 14). They climb to increase their visual field (Williams, 1994). They climb for excitement and to get close to nature (Moore & Wong, 1997). They climb to experience basic physics—gravity, inertia, pendulums, and optics (Rivkin, 1995). They climb to overcome challenges, test their abilities, show off to and compete with their peers, engage in pretend games, and retrieve objects. They climb and swing to stimulate kinesthetic perceptions and vestibular sensations. They climb because their bodies are built for climbing and they have inherent tendencies to do so.

Ability to climb follows a developmental pattern, beginning with exploration of potential climbing objects with observable curiosity and progressing through ever more complex and refined stages. Some children begin to climb even before they are able to walk. By 17 months, half of all toddlers are climbing; by 22 months, 90 percent are climbing (Frankenburg & Dodds, 1967; Readdick & Park, 1998).

Play materials (or equipment) are selected and used for the stimulation they provide (Frost, 2001). Equipment should increase in complexity with accumulation of skill, knowledge, and experience. As experience increases, uncertainty regarding use of the equipment is reduced (Ellis, 1973, p. 135) and interest declines (Frost, 1992; Frost, Wortham, & Reifel, 2001); as familiarity with equipment increases, children naturally seek novel ways to play with it (Crawford, 1989). Novelty in movement and stunting behaviors are a natural progression of familiarity. We know from descriptive and observational research and experience that children love to climb and will attempt to climb and play at the highest possible level. Consequently, steps must be taken to protect the very young, who may not have sufficiently developed skills to play safely at heights. Unfortunately, much play equipment has been designed and installed in direct opposition to the play patterns that theorists and researchers conclude can be expected from children.

The best playthings provide novelty, but experience reduces novelty and children seek new challenges by using materials or equipment in ways not initially proposed or expected. The best playthings are sufficiently complex to stimulate, indeed require, investigation of physical properties, yet are not so complex (e.g., excessive heights) as to pose unwarranted hazards. They are responsive, producing effects that are under the control of the child. They may be manipulated, thus allowing discovery of physical properties. They produce arousal, excitement, and enjoyment in child users. Heavy-duty playground equipment, such as slides and climbers, fulfills some of these provisions in initial stages of use, but is limited in response and manipulation.

A reasonable level of risk is inherent, indeed necessary, in play if children's development is to be served. While the degree of risk must be limited, we also must ensure that children have access to play environments that challenge and even pose some degree of danger (Frost, Wortham, & Reifel, 2001). "All healthy mammals play, and their play includes leaping, defying gravity, climbing, jumping, horsing around—all activities that place the player at risk" (Brown, 1997, 1998). Playgrounds are risky places and children are often encouraged to take risks by their peers and also by adults who take them there (Smith, 1998).

"Children can be helped to take risks in relative safety through the encouragement we are able to give them and through the way we [adults] encounter playground challenges with them" (Smith, 1998, p. 21). Most public park playgrounds do not have regular adult supervisors, and parents, teachers, and other caretakers have little or no training in playground safety. Consequently, adults commonly allow, even encourage, very young children, including toddlers, to use equipment designed for elementary school-age children. They stand by while children engage in dangerous activity on poorly designed and maintained equipment. Helping children learn to take risks is in large part a matter of adults learning how to present and take such risks. Only then can they engage in the positive pedagogical relations proposed by Smith (1998) in terms of how to make playgrounds better for children and how to help children as they encounter the "riskiness of the playground" (p. 26).

Lack of flexibility or options for change greatly reduces the overall play value of heavy-duty equipment. Ironically, these same features increase hazards and risk of injury as children seek stimulation through using equipment in unintended ways, or by engaging in horseplay, stunting, and aggression. Both the National Program for Playground Safety (NPPS) and the Consumer Product Safety Commission (CPSC, 1997) point out the unintended ways that children use slides. The NPPS (1999) contends that "certain equipment pieces, like high tube slides, can put the child in risk if they can easily climb on the outside of the piece" (p. 2).

> *Children can be expected to descend slide chutes in many different positions, rather than always sitting and facing forward as they slide. They will slide down facing backward, on their knees, lying on their backs, head first, and will walk both up and down the chute. Younger children in particular often slide down on their stomachs, either head or feet first.* (CPSC, 1997, p. 24)

The observation that children use equipment in unintended ways "should be viewed as an inappropriate 'adult' concept of how children play and not at all representative of how we can expect children to behave" (Crawford, 1989, p. 46). Crawford concludes that "extensive retrofits of existing playground structures with excessive heights and hard undersurfaces simply must take place" (p. 47).

Playground climbers, overhead apparatus, and slides, all frequently designed and installed for achieving heights, are created primarily to facilitate motor development. However, the available studies do not support high use patterns for this equipment beyond the primary grades (Gabbard & LeBlanc, 1980; Parnell & Ketterson, 1980). As children enter the primary grades they increasingly choose organized games, occupying open spaces, and abandon over-sized playground equipment to younger children or begin using equipment in unintended ways. For example, when allowed by adult supervisors, children integrate playground equipment, especially composite or super-structures, into their chase games (Frost, Wortham, & Reifel, 2001).

While older children outgrow playgrounds, some younger children find playgrounds intimidating (Smith, 1998). Both "outgrowing" and "intimidation" can result from lack of developmentally appropriate playgrounds. Children of like chronological ages differ widely in the difficulty, danger, and challenge they are prepared to take on, and in the fears and frustrations they face on the playground. Adults must bear in mind that a child's view of risk is not the same as an adult's view. Consequently, adults must consider carefully a view of risk that is beneficial for children, and they must consider how to enable children to take risks in relative safety (Smith, 1998).

## Fear of Heights

Beginning early in infancy, fear is a powerful variable in assessing value of heights and implications of height for development. There are two major explanations for the evolution of fear. One group of scholars proposes maturational explanations for developmental changes in emotions, such as fearfulness, among children. For such theorists, the development of the neuro-physiological structures of the brain's frontal lobe precedes and accounts for changes in affect, including fear (Campos, Bertenthal, & Kermoian, 1992).

In an extensive review and analysis of the development of normal fear in children and animals, Marks (1987) found that fear in normal young children occurs in a predictable sequence, depending upon genes interacting with environment. Infants worldwide begin to experience fears at about 6 months of age. These include fears of heights, separation, strange objects, and persons. Fear of heights depends upon age and locomotion experience. With young children, fears come and go without obvious reason. The objects feared vary with development and exposure, but fears generally decline and change during the preschool years.

By age 2 months, infants perceive depth, determined by heart rate slowing, when placed on the deep side of a visual cliff (contrived for experiment). Height fear emerges at about 6 months, evidenced by speeding up of heart rate response and avoidance of height or depth. Fear appears to be related to locomotion as children begin crawling and exploring, using caregivers as secure bases. Walking also enhances fear of heights (Bertenthal, Campos, & Caplovitz, 1983).

Gottlieb (1983, 1991) proposed that psychomotor experiences, such as crawling, and other locomotor and vestibular experiences help account for emergence of fear in young children. Campos, Bertenthal, and Kermoian (1992) investigated Gottlieb's proposition of influential environmental factors and concluded that when age is held constant, locomotor experience accounts for wariness of heights, and that locomotor experience is a better predictor than age of wariness of heights. In both animals and humans, locomotion experiences may generate and refine skills, leading to wariness of heights. These skills include increased sensitivity to heights, improved ability to judge height and distance, and improved visual and vestibular coordination (Campos, Bertenthal, & Kermoian, 1992).

Infants appear to experience a phase when they show no avoidance of heights; following locomotor experiences, however, they may develop quite intense wariness of heights. Individual differences in experiences and development enter the equation for both patterns seen among infants and toddlers. These differences among children are evidenced by some children stepping off beds and furniture or even into pools of water or off vertical heights without apparent fear, while others climb to the top of playground equipment and "freeze" and scream. Experience appears to help children develop a sense of the efficacy and limitations of their actions. Children appear to need many locomotor experiences to help them cope with hazards such as heights. Yet locomotor experiences can lead to both positive and negative emotions—positive due to increased ability to succeed in locomotor tasks, and negative due to inability to cope with locomotor challenges and prohibitions from adults (Campos, Bertenthal, & Kermoian, 1992).

As locomotion becomes coordinated with the environment, infants begin to show fear of heights. Falls and near falls that occur during locomotion are important because they happen frequently, they elicit powerful emotional reactions from adults, and they set the stage for long-term affect, such as fear in future locomotor contexts (Campos, Bertenthal, & Kermoian, 1992). An apparent implication of this tenet is that children must be allowed to assume reasonable risks in order to develop cognitive and locomotor skills, yet be protected from extreme hazards due to their immaturity (Frost, 2001; Frost, Wortham, & Reifel, 2001). Even the approximately 90 percent of falls that do not result in injury may have serious consequences, possibly leading to reduction of climbing due to a resultant psychological fear of falling (Kingma & Ten Duis, 2000; Tinetti & Speechley, 1989).

Children with disabilities generally require more supervision and attention to safety than do other children. Levinson's (1989) quantitative and qualitative studies of 4,000 learning disabled children, adolescents, and adults with cerebellar-vestibular (CV) dysfunction "clearly suggests a CV determined phobic predisposition" (p. 68). Overall, 64 percent of children (7-12 years) and 57 percent of adolescents (13-18 years) expressed fears. Among children 7 to 12 years old, the number who exhibited fear of height (17 percent) was exceeded only by the number who exhibited fear of darkness (22 percent). For adolescents, fear of heights exceeded all other fears (19 percent). The findings indicated that vestibular dysfunction of learning disabled children may lead to imbalance-related fear of heights.

When attention-deficit disorder (ADD) was officially accepted in 1980 as a disorder by the American Psychiatric Association (APA) in their *Diagnostic and Statistical Manual of Mental Disorders*, thousands of mental health professionals, millions of patients, and society at large were affected (Diller, 1998). Whether one accepts biological or cultural explanations for ADD, changes are taking place among children and youth that are leading to increasing diagnoses of ADD (DeGrandpre, 1999). Growing agreement exists among health professionals that ADD places children at greater risk for accidental injury. For example, highway crashes are the biggest killer of adolescents ages 15 to 20 in America, accounting for 6,000 annual deaths (Children and Adults with Attention-Deficit/Hyperactivity Disorder, 2001). Those with ADHD are involved in traffic accidents four times more often than control subjects without the disorder and are over four times more likely to be at fault in the accidents.

The accepted symptoms of ADD indicate that children of all ages with the disorder are easily distracted, often have difficulty playing, experience trouble waiting their turn, often interrupt or intrude on others, and in general have difficulty sustaining attention (short attention spans) and controlling impulses (Diller, 1998). These characteristics of children with ADD, combined with their propensity to run and climb excessively in situations where such activity is inappropriate, place the child with ADD at greater risk for injury on playgrounds.

Both research and experience point to several levels of fear of heights among children:

abnormal fear (phobias), normal fear, and abnormal lack of fear. For very young children (e.g., infants), virtual lack of fear may be observed. Children with ADD and other disorders may be distracted or fail to perceive hazards. Such variation places considerable responsibility on adults who design, install, supervise, and maintain playgrounds used by large groups of children. Children with disabilities who are mainstreamed or placed in "least restrictive settings" may be exposed to extreme heights on playgrounds.

## History: Heights As Hazards

Awareness of the hazards presented by excessive playground equipment heights emerged shortly after manufacturers began marketing equipment to schools and public park systems during the early 1900s. This early manufactured equipment, modified from outdoor gymnastic equipment of the earliest playgrounds, consisted primarily of swings, slides, climbers, see-saws, giant strides, and horizontal bars. Much of the early equipment included slides, swings, and climbers up to 15 feet in height, many still existing on today's playgrounds.

> *The great metal structures of playgrounds from previous eras, the tall slides, the high climbers, the 20-foot swings, create unreasonable hazards for young children. Falls from these structures are long falls in which the child's speed increases, such that the resulting sudden stop on the ground is very forceful.* (Rivkin, 1995, p. 49)

As playgrounds expanded, falls and injuries became common. Hard surfacing was replacing dirt as a ground cover and serious injuries were resulting. As early as 1915, parents of a young boy sued the school board of Tacoma, Washington, over an injury their child sustained in a fall from a swing. By 1917, Curtis described American playgrounds as being in a "miserable state," and "a disgrace to the systems to which they belong" (p. 121). The surfaces were covered with pieces of bricks, piles of ashes, and gullied by rain.

In 1928, the Playground and Recreation Association of America (1928), later renamed the National Recreation Association, published *Play Areas; Their Design and Equipment*, which suggested that the height of play apparatus should be limited, especially that to be used by very small children. In response to a request by recreation authorities, the National Recreation Association (1931), a precursor of the National Recreation and Park Association, published the first standards for playground apparatus. The essential elements of these standards prescribed care of ground under equipment, dedicated equipment for the exclusive use of younger children, and heights of 8 feet for slides and 6 feet for swings for younger children.

During the 1940s and 1950s, extensive areas for play were hard-packed dirt with protruding rocks and "dust bowls." Entire park and school systems were turning to asphalt surfacing.

> *In 1951, a six-year-old boy fell from a swing onto an asphalt surface of a Los Angeles city school playground and died of head injuries. This was the last of 11 playground deaths in that school system over a twenty year period. In 1955, the Los Angeles school system purchased rubber surfacing for its playground equipment, and as of 1965 had had no further fatalities.* (Butwinick, 1974, p. 8)

In 1972, the U.S. Consumer Product Safety Commission (CPSC) was created with the passage of the Consumer Product Safety Act. The National Electronic Injury Surveillance System also was established. In that same year, a Bureau of Product Safety (1972) report, *Public Playground Equipment*, painted a dismal picture of American playgrounds; playground equipment ranked 8th on the CPSC hazard list. The CPSC commissioned the University of Iowa to collect and analyze accident/injury data from the NEISS and the National Safety Council, commissioned the University of Michigan to prepare anthropometric data, and commissioned the Franklin Institute to conduct impact tests of surfacing.

In 1974, Elayne Butwinick, an elementary school teacher and member of the National Recreation and Park Association's National Task Force on Park and Recreation Playground Equipment Safety Standards, petitioned the CPSC to issue a consumer product safety standard for public playground equipment. Based on her evaluation of 30 public school and recreation playgrounds and an analysis of 1,100 equipment accidents, she concluded that 85 percent of all accidents on climbing equipment (460 accidents) involved falls from the equipment. The few cases of death all occurred on asphalt or pavement. Sixty-three percent of slide injuries resulted from falls.

Also in 1974, Theodora Sweeney, at that time a PTA chairperson and later a playground safety consultant, petitioned the CPSC to "write a strict set of mandatory guidelines for playground equipment and surfaces." Sweeney's petition (1974) incorporated data compiled by the U.S. Bureau of Product Safety, studies by the University of Iowa, and her own research. She addressed the issue of equipment heights, stating that she was unable to locate height guidelines and concluding that the playground industry had none. She speculated from perusing equipment catalogues that "the profit motive, rather than concern for children's safety, rules the industry.... The bigger and higher the equipment, the more it costs, and the greater the profit" (p. 4). In the absence of guidelines, she devised a rule of thumb that equipment (overhead apparatus excluded) should not exceed the average height of the intended child user.

The CPSC commissioned the National Recreation and Park Association (NRPA) to develop a safety standard for playground equipment. The NRPA *Proposed Safety Standard for Public Playground Equipment* (1976) proposed that surfaces with direct fall heights of more than 8 feet and up to 12 feet have a protective barrier at least 38 inches high, completely surrounding the surface, except for necessary entry and exit openings.

## National Standards and Guidelines for Surfacing and Heights

Two primary factors are largely responsible for injuries in falls: acceleration from a height and nature of surfacing material. The topic of surfacing material is extensively reviewed in many documents, including those published by CPSC and the American Society for Testing and Materials (ASTM, 1995). Acceleration from heights should be given careful consideration because surfacing under and around equipment of heights greater than about 6 feet is frequently improperly designed, improperly installed, and/or poorly maintained. As height increases, speed of fall increases and the risk of injury increases.

The formula for acceleration from a height is:
Final Velocity = the square root of Initial Velocity + 2(Acceleration) (Distance)

The Initial Velocity may be zero. If the child is already moving, the Initial Velocity will be greater. Distance is the vertical distance from point of fall to surface impacted.

The following represents a fall from 3 feet:
Final Velocity = the square root of [2 (32' / s2) (3')] = 13.8' per second or 9.41 mph (miles per hour).

A fall from 9 feet yields 24 feet per second or 16.36 mph.

A fall from 12 feet yields 27.7 feet per second or 18.8 mph.

"It's a matter of physics. The higher the fall and harder the surface, the worse the injury" (Henzy, 2001, p. 1). The evidence that increasing height increases probability for serious injury or death in falls leads virtually every major agency responsible for playground safety to recommend meeting the CPSC Head Injury Criteria (HIC), and/or to restrict the height of equipment.

The CPSC (1997) and the ASTM (1995) focus on provision of resilient surfacing under and around playground equipment to reduce the likelihood of head injuries in falls. Two methods were established to estimate the threshold tolerance of the human head to an impact injury. One holds that if the peak deceleration of the head during impact does not exceed 200 times the acceleration due to gravity (200 G's), a life-threatening injury is not likely to occur. The second method holds that both the deceleration of the head during impact and the time duration over which the head decelerates to a halt are significant in assessing potential for head impact injury. This value, derived by mathematical formula, is called the Head Injury Criteria (HIC). If the HIC is less than 1,000, the impact injury is not believed to be life threatening.

The CPSC (1997, pp. 4) defines "critical height" as: "The fall height below which a life-threatening head injury would not be expected to occur." This term is used to describe the shock absorbing performance of a surfacing material. The critical height of a surfacing material is defined (CPSC, 1997, p. 6) as the maximum height from which an instrumented headform, upon impact, yields both a peak deceleration of no more than 200 G's and a HIC of no more than 1,000. The headform is an instrument shaped like a human head that measures the force of impact when it hits the ground. The procedure for this test is described in ASTM F355-95.

The CPSC (1997) identifies the fall heights, the distance from the intended playing surface, for various types of playground equipment. For example, the fall height of a swing structure is the height of the pivot point where the swing's suspending elements connect to the supporting structure. The fall height of a composite structure or superstructure is the height of the platform or deck, and the fall height of overhead equipment (e.g., horizontal ladder) is the maximum height of overhead apparatus from the ground or surfacing below. There are certain problems with these estimates, however. For example, identifying the fall height of slides as the height of the platform or deck (designated play surface) leading to the entry of the slide is misleading, for the platforms and decks are enclosed by protective barriers, typically 38 inches high, except for entry stairs. Consequently, the actual fall height of slides, including the taller ones (e.g., 12 feet to 14 feet), is the height of the platform or deck plus 38 inches. This results in an actual fall height of 15 feet 2 inches from a 12-foot slide.

The CPSC (1997) commissioned independent testing laboratories to conduct tests for critical heights (in feet) of various surfacing materials. The testing laboratories tested seven materials at 6-inch, 9-inch, and 12-inch uncompressed depths and 9-inch compressed depths. In practice, only compressed depths are relevant because "uncompressed" materials quickly become "compressed" materials as children play on them. Only two materials, wood chips and double shredded bark mulch, had critical heights of 10 feet when installed 9 inches deep in a compressed state. That is, during falls onto these materials from heights greater than 10 feet, a life-threatening injury could be expected to occur. The most common surfacing materials, sand and gravel, had critical heights ranging from 4 feet to 6 feet for surfacing of 9-inch compressed depths.

The CPSC also provides test results for shredded tires at 6-inch uncompressed depths. Shredded tires, unlike wood chips, sand, and gravel, tend to suffer less compression during use. The critical height of 10 to 12 feet makes shredded tires the top performer in CPSC tests. Shredded tires are rarely seen in park, school, and child care center playgrounds.

Manufactured materials (e.g., mats, poured surfaces) were not tested by CPSC, but some manufacturers have conducted laboratory tests for their materials (e.g., No Fault Industries, Inc.). Most manufacturers offer to help consumers/purchasers develop a surfacing plan that complies with CPSC and ASTM surfacing guidelines. A sample plan by a major manufacturer specifies 2-1/2-inch-thick mats for falls up to 6 feet and 1-5/8-inch-thick mats for falls up to 4 feet (Kompan, Inc., 1996). Robertson Industries, Inc., states that their resilient rubberized "TotTurf" "reduces the impact of a falling child at 5 to 10 feet, yet is firm enough to support wheelchair access." Such manufactured materials are so expensive, however, that they are most frequently seen in theme parks and selected city parks. Their use in public schools and child care centers generally is restricted to limited areas for wheelchair access.

The Consumer Federation of America (1992, p. 18) stipulates that the fall height of climbing equipment and slides shall not exceed 7 feet above the protective surfacing for school-age children and 6 feet above the protective surfacing for preschool-age children. Furthermore, they stipulate that the fall height of each play event shall not be higher than the critical height of the protective surfacing under and around the equipment. The CFA later modified these heights to a maximum fall height of 6 feet for school-age children for climbing equipment and slides, and a maximum of 4 feet for preschool-age children (CFA, 1996a). They also recommended that swing heights (height of the crossbeam) be limited to 8 feet (CFA, 1996b).

*Surfacing materials, even though they may be resilient, will not provide adequate protection unless their impact-absorbing qualities are sufficient for the highest accessible part of the play event.* (CFA, 1992, p. 13)

*It is recommended that the Critical Height of a surfacing material exceed the fall height of the equipment under which it is being installed by at least 2 feet, as an added precaution against serious and potentially life-threatening injuries and injuries, such as limb fracture, which may occur with less impact.* (CFA, 1992, p. 14)

*It is recommended that the fall height of swing structures with conventional, to-fro seats not exceed 10 feet above the protective surfacing when designed for school-age children or 8 feet above the protective surfacing when designed for preschool-age children, as an added precaution against serious fall injuries.* (CFA, 1992, p. 19)

The CFA (1996, p. 29) later recommended that all swings—to-fro, infant-tot, and tire swings—not exceed 8 feet above the protective surfacing.

The American Public Health Association and the American Academy of Pediatrics standards (1992) stipulate that the maximum height of playground equipment shall be no greater than 5-1/2 feet for children up to the age of 6 and no higher than 3 feet if the maximum age of children using it is 3 years.

The National Recreation and Park Association (Kutska & Hoffman, 1992) recommends in their Playground Safety Audit Form that slides should be no more than 8 feet high, accessible equipment height (platform, deck, etc.) should not exceed 4 feet for 2- to 5-year-old users, and protective surfacing should pass the 200 G ASTM 1292 test.

## Play Equipment Height Research

Chalmers et al. (1996) evaluated the effectiveness of the height and surfacing requirements of the New Zealand Standard for Playgrounds and Playground Equipment (1986; NZS 5828). Data were collected on 300 children, age 14 years or younger, who had been injured in falls to the ground or surface from playground equipment. Of these, 110 children had received medical attention for their injuries and 190 (controls) had injuries not requiring medical attention. The ages of children were 0-4 (38 cases), 5-9 (220 cases), and 10-12 (42 cases).

Structured interviews were conducted with children, parents or caregivers, teachers, and witnesses. Data were collected on gender, age, height, weight, date and time, place of occurrence, type of equipment, height of fall, type of surface, particle size, depth, retention of loose fill materials, and body part to hit first.

Logistic regression models indicated that the odds of injury increased with increases in height of falls and that a marked increase occurred when children fell 1.5 to 2.0 meters. Increasing risk with increasing height of falls was similar for both impact absorbing and non-impact absorbing surfaces. Falls from heights in excess of 1.5 meters increased the risk of injury 4.1 times that of falls from 1.5 meters of less. Non-compliance with the requirement that no child should fall from a height exceeding the critical drop height of the surfacing material was estimated to increase the odds of being injured by at least 2.13 times.

Chalmers and colleagues concluded that 39 percent of cases failed to meet the New Zealand safe fall height requirements, either through absence of impact-absorbing surface or by exceeding the maximum height (2.5 meters) specified in the standard. They also concluded that the height and surfacing requirements of the New Zealand standard are effective in preventing injury in falls from playground equipment. A significant proportion of playgrounds, however, did not comply with surfacing and height requirements. It was estimated that a 45 percent reduction in injuries requiring emergency room treatment could be achieved by reducing maximum fall height of equipment from the present New Zealand standard maximum height of 2.5 meters to 1.5 meters.

Although Chalmers's study makes a strong case for limiting heights of playground equipment and for meeting the critical drop height of surfacing materials, his recommendation for limiting heights to 1.5 meters begs further study. This limitation would pose significant problems with regard to retrofitting existing equipment that exceeds this height limitation. Furthermore, while such a restriction may be appropriate for preschool children, overhead apparatus (e.g., horizontal ladders, ring treks, track rides) would not function for school-age children at this low height. Studies of the effect of such restrictive heights would be needed to assess the impact on developmental benefits for children, particularly in the areas of controlled risk, motor and cognitive challenge, and novelty. Nevertheless, reducing injuries by meeting the critical drop heights of surfacing remains an important issue to be addressed by consumers, installers, and manufacturers. The available evidence confirms that complying with the commonly ignored critical height standards or guidelines would have the effect of reducing fall heights and, consequently, reducing injuries.

A case control study of children (n =126) injured in falls from playground equipment in 1995-1996 was conducted at the Hospital for Sick Children in Toronto (Macarthur, Hu, Wesson, & Parkin, 2000). Children with severe injuries, predominantly fractures, were compared with controls with minor injuries, predominantly facial lacerations. The median height of falls was 199 cm (6.47 feet) for severe cases and 160 cm (5.20 feet) for minor cases. Children suffering severe injuries were more likely to have fallen from heights greater than 150 cm (73 percent), compared with those suffering minor injuries (54 percent). The majority of all cases fell onto impact-absorbing undersurfaces, but the median depth was only 3 cm (1.17 inches). "Height of fall was an important risk factor for severe injury associated with falls from playground equipment. Above 150 cm (4.88 feet) the risk of severe injury was increased 2-fold" (Macarthur et al., 2000).

All supracondylar humerus fractures in children treated at Children's Hospital and Health Center, San Diego, over an 8-year period (n=391) were reviewed to secure information about the manner in which these injuries occurred. Girls sustained these injuries more frequently than boys and the non-dominant arm was more often injured. Seventy percent of the fractures resulted in falls from heights. Children 3 years old or younger tended to fall off household objects and children 4 years and older tended to fall from playground equipment, such as monkey bars, slides, and swings (Farnsworth, Silva, & Mubarak, 1998).

Researchers conducted a correlational study of the safety of different playground surfaces, and types and heights of equipment, in public playgrounds in the City of Cardiff, United Kingdom. The subjects were 330 children between 0 and 14 years of age treated at the Accident and Emergency Department I Cardiff Royal Infirmary during the summers of 1992 and 1993. Children's hospital records and interviews with parents indicated that playgrounds with rubber surfaces had the lowest rate of injury, with a risk half that of bark and one-fifth that of concrete. "The height of the equipment correlated significantly with the number of fractures ($p<0.005$) from falls. . . . Our data suggest that the proposed raising of the maximum fall height from 2.5 m (8.20 feet) to 3.0 m (9.84 feet) in Europe is worrying" (Mott et al., 1997).

Laforest, Robitaille, Lesage, and Dorval (2001) evaluated conformity of play equipment to Canadian standards in a random sample (102) of Montreal public playgrounds. Height of equipment was measured and surface absorption (g-max) was tested, using a Max HIC instrument. During the study period, injuries at two children's hospitals in Montreal were recorded and parents of the injured children were interviewed. The conclusions follow:

*This study confirms the relationships between risk of injury, surface resilience, and height of equipment, as well as between type of material and severity of injury. Our data suggest that acceptable limits for surface resilience be set at less than 200g, and perhaps even less than 150g, and not exceed 2 meters for equipment height.* (Laforest et al., 2001, p. 9)

## Conclusions of Playground Safety Professionals in Professional Books and Journals

A number of playground safety professionals who work extensively throughout the United States and in foreign countries have published conclusions about playground equipment heights. These professionals work with cities, schools, and agencies in playground evaluation and design, speak at national and international conferences, help develop national playground standards, and assist law firms in child injury and fatality litigation resulting from playground accidents.

The records of playground safety professionals who work in child injury litigation represent the most extensive case studies available, because many have served as consultants and/or expert witnesses in 100 to 500 lawsuits. In a single injury case, each expert routinely reads numerous depositions, police reports, eyewitness reports, maintenance records, design and installation records, and conducts extensive inspections of injury sites, interviews adult witnesses and injured children, writes reports, and testifies in deposition and at trial. The National Electronic Injury Surveillance System (NEISS) collects data for a greater number of injuries, but their process does not approach the depth of the analyses conducted by litigation experts.

Frost and Sweeney (1996) conducted case studies of 177 injuries and 13 fatalities occurring on playgrounds in 38 states and the District of Columbia. They were consultants to law firms involved in these cases and had access to a very broad array of data for each case. Typically, injuries leading to lawsuits are very serious injuries involving long-term or permanent impairment. Specific data are available in the published document, but a typical, generalized case profile follows:

*A seriously injured male child between the ages of 2 and 8 who fell from a slide, swing or climber onto concrete, asphalt or hard-packed earth while playing at a public school, public park or child care center playground. The child suffered a broken limb or head injury, resulting in litigation that endured for two to four years before being settled out of court. The agreement usually favored the plaintiff.* (Frost & Sweeney, 1996, p. 14)

The factors most commonly implicated in these very serious injuries and fatalities were excessive heights and inappropriate surfacing. That is, heights of falls exceeded the ability of surfacing to protect children in falls. This hazardous ratio resulted from improper surfacing, insufficient depth, inadequate maintenance, and excessive heights. Ninety-three percent of the cases represented violations of CPSC and ASTM recommendations. While supervision was an issue in most of the cases, the apparent primary cause of injuries was violation of equipment and surfacing safety fundamentals.

A wide range of variables affecting potential injury resulting from falls from heights precludes clear agreement among professionals regarding maximum heights of climbing structures. These include chronological age, skill development, type of equipment, and nature of surfacing. Readdick and Park (1998) specify one foot of height for every year of age. For example, 3-year-olds can climb three feet and 5-year-olds can climb five feet. For older children, they propose that the adult's comfort level and children's level of movement competence and confidence be the primary determinants of equipment height.

Prior to the first publication of the CPSC *Handbook for Public Playground Safety* (1981), commentaries on the handbook were invited. With respect to height, the review and commentary by Frost (1980) on a proposed photograph of a slide stated:

> *The structure in Figure 13 is of extremely poor design from a safety perspective. The child must climb poorly protected steps for a considerable height (12' to 18') to reach an enclosure that has no function except as a holding area for sliding. There is no apparent play or exercise advantage in utilizing heights that exceed the child's jumping reach from ground level. Climbing a six-foot ladder twice equals climbing a twelve-foot ladder once and does so minus the hazard of falls from extreme heights.* (Frost, 1980, p. 6)

> *There appears to be no useful purpose in manufacturing equipment with use areas (e.g., decks) that far exceed the users' reach when standing on the ground. Decks need to be high enough for taller users to walk under without stooping over. (Decks also cover space to be used for dramatic play.) Slides attached to such heights provide sufficient height (given appropriate angle of decline) to provide excitement and challenge. The only apparent factor added by increasing slide heights is* extended *excitement. Children have the option of repeating the slide action if additional excitement is desired. Because of the increase in hazards with increased height and the absence of any meaningful rationale for extreme heights, the maximum height of equipment should not exceed the standing reach height (arms vertically extended) of the taller expected users. Height of equipment as used here means the tallest point where children would stand or walk (e.g., platform or deck) and does not refer to the height of guard-rails. Equipment height for devices that require jumping (e.g., horizontal ladders) would obviously be a few inches taller than this maximum. The maximum height for equipment use zones (platforms, decks, etc.) should be about seven feet regardless of age group.* (Frost, 1980, p. 15)

The data suggest that the height/surfacing issue is the most important factor in ensuring safe play on playgrounds:

> *The farther the child falls, the faster he falls and, potentially, the more damaging the result. The addition of shock-absorbing surfacing helps to protect children in falls, but the best surfacing loses its protective qualities under equipment exceeding a certain height. Consequently, climbing equipment must not encourage or allow climbing heights that exceed the cushioning properties of the surface below.* (Frost, 1992, p. 228)

Despite virtually universal acceptance of these tenets and their application to guidelines and standards worldwide, the combined hazard of excessive heights and excessive surface hardness (too high, too hard) continues to be the most common error in playground safety.

*Given the injury data for falls, the great variation in protection offered by protective surfaces, and the virtually universal disregard for playground maintenance, the fall height limit of 8 feet seems more reasonable than greater heights for older children (school age). For pre-primary school age, heights should be more severely limited. In general, potential fall heights from equipment should not exceed by more than a few inches the reaching height of child users when standing erect on the protective surface underneath the equipment. In addition to reduction of likelihood of injury, this specification would also allow decks of sufficient height for children to stand erect underneath and use the under-deck areas for dramatic play.* (Frost, 1992, p. 229)

The most extensive review of playground safety research and expert opinion on record was conducted by the Comsis Corporation (Ratte, Denham, & Johnson, 1990). Having reviewed the research available prior to 1990, Comsis recommended conforming to the ASTM standards for testing playground surfacing. They concluded that the highest accessible part of swings should be equivalent to the maximum height of its support structure. The highest accessible part of slides and climbers should be the maximum height above ground of the guardrail or protective barrier, rather than the maximum height of the platform itself. For older and younger children, the recommended maximum heights for upper body devices are 6.7 feet and 4.7 feet, respectively.

Comsis (Ratte et al., 1990) recommended that the highest accessible part of equipment as defined above (e.g., ground to top of protective barrier) not exceed 10 feet above the surface for school-age children (ages 5-12) or 7 feet for preschool-age children (ages 2-5). The maximum fall heights recommended would effectively limit the height of elevated surfaces to 82 inches for older children and 55 inches for younger children. These heights correspond to the vertical grip reach of the maximum reaching height for each age group (78.2 inches for a 95th percentile 12-year-old; 53.9 inches for a 95th percentile 5-year-old). The most conservative method for determining the maximum fall height from equipment, adding the maximum user's height to that of the highest accessible part of the equipment, was rejected by Comsis. This method would leave insufficient deck height or overhead apparatus height for play function.

With respect to the issue of whether height, per se, is an important factor in determining play value or promoting development, Comsis concluded that "additional height is not necessary for the play or developmental value of equipment" (p. 5.1-31).

## National Surveys of Playgrounds

National surveys of playgrounds have been conducted and published by three different organizations: the American Alliance for Health, Physical Education, Recreation, and Dance (AAHPERD), the Consumer Federation of America (CFA), and the National Program for Playground Safety (NPPS). Volunteer professionals were trained at national professional conferences, and interrater reliability was established before the surveys.

The AAHPERD published three surveys in book form: one of elementary school playgrounds (Bruya & Langendorfer, 1988), a second of public park playgrounds (Thompson & Bowers, 1989), and a third of preschool playgrounds (Wortham & Frost, 1990). The elementary school playground survey included 206 playgrounds in 23 states. The average maximum height for climbing equipment (944 structures) in this survey was 9.3 feet, with

30 percent of the structures over 12 feet in height. Thirty percent of the 300 slides had maximum heights of 10 to 11 feet and 10 percent were higher than 11 feet.

The AAHPERD survey of community park playgrounds included 198 playgrounds in 18 states. The average maximum height of climbing equipment (426 structures) was 7.4 feet, with 18 percent more than 10 feet high. Eight percent of the slides were more than 11 feet high, 14 percent exceeded 10 feet high, and 32 percent were more than 8 feet high. "This information regarding excessive height when coupled with the under surface data . . . represents a troubling scenario. . . . Slide heights of ten feet and greater and hard impact surfaces underneath slide structures seem unnecessarily precarious and negligent" (Thompson & Bowers, 1989, p. 41). Crawford (1989), a contributor to this AAHPERD volume, concluded, "Extensive retrofits of existing playground structures with excessive heights and hard undersurfaces simply must take place. Today's generation of children are clearly at physical risk from these high structures and hazardous installations" (p. 4).

The AAHPERD survey of preschool center playgrounds (Wortham & Frost, 1990) was conducted by trained professionals on 349 playgrounds in 31 states. The average maximum height of climbing equipment (1,046 structures) was 5 feet 4 inches. Thirty-nine percent of the climbing equipment was more than 6 feet high and 14 percent was more than 8 feet high. The average maximum height of slides was 5 feet 5 inches. The researchers concluded:

> Height is a critical factor because the farther the child falls, the more likely the child will be injured. . . . The height of equipment should not exceed the capacity of the installed surface to protect the child in a fall. European standards restrict climbing heights to 8 to 9 feet. [Author's note: The later European Standard (CEN, 1998) limited free fall heights to 3 meters.] The CPSC guidelines do not specify a maximum height. Given the number of injuries resulting from falls, the poor maintenance of playgrounds, and the improper surfacing existing on playgrounds, the maximum fall height for children should not exceed the European standard. Fall heights should be reduced for younger age groups. A general rule of thumb is that equipment fall heights should not exceed by more than a few inches the reaching height of children when standing on the protective surface underneath the equipment. (Wortham & Frost, 1990, p. 35)

National surveys of playgrounds conducted by the U.S. Public Interest Research Group and the Consumer Federation of America (Mierzwinski, Fise, & Morrison, 1996; Sikes, Fise, & Morrison, 1992; Wood, Fise, & Morrison, 1994), examined whether limiting heights would limit fun, challenge, and play value. Wood et al. (1994) concluded that "increasing the height of the equipment does not necessarily increase challenge or play value, it always increases hazard" (p. 10). They warn that older children's boldness in experimenting with creative climbing techniques may explain in part the finding that children over 6 are the group most frequently injured in falls from climbers. Falls from the top of slides, from slide platforms, from the top portion of slide chutes, and from slide ladders are also common. Slides have higher rates of head injuries than other types of equipment.

Taking play value into account, the CFA Parent Checklist (Wood et al., 1994) states: "Platforms for climbing equipment and slides should not exceed 7 feet for school-age children or 6 feet for preschool-age children" (Appendix C). In their *Fifth Nationwide Survey of Public Playgrounds* (Press Release, 2000), the CFA concluded:

*In 2000, 48% of playgrounds had climbers and 36% had slides where the height of the play equipment is greater than 6 feet high, which is higher than necessary for play value, and only serves to increase the risk of injury.*

Between 1998 and 2000, the National Program for Playground Safety (NPPS) (Hudson, Mack, & Thompson, 2000) conducted surveys of 3,052 school, park, and child care playgrounds in all 50 U.S. states. Overall, the nation's playgrounds received a grade of C, with the best (in Arizona) receiving a grade of B+ and the two worst (in Florida and Michigan) receiving grades of D-. The surveys concluded that surfacing was not at the proper depth or in the proper use zones in over half the playgrounds, thus increasing the probability of injuries in falls. In personal interviews, Thompson and Hudson of the NPPS recommended that the maximum height of play equipment should not exceed 8 feet.

## INTERVIEWS OF PLAY EXPERTS ON HEIGHT ISSUES: STUDY ONE

In 2001, experts from the fields of education, child development, kinesiology, playground design, and play-related litigation provided their opinions regarding the relationship between children's play and the heights of outdoor manufactured playground equipment. They were asked, either during one-on-one interviews in person, over the phone, or through E-mail, to answer these questions:

- Why do children climb? (e.g., peer pressure, inherent need)
- Should there be a maximum climbing height for play equipment?
- Should height be measured from the top of protective barriers?
- How does height influence degree of injury?

The interview participants presented a wide range of opinions as to why children are motivated to climb to higher and higher places. David Gallahue, a professor at Indiana University, explained that children, much like adults, climb for the sheer pleasure of the challenge that the activity presents. As a former mountain climber, he recalled that he spent his childhood trying to climb any and all objects. Children, Gallahue said, "choose to climb because of the challenge, the sense of danger, and the sense of being able to survey all about them from the 'top of the mountain.'" Rusty Keeler of Planet Earth Playscapes stated that children climb for challenge, new perspectives, testing their physically developing skills, and the feeling of accomplishment they receive from reaching climbing milestones. Thomas Bowler, a specialist in playground litigation, also believes that children climb for the risk and thrill of it, and for the different perspectives that height can offer. He pointed out that some children climb as high as they can because they are forbidden to do so.

Peter Heseltine, Vice President of the International Play Association and the England representative for the Association, agreed with Gallahue about the sense of danger: "Children love to climb and be high because it is scary and it presents them the feeling of danger and risk." On the other hand, Paul Hogan, consultant and former President of the International Play Association USA, stated that children actually climb for security and curiosity. He believes that "all animals climb when they have the ability. This is a basic inherent instinct to rise above the perils of the jungle floor. All animals who can climb do so to observe their terrain, look for enemies, food, and new adventurers."

Others interviewed expressed the opinion that children possess not only a propensity but also a need to climb. Carl Gabbard, a health and kinesiology professor at Texas A&M University, stated that climbing is an "inherent exploratory event" and is "part of their need to seek and explore the environment." Similar opinions were presented by Donna Thompson and Sue Hudson, both from the National Program for Playground Safety: Children possess a natural inclination to climb. Thompson and Hudson further explain that children have no fear of going up. The fear is in coming down. Children, they say, lack the cognitive ability to know how to get down from the exciting heights to which they are able to climb.

Just as explanations as to why children climb vary, there is no consensus in opinion regarding whether there should be maximum climbing heights for outdoor play equipment. Gabbard and Gallahue both answered "certainly," and gave explanations of safety needs to support their answer. Neither indicated what that maximum height should be. Thompson, Hudson, and Bowler specified a maximum height of eight feet, citing data demonstrating a dramatic increase in serious injuries sustained by children falling from greater heights. Hogan expressed the opinion that those manufacturing equipment over 12-feet high are "out of their heads."

Conversely, Heseltine answered that height is irrelevant and it is the fall that should be discussed. "Play structures should be designed in a way that prevents falls of greater than a meter and a half (i.e., 4.5 feet). A slide can be as high as this ceiling (approximately 40-50 feet) as long as a child falls no farther than a meter and a half." Tom Jambor, a consultant and retired Associate Professor of Early Childhood Development from the University of Alabama at Birmingham, stated that "height is perception." For example, a structure 20-feet high with graduated landscaping might be no more than 4 feet off the ground at any point. Keeler also believes that high equipment can be designed to be very safe for children, and that a maximum height for equipment does not need to be imposed.

The above responses represent different perceptions of the question: Should there be a maximum climbing height for play equipment? Some responses were addressed to fall height (vertical distance of highest possible fall from equipment) and others related to equipment height (difference in elevation from ground entry to highest point on equipment). Despite these differences in interpretation, none of the responses indicated that children should be exposed to extreme fall heights.

The third question posed to the participants closely mirrored the question regarding maximum heights. Currently, ASTM standards and CPSC guidelines require fall height or critical height to be measured vertically from the ground surface to the play structure's deck or platform. However, if children are naturally inclined to climb to the highest point possible, it seems more accurate to measure the height of playground equipment from the ground to the uppermost part of the protective barrier or railing. Gallahue and Keeler agreed. "Children," Gallahue said, ". . . will find new and ever more challenging ways of using the equipment, making measurement from the top-most possible point a realistic means of calculating height."

Keeler stated that the rail is "where the children are falling from, and that [height] should determine what kind of surfacing is necessary for the play area." Bowler agreed, although he gave another caveat. Throughout the years he has been involved in playground litigation, he has experienced cases in which falls could have permanent results. He explains that "the true fall height when we're talking about head injury is the height of the platform, plus the height of the railing, plus the height of the child." He maintains that this measurement would give the most accurate indication of how far a child's head falls before it impacts the ground.

Thompson and Hudson, however, disagree. According to them, the protective barriers that enclose decks and platforms above ground level are not considered play spaces and therefore should not be included in the height measurement. They believe that railings should be built so that children cannot climb on them. They agree with the current ASTM standards and CPSC guidelines regarding calculating height. Furthermore, they contend that falls from protective barriers are most likely the result of poor supervision rather than poor safety regulations.

Finally, interview participants commented on how height influences the degree of injury sustained in falls. All responses were similar: added height increases impact of force; the higher the height, the more protective surfacing is needed (although at some point surfacing becomes ineffective for protection against serious injury); and the greater the height, the greater the risk for more severe injury. As Bowler states, "There is a direct relationship between height and injury."

In summary, experts agree that:

- Children, when given the opportunity, will climb as high as possible.
- Increasing heights increases the potential for serious injury ("the higher you climb, the harder you fall").
- There was no clear agreement among those interviewed on whether the height of manufactured play equipment should be limited. Some focused on fall heights, contending that they should be limited. Others focused on equipment heights, contending that equipment height could be unlimited—assuming that fall height was controlled. None of the experts contended that fall height should be unlimited.

Sue Hudson explained that increasing the height of playground equipment does nothing to increase its play value. "A slide is still a slide at 4, 8, or 28 feet." It is better, she says, to make tasks more complex and challenging at safe heights than to simply increase the height of equipment, which does nothing to increase its complexity. She stated that each piece of equipment must be analyzed for the specific challenge it presents, and that more complex challenges are needed. From the NPPS perspective, simply making play equipment taller instead of making it more innovative and challenging is not beneficial for children, and increasing heights increases risks for serious injury.

## OBSERVATIONS OF CHILDREN ENGAGED IN CLIMBING: STUDY TWO

### PURPOSE

Children often play in play environments with manufactured play equipment. Over the last three decades, parents and safety advocates collaborated to reduce the number of injuries and deaths associated with play equipment. One area of ambiguity relevant to children's safety is the issue of height for playground equipment. The purpose of this study

Jonesville City Park

LaPorte City Park

Baker Municipal Water Park

Beau's Seafood

was to examine children's free play behaviors while using high playground components (often in excess of 10 feet) in naturalistic play settings.

## QUESTIONS

In order to determine appropriate height for playground equipment, it is important to know whether the play value of height is overcome by the risk associated with increased height. The questions for this study were based on two central tenets: 1) there is play value in climbing on playground components, and 2) there is risk associated with climbing. These two central tenets were explored by answering the following questions:

> Why do children climb? (Peer pressure? Inherent tendency?)
> How do children use (and misuse) high equipment?
> What emotions do children express while climbing very tall equipment?
> What is the nature of adult involvement on playgrounds?
> What hazards are present when children climb very tall equipment?
> Should height be measured from the top of guardrails and protective barriers?
> Should there be a maximum climbing height for play equipment?

## METHODOLOGY

### Observations

In order to answer the questions above, observations were conducted of children on playground equipment with higher than typical equipment (upper decking 10 feet or more high). The observations were conducted by two trained graduate student observers. A coding sheet was developed to structure the observations (see Appendix). An observation session was conducted using the common coding sheet to calibrate interrater reliability between the two observers (95 percent reliability was reached). The observations were recorded as anecdotal notes on the children's use of the target equipment. The observations were conducted over a three-week period, with a total of 14 observations completed at four different sites.

### Settings

Four sites with tall play equipment were selected: 1) a modern restaurant play structure, 2) a modern city park play structure, 3) a 30-year-old city park play structure, and 4) a modern water slide. Of the 14 observations, randomly scheduled, six were conducted at the restaurant play structure (Beau's Seafood), four at the modern city park play structure (Jonesville City Park), two at the older city park (La Porte City Park), and two at the water slide (Baker Municipal Water Park).

Beau's Seafood featured a play structure with two 10-foot (deck height), 720-degree, enclosed tube slides connected via an enclosed tube bridge. The surfacing was sand, mostly compacted, at a depth of 4-10 inches, on top of compacted earth. The structure was designed as an enclosed play structure (with upper decks surrounded by 5-foot vertical pole barriers spaced 3 inches apart). Once the upper deck is entered, the children cannot egress except to go down the slide or return down a 5-foot vertical ladder. Two 5-foot straight slides are positioned at the lower decks on either end of the play structure.

Children accessed unintended parts of the play structure.

The Jonesville City Park consisted of several play areas: 1) a toddler play area containing three spring rockers, tot swings, two composite structures, and a merry-go-round; 2) an organized game area of volleyball courts, tennis courts, and a basketball court; 3) a primary-age play area with a merry-go-round, tire swing, a series of overhead ladders, and a composite structure with four climbers (two ladders, an arch climber, and a chain climber) and four slides (two open spiral slides, a straight slide, and a tube slide). The tallest slide and the focus of this play structure was an enclosed tube slide, measured at 12 feet to the bottom of the deck from the surfacing in place (pea gravel averaging 6-8 inches in depth).

The Baker Municipal Water Park play area consisted of a number of pools and diving boards, water guns, a composite structure with climbers, and open decks with such water equipment as dumping buckets and water geysers. The focal piece of equipment was a 30-foot-tall water slide. The entrances to the slides were reached by climbing a set of stairs to the top deck. From the deck there were two possible slide options: a closed tube slide and an open spiral slide. A lifeguard was stationed at the top and bottom of the slides. There were no fall zones or surfacing around any of this equipment.

The LaPorte City Park consisted of three separate play areas: 1) a toddler play area with an accessible play structure, toddler swings, and a stand-alone slide; 2) an organized games area, which consisted of baseball fields and tennis courts; and 3) an older play structure area. The primary observation was of the older section (around 30 years old), which consisted of four pieces of large cast iron equipment in the shape of a flying saucer, a submarine, a satellite station, and a 25-foot-tall rocket with an 8-foot-tall slide. The equipment was freshly painted in red and white, in good condition, surrounded by a fall zone of sand about 8 inches deep. The rocket slide had four levels connected by ladders that rose through holes cut in the floor. Each deck was about 5 feet tall and about 4 feet in diameter. The second deck had a straight metal slide that exited from one side. The top level had a steering device, which presented a pinch and crush hazard because of wear over the years.

## FINDINGS

### Why Do Children Climb?

Children climbed the equipment at all settings. They appeared to find great play value in climbing. They seemed to enjoy observing from extreme heights and derived satisfaction from the climbing experience itself. They also enjoyed sliding because of the feeling of falling that is associated with slides. The motivation behind climbing appears to change as the child experiences climbing the particular equipment. Generally, three climbing phases may be identified: climbing to explore, climbing with a purpose, and climbing to play.

The first phase of climbing is exploration. Generally, younger children would climb without any apparent goal in mind except to climb to the highest level possible. Frequently, children as young as 20-24 months old climbed the equipment to the maximum height in this exploratory manner. Exploration also occurred with older children when encountering a piece of equipment for the first time. The rocket slide at LaPorte City Park was fairly unique to the children. As children climbed the structure in an exploratory manner, they would reach the top and then climb back down. Exploration also occurred as children tried to climb equipment in more challenging ways: climbing up the slides, climbing on top of the tube slides, or climbing on the outside of the equipment. Such exploration often happened when a child who was engaged in solitary play tried to find a more challenging way to climb the equipment.

The second phase of climbing, climbing with a purpose, typically was observed as the children attempted to reach a play event like a slide. Climbing for a purpose was common on all play structures. Climbing the steps to the top of the water slide was more a function of reaching the slides than part of the play experience. This occurred on the other equipment as well; the tube slides and the rocket slide were all placed at a point where the children had to climb to reach them. Climbing at this point became secondary to the end result of sliding down the slide.

Finally, children would climb as part of a play experience. This play experience could be dramatic in nature. One child spoke of climbing "to outer space" while climbing the rocket slide, and then said, "I'm going to outer space and driving." This was an example of reaching a height in order to achieve a dramatic experience. In another example, children at the Jonesville City Park brought a sword and scabbard to the playground and climbed the play structure to pretend while fighting with the sword. Climbing added to the dramatic experience by increasing the excitement of the sword fighting game.

Children frequently climbed the play structure as part of a chase game. Chase was common on all of the play structures except the water slide, where chasing was stopped by the lifeguards. Generally, children older than 4 had enough experience on the play equipment to participate in chase games. The chase games usually involved children climbing the equipment and sliding down in order to escape other children. See Clarke (1999) for an exploration of the developmental levels of chase games.

**Peer Pressure and Climbing**

Peer pressure occurred in all three phases of climbing. There was pressure for children to climb higher in order to explore the equipment; this occurred on the Beau's Seafood slide, where children imitated other children's climbing. Peer pressure also influenced the use of a particular slide. At the Baker Municipal Water Park slide, two 6-year-old boys who enjoyed the slide challenged a third to use the slide, although he was uncertain that he wanted to do so. Peer pressure was observed frequently in chase games as children climbed to escape the chaser. This also involved climbing up slides or stopping in the middle of sliding and climbing back up the slide. In one case, a child climbed the outside of a tube slide in order to be at a place where the chaser could not reach him. Interestingly, parents sometimes encouraged children to climb equipment. Parents appear to be interested in having their children become experienced climbers and pressured their children to try climbing to higher parts of the equipment.

Based on the review of existing research and field observations, children have some degree of innate desire to climb to the highest possible point, whether in a tree or on playground equipment. This climbing occurs in developmental phases as the child gains experience. Competition with peers also influences and promotes climbing.

## How Do Children Use (and Misuse) Equipment?

Children used the equipment as intended at all the play spaces. Intended use is defined as the types of use for which the manufacturer designed the play equipment. Unintended use, or misuse of equipment, also occurred at all play spaces except the water park. Unintended use is defined as the types of use for which manufacturers did not design the play equipment. At the water park, close supervision by the lifeguards kept the children from using the equipment in unintended ways.

Unintended use of the equipment included very young children accessing the equipment, as well as older children climbing up the slides, stopping in the middle of 720-degree tube slides, sliding down the slide at the same time as another child, climbing on the outside of the slides, climbing the support or enclosure structures on the outside of the equipment, sitting on the protective barriers, and sliding down the protective barriers.

The enclosed play structure at Beau's Seafood offered numerous opportunities for children to access the outside of a structure by climbing components that were designed to eliminate such usage. In six out of six randomly scheduled observations, children were climbing on the outside of this play structure to the highest point (13 feet), where they could sit or lie down. They would climb the exterior of the tube slide and lie down at the top or, without any footholds, shimmy up the outside of the enclosed upper deck with alternating hand grips on the vertical bars of the protective barrier. They then would climb laterally to access the top of a tube bridge, the highest point where they could sit down. The youngest children observed climbing in such a way were 7 years old. A 5-year-old also was observed several times shimmying up the vertical bars in like fashion for four feet with relative ease, but did not climb to the highest point. One 4-year-old was seen shimmying, with hands and legs, up and down an eight-foot vertical pole that supports the tube slide. Any falls from the equipment almost certainly would be onto the structures protruding below, or, in some cases, onto children playing with sand and/or water on the ground surface.

Such unintended use often occurred under the observation of parents or guardians who displayed no concern that such behavior on the slides was a hazard. On the other hand, the children were warned about sitting on the protective barriers and sliding down the protective barriers. So parents appeared to consider some unintended use activities safe and others unsafe.

Children used playground equipment in ways that are intended by the manufacturer and also in unintended, riskier ways. The children roughhoused and played chase games at the highest deck, increasing the chances for someone to be accidentally pushed or chased over the protective barrier. Manufacturers need to expect that children will use all play equipment on the playground in unintended ways, as both children and their caregivers clearly see unintended use of equipment as appropriate.

## What Is the Nature of Adult Involvement?

In most cases, the children at these play spaces were supervised by a parent or guardian. The most stringent monitoring occurred at the water park, where the lifeguards carefully monitored all play activities on the water slide. The lifeguard at the top would allow only one child to slide at a time, while the lifeguard at the bottom would make sure the children had cleared the shoot at the end before signaling that another child could enter the slide.

Parents monitored younger children more closely than older children on the play equipment. Children under 4 years of age usually were closely monitored. In some cases, parents climbed the equipment with younger children in order to make sure they were not at risk. On the other hand, some parents would take young children up to the top of slides in order to have them slide down, thus encouraging them to access heights on equipment meant for older children.

The least-monitored children were elementary age and older children. This group was the most skillful at climbing and also the most likely to take chances; parents appeared to allow them to take risks with little or no supervision. In some cases, parents were engaged in eating or playing an activity like basketball while the children were playing on the equipment. In other cases, they sat on benches, engaged in conversation, and only periodically looked to see where the children were.

Supervision varied with the age of the children. Young children were closely supervised, while elementary and teenage children were lightly supervised or not supervised at all. In addition, supervision varied by site. Some higher equipment can be used safely if a high level of supervision is present (e.g., the water slide).

## What Hazards Are Present?

Generally, the equipment itself met ASTM standards and CPSC guidelines. The most common hazards were surfacing of inadequate depth and compaction due to poor maintenance, or surfacing of improper type (sand and pea gravel) for the height to be protected. Use zones were not clear of obstructing elements, presenting the danger of falling onto lower components or onto children playing below. Finally, some of the equipment included outside elements or support structures that were easy to climb.

The range of maintenance on play structures varied from location to location. The water slide was new and well-maintained. There was surfacing under all of the play equipment; however, the level of maintenance of that surfacing varied. For example, the surfacing at the city parks lacked maintenance. Although it was close to CPSC depth guidelines in most places, it did not meet CPSC guidelines in the most critical areas—immediately under swings and tall structures. The seafood restaurant had the most poorly maintained surfacing among the sites studied. None of the sites had surfacing that would meet CPSC/ASTM criteria for the heights of equipment in place.

## What Emotions Do Children Experience When Climbing?

Most children appeared to use and enjoy the play structures in a variety of ways. They were excited to explore the different pieces. Their enjoyment of the chase games was evident in the amount of laughter they exhibited. In these cases, it was obvious that the children were becoming less focused on the equipment itself and more on the excitement of the play experience. In the exploratory condition, children would display a "climbing face" that reflected their intense focus on the activity of climbing.

In some cases, the difficulty of climbing caused toddlers and preschool children to become frightened. The children might freeze at the top of equipment; in one case, a child began crying and stamping his feet until a parent came and helped him down from the equipment. Such behavior was not observed at lower heights. When children became frightened, parents often would have to scale narrow ladders or staircases to reach the child and then climb down these same ladders backwards while holding the child. In three observations of children freezing on equipment, the parents encouraged the child to continue climbing even though the child was frightened.

Finally, a third level of emotion observed could be classified as rebelling. In one case, a child appeared to be challenging his father's authority by intentionally taking risks at the top of the equipment. The father eventually took the boy home after warning him several times to climb down from protective barriers. In these hazardous climbing situations, parents and caregivers are relying on children to use good judgment, while children may be deliberately rebelling against their parents' wishes.

Although most of the emotions expressed on the play structures appeared to be pleasurable, it was not uncommon for very young children to be frightened by high play equipment or for a child in any age group to misuse the equipment. The outside areas of the highest points of equipment were scrawled with graffiti, showing that children frequently climbed on the outside of the equipment. The height of the equipment then became an opportunity to express either creativity or negative, rebellious emotions.

### Should Height Be Measured From the Top of Protective Barriers?

In several observations conducted for this study, a child scaled the protective barrier of the equipment or climbed the outside of a slide from the ground. If a child fell from the top of the protective barrier, the child's head would be at a fall height of an additional two feet (sitting) or five feet (standing) above a barrier or guardrail. Although safety organizations have considered measuring critical heights from the top of protective barriers rather than the top of decks, and children do indeed place themselves at risk by climbing on the top of such barriers, using that point as the critical height criterion would in many cases reduce the height of decks, slides, and other play events to non-functional status. Such reduction in height also would prevent children from using the space under decks for social and dramatic play.

### Should There Be a Maximum Climbing Height for Play Equipment?

Based upon the observations in this study, it appears that a maximum potential climbing height (fall height) should be carefully considered. For the most part, children were readily able to access and climb the outside of self-contained equipment. Children as young as 5 years old were observed taking considerable risks in climbing toward the highest point of the play structure. Supervision may make for greater safety, but parents or responsible adults cannot be relied upon to supervise adequately. Manufacturers and installers who exceed CPSC and ASTM recommendations for type and depth of surfacing material, and users who fail to maintain surfacing at the proper depth and condition, also share responsibility for protecting children in falls from equipment. Based on this study, the investigators see no logical reason for designing or installing climbing equipment with critical fall heights of greater than 8 feet for school-age children or 5 feet for preschool children. Swing heights are considered in Chapter 5.

## CONCLUSIONS

A number of hazards were found on the play structures observed in this study. The importance of maintenance and design of play spaces was evident, as surfacing materials were frequently inadequate under tall play structures. Children appeared to enjoy climbing to the top of play structures. The emotional benefit of climbing was evident, as children appeared to feel a sense of accomplishment from climbing. Some children also enjoyed risk-taking and challenging themselves to reach hard-to-access spaces. Other children showed great discomfort on climbing structures, perhaps because they lacked climbing experience.

Although no serious falls were witnessed during the observations, it appeared that children on the outside of the equipment could easily fall from excessive heights. The children on the public playgrounds studied were not closely supervised, the surfacing in place did not meet CPSC/ASTM impact tests for heights of equipment, and the maintenance on and around play structures was infrequent.

The following conclusions about equipment height on playgrounds can be made:

• Falls are by far the leading cause of injuries on playgrounds. Most injuries result from falls to the surface below equipment. Sixty to 70 percent of all injuries on playgrounds result from falls, and approximately 90 percent of serious injuries result from falls. Most serious injuries to the head tend to occur in falls greater than 4-1/2 feet.

• Children climb for many reasons, resulting from both innate and experiential factors. They climb for excitement, to overcome challenges, to experience basic physics, to engage in pretend games, to show off for peers, to get close to nature, to achieve the highest possible level, to test their abilities, and to stimulate kinesthetic perceptions and vestibular sensations. Climbing follows a developmental progression, beginning with exploration and progressing through increasingly complex and refined stages. Climbing down is more difficult than climbing up, yet children frequently attempt to climb to the highest possible level of equipment, regardless of the designer's intent. Their creative and sometimes hazardous use of play equipment supports the notion that the concept of intended use is an inappropriate adult concept (Crawford, 1989). Using play equipment in unintended ways is normal behavior of children, although contrary to adult concepts of how children play.

• The literature review and interviews with professionals indicated that play value is not merely a function of height, but also a function of many variables that can make equipment more exciting and challenging without increasing height above levels recommended by playground specialists and national safety organizations.

• Both maturational and experiential views exist regarding children's fear of heights. One view holds that development of neuro-physiological structures of the brain precedes and accounts for fear of heights. The second view holds that fear appears to be related to experience in locomotion: exploring, crawling, walking, and climbing. Yet a third view posits that interaction between development and experience accounts for the fear response. The levels of fear include abnormal fear (phobias), normal fear, and abnormal lack of fear. Lack of fear is frequently observed among infants.

• The subject of hazardous heights has been discussed in professional literature throughout the history of manufactured playground equipment. During the 20th century, most manufacturers gradually decreased the maximum heights of their equipment. The first national standards for playground apparatus, published in 1931, recommended restricting equipment heights. Systematic collection of injury data by the National Safety Council and the National Electronic Injury Survey System and petitions by private citizens spurred the Consumer Product Safety Commission to publish the first *Handbook for Public Playground Safety* in 1981.

• Every major national playground safety organization recommends restricting fall heights of playground equipment. This can be done in two ways. The most authoritative documents (from CPSC and ASTM), now recognized as the "national standard of care," do not specify maximum equipment or fall heights for equipment, per se, but effectively limit heights by recommending resilient surfacing that accommodates limited heights according to prescribed criteria (Head Injury Criteria [HIC] and G-forces). Only two tested materials among eight types, namely wood chips and double shredded bark mulch, installed 9 inches deep (uncompressed material rarely occurs after play begins), are recommended for heights over 6 feet. This recommendation, if applied, would limit fall heights (as defined by CPSC and ASTM) to 6 feet for most common surfacing materials. National surveys by three major professional organizations (AAHPERD, CFA, and NPPS) show widespread violation of CPSC/ASTM recommendations for heights and surfacing.

All other major organizations concerned with playground safety reviewed for this study recommended stipulated maximum fall heights (potential vertical height of fall from equipment to surface below) for playground equipment. The Consumer Federation of America recommends limiting climbing equipment fall heights to 6 feet for school-age children and 4 feet for preschool-age children. They recommend limiting swing beam heights to 8 feet. The American Public Health Association and the American Academy of Pediatrics recommend that the maximum height of playground equipment be no greater than 5-1/2 feet for children up to the age of 6 and no higher than 3 feet for children 3 and under.

Audit forms published by the National Recreation and Park Association stipulate that slides should be no more than 8 feet high, that accessible equipment height (platform, deck, etc.) should not exceed 4 feet for 2- to 5-year-olds, and that protective surfacing should pass the 200 G ASTM 1292 test. Conclusions drawn from the National Program for Playground Safety's 50-state survey of playgrounds specified that the maximum height of playground equipment should not exceed 8 feet.

• While adult involvement greatly reduced the risks of heights on playgrounds, adult supervision was not regular for any age group and decreased for older children. Children and their parents were unaware of, or unconcerned about, using play equipment as it was intended to be used. Younger children were usually more closely supervised on tall structures; even then, parents sometimes urged them to use equipment that was not designed for their age group. Older children were usually lightly supervised or completely unsupervised, and created their own challenges on all types of equipment.

• Playground safety experts point to children's natural propensity to climb, and explain that they will climb for risk, thrill, feeling of accomplishment, feeling of risk and danger, and to reach visual vantage points. None of the experts proposed that children should be prohibited from climbing. The general view was that children will climb as high as possible. Some of the experts recommended maximum fall heights. Others held that height of equipment (not potential fall height) was manageable through innovative design. None of the responses indicated that children should be exposed to excessive heights.

• No evidence could be found in the literature, the interviews, or the observations of children contrary to this principle: the farther a child falls, the faster he or she falls and the greater the likelihood for serious injury.

• Observations of the writers at playgrounds throughout the United States and planned observations at selected sites indicate that some manufacturers market equipment with fall heights that exceed recommendations by safety organizations and safety experts as well as the criteria established by ASTM and CPSC. Slides that are 10 to 12 feet in vertical height from entry point to surface are common. The most commonly observed surfacing is sand and pea gravel. Neither of these surfaces meets CPSC/ASTM criteria for falls from these heights. Attempts to protect children from falls by totally enclosing slide entries fail, because children commonly climb on the outside of tube slides and on the support structures.

## RECOMMENDATIONS

Based on the observations of this study, a number of recommendations can be made to designers, manufacturers, and purchasers of outdoor play equipment. Children enjoy climbing and the sensation of height. They will climb the highest components of play equipment in order to experience a challenge and the sensation of height. Children enjoy the success of climbing structures and benefit from the risk-taking inherent in climbing. Playground equipment should be designed, manufactured, and selected to give children a sense of height, a variety of climbing challenges, and opportunities to develop a range of motor skills. The level of risk to children should be carefully weighed to guard against unacceptable hazard levels.

The normal pattern is for children to use play equipment in diverse and unintended ways. Equipment designers, manufacturers, and purchasers should assume that children will access unintended parts of the play structure. They should take into consideration how children place themselves at risk, even if equipment is designed to be enclosed. In addition, children's play on play structures often is not supervised. Responsible parties should assume that the play structure will not be supervised and it is likely that children will misuse equipment in ways that increase their risk of falling from tall equipment.

Resilient surfacing greatly reduces the risk of injury from falling. On the three public playgrounds that were observed, however, proper surfacing was not installed and the surfacing had not been properly maintained. The surfacing material was sand, which does not meet CPSC and ASTM specifications for falls from the heights of the equipment studied. Manufacturers and installers should take into consideration the reality that many play-ground equipment purchasers, installers, and even manufacturer's representatives do not always insist on appropriate surfacing under newly installed play structures.

Responsible parties also should understand that wariness of heights and skill in climbing is learned and that children's experience with heights will help them develop a wariness of heights and skill in climbing. Not all children will have the same wariness of heights. Some will have a lower sense of risk, which may lead them to take greater risks on play equipment than they are sufficiently developed to handle safely. Other children will have an abnormal phobia or fear of heights, which will keep them from using play equipment unless they are encouraged and assisted by caring adults.

Designers and manufacturers can help prevent fall injuries from extreme heights on playground equipment by carefully examining children's climbing patterns. They climb on the outside of very tall equipment, using any protruding element as a hand-grip or foot-step. Specifically, they use bulging connections of tube slides for both hand-grips and foot-holds, they use vertical bars of protective barriers for hand grips, they shimmy up vertical or near-vertical support posts, and they use the exposed outer edges of decks for hand-grips and foot-holds. Attention should be directed to minimizing access to such structural elements. Similar climbing experiences can be provided by installing "climbing walls" with well-designed hand- and foot-holds, properly installed over resilient surfacing and limited in height.

Some specific recommendations are:

• The wide range of individual differences in development among children of like chronological age leads to the conclusion that levels of development as well as chronological age should be carefully considered in matching children to playground equipment sizes and types. The current designations of two broad chronological age designations (2-5 and 5-12) adopted by CPSC and ASTM compresses a wide range of developmental levels into only two categories. Such chronological age designations could be improved by considering the development of individual children, as expressed in the National Association for the Education of Young Children's guidelines for developmental appropriateness of materials, curriculum, and instruction for young children (Bredekamp & Copple, 1997). Indeed, even the degrees of daring, audacious, and risky responses to the playground differ widely among children of like age groups. Chronological age, experience, and skill development all should be considered when making decisions about the appropriateness of playground equipment and the nature of play to be accommodated.

• Concerns about height, hazards, and injuries are not simple issues of restricting the maximum height of equipment. For example, rotating tire swings must be installed with swivel or beam heights sufficient to avoid injuries to children's heads from impacting overhead beams when pushed very vigorously. Decks or platforms need to be sufficiently high to accommodate young children engaging in make-believe or dramatic play underneath the structure, and thus enhance play value, conserve space and material, and provide shade. On the other hand, no reasonable rationale can be made for manufacturing and installing slides and climbers that violate national guidelines and standards for heights with respect to protective surfacing.

• All the national surveys, guidelines, and standards (AAHPERD, CFA, NPPS, CPSC, and ASTM) reviewed in this document conclude that equipment designed for older groups is anthropomorphically unsuitable for younger children's play. Despite this common conclusion, toddlers and preschool children commonly play on excessively high structures designed for the sizes and skills of older children. Excessive heights of older children's play equipment means extreme hazards for younger children with undeveloped skills using that equipment. Playground sponsors should ensure that signs are posted regarding the age or developmental ranges for which playgrounds are designed. Educational programs are needed to help adults make wise decisions about selecting and supervising playgrounds for children.

• Despite recommendations, warnings, and admonitions regarding maximum equipment heights, some manufacturers commonly advertise and sell slides that exceed peak G and HIC values of the protective surfacing that they install or that is installed by consumers. For example, some manufacturers market both open and enclosed tube slides that are 10 to 12 feet in vertical height. The commonly used protective surfacing materials are not rated to protect children in falls from this height. The problem is even more serious when taking into account that the overall climbing (fall) height of these slides may exceed 15 feet (i.e., when children climb on and fall from the top of protective barriers, support members, or the top of slide chutes).

The CPSC/ASTM recommendations for height of overhead apparatus are appropriate when loose surfacing or a composite surface is installed and maintained per established criteria. However, fall height of apparatus installed over protective surfacing commonly exceeds the designated fall height. This is due to a number of variables, including poor design of equipment, improper initial installation of surfacing, and lack of maintenance following installation.

• Height is a critical variable for ensuring fun, challenge, and development for children. Innovative design of playground equipment can help ensure these qualities without increasing potential fall heights (not equipment heights) beyond criteria recommended by safety experts, research evidence, and the criteria established by ASTM/CPSC and other national professional organizations concerned with child safety.

• Taking all the evidence reviewed into account, the writers recommend the following:
  - Maximum fall height (per CPSC/ASTM criteria) of to-fro swing beams should not exceed 8 feet for school-age children or 7 feet for preschool children.
  - Maximum fall height on overhead apparatus should not exceed 6-1/2 feet for school-age children or 5 feet for preschool children.
  - Maximum height for platforms, decks, slides, and climbers should not exceed 6-8 feet for school-age children or 4-5 feet for preschool children. All equipment with fall heights exceeding these recommendations should be designed to prevent climbing on the outside of the equipment. Height ranges are recommended to allow for innovation in design, diversity of challenges, and different age and developmental levels of the children expected to use the equipment.
  - Overhead beams of rotating tire swings should not be installed lower than 7 feet for preschool-age children or 8 feet for school-age children, to help avoid contact of children's heads with overhead beams during extreme swinging.
  - Manufacturers should take steps to ensure that upon initial installation of their equipment, surfacing meets CPSC/ASTM recommendations for type, HIC, and G rating.

The recommendations above are general in nature, intended to address common design, manufacturing, and use patterns, and are subject to change resulting from a range of factors. During the early years of the 21st century we are seeing a growing movement by designers and manufacturers to create variation and challenge in playground equipment. Manufacturers are researching, designing, and marketing playground equipment with greater diversity in their equipment options. The authors anticipate that such creativity and ingenuity may lead to safer equipment and surfacing options without relinquishing play value and complexity. For example, the hazards of height, per se, may be diminished by modifying equipment elements onto which children can fall (e.g., broad surfaced or flexible climbing components instead of narrow, rigid bars); by creating surfacing options with greater resiliency yet requiring less maintenance; and by configuring equipment to provide greater challenge and play value within limited heights.

## References

American Public Health Association and the American Academy of Pediatrics. (1992). *Caring for our children: National health and safety performance standards: Guidelines for out-of-home child care programs.* Washington, DC: Authors.

American Society for Testing and Materials. (1995). *Standard test method for shock-absorbing properties of playing surface systems and materials.* Philadelphia: Author.

Baker, S. P., O'Neill, B., Ginsburg, M. J., & Li, G. (1992). *The injury factbook.* New York: Oxford University Press.

Bertenthal, B. I., Campos, J. J., & Caplovitz, K. S. (1983). Self-produced locomotion: An organizer of emotional, cognitive, and social development in infancy. In R. N. Emde & R. Harmon (Eds.), *Continuities and discontinuities in development* (pp. 175-220). New York: Plenum.

Bredekamp, S., & Copple, C. (Eds.). (1997). *Developmentally appropriate practice for early childhood programs* (Rev. ed.). Washington, DC: National Association for the Education of Young Children.

Brown, S. (1997). *Discovering the intelligence of play: A new model for a new generation of children* (videotape). Touch the Future (4350 Lime Ave., Long Beach, CA, 90807).

Brown, S. (1998). Play as an organizing principle: Clinical evidence and personal observations. In M. Befoff & J. Byers (Eds.), *Animal play: Evolutionary, comparative, and ecological perspectives* (pp. 243-259). Cambridge: Cambridge University Press.

Bruya, L. D., & Langendorfer, S. J. (1988). *Where our children play: Elementary school playground equipment.* Reston, VA: American Alliance for Health, Physical Education, Recreation, and Dance.

Bureau of Product Safety. (1972). *Public playground safety.* Washington, DC: U.S. Food and Drug Administration.

Butwinick, E. (1974). *Petition to the Consumer Product Safety Commission.* Washington, DC: Author.

Campos, J. J., Bertenthal, B. I., & Kermoian, R. (1992). Early experience and emotional development: The emergence of wariness of heights. *Psychological Science, 3*(1), 61-64.

CEN European Committee for Standardization. (1998). *European standard for playground equipment - EN1176-1.* Brussels, Belgium: Author.

Chalmers, D. J., Marshall, S. W., Langley, J. D., Evans, M. J., Brunton, C. R., Kelly, A. M., & Pickering, A. F. (1996). Height and surfacing as risk factors for injury in falls from playground equipment: A case-control study. *Injury Prevention, 2,* 98-104.

Children and Adults with Attention-Deficit/Hyperactivity Disorder. (2001). *Parents of teen drivers with ADHD: Proceed with caution.* Retrieved June 20, 2001, from www.chadd.org

Clarke, L. (19998). Development reflected in chase games. In S. Reifel (Ed.), *Play and culture studies, 2* (pp. 73-82). Stamford, CT: Ablex.

Consumer Federation of America. (1992). *Report and model law on public play equipment and areas.* Washington, DC: Author.

Consumer Federation of America. (1996a). *Report and model law on public play equipment and areas.* Washington, DC: Author.

Consumer Federation of America. (1996b). *Action alert: Comments on improving the Consumer Product Safety Commission Handbook for Public Playground Safety.* Washington, DC: Author.

Consumer Product Safety Commission. (1981, 1997). *Handbook for public playground equipment.* Washington, DC: Author.

Crawford, M. (1989). In D. Thompson & L. Bowers (Eds.), *Where our children play: Community park playground equipment* (pp. 37-49). Reston, VA: American Alliance for Health, Physical Education, Recreation and Dance.

Curtis, H.. S. (1917). *The play movement and its significance.* Washington, DC: McGrath Publishing.

DeGrandpre, R. (1999). *Ritalin nation.* New York: W. W. Norton.

Dietz, W. H. (March 19, 1999). *Kids' obesity linked to TV. American Medical Association Press Conference.* Report by U.S. Centers for Disease Control and Prevention. Retrieved from http//onhealth.webmd.com.

Diller, L. H. (1998). *Running on Ritalin.* New York: Bantam Books.

Ellis, M. J. (1973). *Why people play.* Englewood Cliffs, NJ: Prentice-Hall.

Epstein, L. H. (2000). To get obese kids to exercise, turn off the TV. *Archives of Pediatrics and Adolescent Medicine, 154,* 220-226.

Farnsworth, C. L., Silva, P. D., & Mubarak, S. J. (1998). Etiology of supracondylar humerus fractures. *Journal of Pediatric Orthopedics, 18*(1), 38-42.

Frankenburg, W. K., & Dobbs. (1967). The Denver developmental screening test. *The Journal of Pediatrics, 71*(2), 181-191.

Frost, J. L. (1980). *Commentary: Public playground equipment.* Washington, DC: U.S. Consumer Product Safety Commission.

Frost, J. L. (1992). *Play and playscapes.* Albany, NY: Delmar.

Frost, J. L. (Ed.). (2001). Children and injuries. Tucson, AZ: Lawyers and Judges Publishing Co.

Frost, J. L., & Henniger, M. L. (1979). Making playgrounds safe for children and children safe for playgrounds. *Young Children, 34*(5), 23-30.

Frost, J. L., & Jacobs, P. (1995). Play deprivation and juvenile violence. *Dimensions, 23,* 14-20, 39.

Frost, J. L., & Sweeney, T. B. (1996). *Cause and prevention of playground injuries and litigation: Case studies.* Olney, MD: Association for Childhood Education International.

Frost, J. L., Wortham, S., & Reifel, S. (2001). *Play and child development.* Columbus, OH: Prentice-Hall/Merrill.

Gabbard, C. (2000). Should quality physical education be part of the core curriculum? *Principal, 79*(3), 29-31.

Gabbard, C. P., & LeBlanc, E. (1980, May). *Movement activity levels on traditional and contemporary playground structures.* ERIC/EDRS, #198-082.

Gottlieb, G. (1983). The psychobiological approach to developmental issues. In P. Mussen (Ed.), *Handbook of child psychology: Vol. II* (pp. 1-26). New York: Wiley.

Gottlieb, G. (1991). Experiential canalization of behavioral development: Theory. *Developmental Psychology, 27,* 4-13.

Henzy, E., & Connecticut Safe Kids and Connecticut Children's Medical Center. (2001). *Press release: CT offers playground safety advice.* Hartford CT: Connecticut Children's Medical Center.

Hudson, S., Mack, M., & Thompson, D. (2000). *How safe are America's playgrounds? A national profile of child care, school and park playgrounds.* Cedar Falls, IA: National Program for Playground Safety.

Kingma, J., & Ten Duis, J. (2000). Severity of injuries due to accidental fall across the life span: A retrospective hospital-based study. *Perceptual and Motor Skills, 90,* 62-72.

Kompan, Inc. (1996). *Kompan.* Marathon, NY: Author.

Kutska, K. S., & Hoffman, K. J. (1992). *Playground safety is no accident.* Arlington, VA: National Recreation and Park Association.

Laforest, S., Robitaille, Y., Lesage, D., & Dorval, D. (2001). Surface characteristics, equipment height, and the occurrence and severity of playground injuries. *Injury Prevention, 7,* 35-40.

Levinson, H. N. (1989). A cerebellar-vestibular explanation for fears/phobias: Hypothesis and study. *Perceptual and Motor Skills, 68,* 67-84.

Macarthur, C., Hu, X., Wesson, D. E., & Parkin, P. C. (2000). Risk factors for severe injuries associated with falls from playground equipment. *Accident Analysis & Prevention, 32*(3), 377-382.

Marks, I. (1987). The development of normal fear: A review. *Journal of Child Psychology, 28*(5), 667-697.

Marotz, L. (2001). Childhood injury in early care and education programs. In J. L. Frost (Ed.), *Children and injuries* (pp. 171-197). Tucson, AZ: Lawyers & Judges Publishing Co.

Moore, R. C., & Wong H. H. (1997). *Natural learning: Creating environments for rediscovering nature's way of learning.* Berkeley, CA: MIG Communications.

Mott, A., & Rolfe, K., James, R., Evans, Kemp, A., Dunstan, F., Kemp, K., & Sibert, J. (1997). Safety of surfaces and equipment for children in playgrounds. *Lancet, 349*(9069), 1874-1876.

Mierzwinski, E., Fise, M. E., & Morrison, M. (1996). *Playing it safe: A third nationwide safety survey of public playgrounds.* Washington, DC: U.S. Public Interest Research Group and Consumer Federation of America.

National Program for Playground Safety. (1999). *America's playgrounds safety report card.* Cedar Falls, IA: Author.

National Recreation Association. (1931). *Report of committee on standards in playground apparatus* (Bulletin 2170). New York: Author.

National Recreation and Park Association. (1976). *Proposed safety standard for public playground equipment.* Arlington, VA: Author.

Parnell, J., & Ketterson, P. (1980). What should a playground offer? *The Elementary School Journal, 80*(5), 233-239.

Perry, P. (2001). Sick kids. *American Way, 4,* 64-65. Dallas, TX: American Airlines.

Playground and Recreation Association of America. (1928). *Play areas: Their design and equipment.* New York: A. S. Barnes and Company.

Playground Association of America. (1910). *Proceedings of the Third Annual Congress of the Playground Association, 3*(3).

Ratte, D. J., Denham, S. A., & Johnson, D. M. (1990). *Development of human factors criteria for playground equipment safety.* Silver Spring, MD: Comsis Corporation.

Readdick, C. A., & Park, J. J. (1998). Achieving great heights: The climbing child. *Young Children, 53*(6), 14-19.

Rivkin, M. S. (1995). *The great outdoors: Restoring children's right to play outside.* Washington, DC: National Association for the Education of Young Children.

Sikes, L., Fise, M. E., & Morrison, M. (1992). *Playing it safe: A nationwide safety survey of public playgrounds.* Washington, DC: U.S. Public Interest Research Group and the Consumer Federation of America.

Smith, S. J. (1998). *Risk and our pedagogical relation to children.* Albany, NY: State University of New York Press.

Standards Association of New Zealand. (1986). *General guidelines for new and existing playgrounds equipment surfacing, NZS 5828, part I.* Wellington, NZ: Standards Association of New Zealand.

Sweeney, T. (1974). *Petition to the Consumer Product Safety Commission.* Cleveland Heights, OH: Author.

Therrell, J. (2001). History, nature and scope of child injuries. In J. L. Frost (Ed.), *Children and injuries* (pp. 23-42). Tucson, AZ: Lawyers & Judges Publishing Co.

Thompson, D., & Bowers, L. (1989). *Where our children play: Community park playground equipment.* Reston, VA: American Alliance for Health, Physical Education, Recreation, and Dance.

Thompson, D., & Hudson, S. (2001). In J. L. Frost (Ed.), *Children and injuries* (pp. 249-312). Tucson, AZ: Lawyers and Judges Publishing Co.

Tinetti, M. E., & Speechley, M. (1989). Prevention and falls among the elderly. *The New England Journal of Medicine, 20,* 1055-1059.

Tinsworth, D. K., & Kramer, J. T. (1990). *Playground equipment-related injuries and deaths.* Washington, DC: U.S. Consumer Product Safety Commission.

Tinsworth, D. K., & McDonald, J. E. (April, 2001). *Special study: Injuries and deaths associated with children's playground equipment.* Washington, DC: U.S. Consumer Product Safety Commission.

Williams, G. M. (1994). Talk on the climbing frame. *Early Child Development and Care, 102,* 81-89.

Wood, B., Fise, M. E., & Morrison, M. L. (1994). *Playing it safe: A second nationwide safety survey of public playgrounds.* Washington, DC: Consumer Federation of America.

Wortham, S. C., & Frost, J. L. (1990). *Playgrounds for young children: National survey and perspectives.* Reston, VA: American Alliance for Health, Physical Education, Recreation, and Dance.

# Appendix:
# Coding Sheet

## CODING HEIGHT OBSERVATIONS

DAY/DATE:_____PLACE:_____STARTTIME:_____ENDTIME:_____

Slide 1        Slide 2        Slide 3      Overhead 1     Overhead 2        Other

Type of Equipment

   Equipment Description

   Surfacing Type/Depth

   Sex/Age

   Typical Use

   Misuse

   Hazards

   Distinct Emotions

   Play Value

Anecdotal Record:

# CHAPTER 4
# The Developmental Benefits and Use Patterns of Overhead Equipment on Playgrounds

*The skill that kids develop on the overhead ladder is called brachiation, and it is one of the very few experiences that are new to children on the playground.*
(Hewes & Beckwith, 1975, p. 123)

Overhead ladders, ring treks, and other types of overhead equipment constitute 10-12 percent of all playground equipment (Bowers & Bruya, 1988). The overall purpose of this study is to review research literature on overhead ladders and the benefits of upper body activity for children. In addition, this study presents new data collected from an empirical study of overhead equipment. Information gathered from the literature and field-based observations is used to formulate a developmental progression chart for children's use of overhead equipment. The history and safety of overhead equipment, the benefits of overhead equipment, the skills needed to use overhead equipment, and the developmental patterns of children's use of overhead equipment also are explored in this study.

## HISTORY OF OUTDOOR OVERHEAD EQUIPMENT

Outdoor equipment designed to promote physical activity has roots back to Germany's post-Napoleonic period, when gymnastics equipment was built for boys and young men to use out-of-doors. This equipment, called outdoor gymnasia, came to the United States around the middle of the 19th century as eastern cities developed outdoor play spaces for young men and boys (Frost, 1992). At the end of the 19th century, the playground movement became related to the Progressive Movement, which was concerned with aspects of overcrowding and poverty in the cities. Playgrounds were developed in cities to give boys and girls places to play away from the streets and pool halls (Brett, Moore, & Provenzo, 1993). Overhead equipment, see-saws, and swings were considered important components of outdoor playgrounds during this progressive era (Mero, 1908).

The equipment in these early outdoor playgrounds generally consisted of swings, giant strides, sliding boards, teeter boards, climbing apparatus, gymnastics equipment, and such upper body equipment as rings and overhead ladders. As manufacturers developed equipment for early playgrounds, they tended to build structures without concern for height; some devices were more than 20 feet tall (Frost, 1992). The basic design for the overhead ladder was two parallel bars with horizontal bars spaced at even intervals. This design for overhead ladders has not changed a great deal in the last 150 years, although modifications have been made to the dimensions and purposes of the equipment.

In the 1950s, manufacturers began developing novelty equipment for playgrounds. Overhead ladders would be based on themes such as space travel or western adventures (Frost, 1992). As playground equipment continued to develop during the 1970s, designers like Paul Friedberg (Friedberg, 1975) and Jay Beckwith (Hewes & Beckwith, 1975) developed innovative playgrounds featuring linked equipment. In traditional playgrounds, stand-alone equipment such as swings, slides, and overhead ladders were scattered around the playground. Linked equipment brought together these components, encouraging movement from one activity to another. Overhead ladders linked equipment together, making them another way of getting to different parts of the playground rather than merely a separate event (Friedberg & Berkeley, 1970).

As equipment evolved during the course of the 20th century, new overhead apparatus designs were implemented for playgrounds. Introduction of new materials and technologies allowed manufacturers to develop innovative types of overhead equipment that incorporated movement and other physical challenges. Typical modern overhead apparatus designs include challenge ladders with unevenly spaced rungs, ring treks, C- and S-shaped overhead ladders (with and without movement elements), track rides, and parallel bars, as well as traditional overhead ladders (Frost, 1992; Ratté, Denham, & Johnson, 1990; Wortham, 1990).

## MOTIVATIONS FOR USING UPPER BODY EQUIPMENT

Free play is the primary method through which preschool children gain experience and learn. As children get older they participate in more group games and organized activities, although unstructured physical activity is still an important part of fitness for school-age children (Ross & Gilbert, 1985). Two factors have been shown to influence children's upper body development: environment and social scaffolding. Children are motivated by both the environment and their peers to engage with upper body equipment.

### Environment

The physical environment is important for physical development. In order to promote physical fitness, the Centers for Disease Control and Prevention call for environments "that encourage and enable safe and enjoyable physical activity" (*Active Youth*, 1998, p. 5). Children need opportunities to interact with equipment that requires them to hang while supporting their entire body weight with their hands and arms.

The type of playground has an influence on children's development of physical skills. In a comparison of traditional and contemporary playgrounds, Barbour (1999) found that the traditional playground featuring heavy, fixed equipment encouraged gross motor skills and favored children with high levels of physical competence, while children with lower levels of physical competence were constrained by this type of playground. The contemporary playground, on the other hand, featuring a range of fixed equipment and portable or loose parts, encouraged children of either high or low levels of physical competence to interact with each other.

The apparatus available on the playground also has an effect on children's endurance. Gabbard (1979, 1983) found that the availability of overhead equipment allowed children more upper body experience on the playground. According to Gabbard (1983), "Young children in a free-play condition with the opportunity to utilize specific apparatus, would produce sufficient activity to increase significantly their level of upper body muscular endurance" (p. 538). Additional opportunities for upper body exercise increased children's endurance on a fixed hang test, demonstrating that the activity enhanced their upper body strength.

The challenge level of overhead ladders is also important. Static pieces of equipment such as overhead ladders often are associated with misuse, as children who have mastered the equipment begin to look for more challenging ways of using it (Frost, Wortham, & Reifel, 2001; Sawyers, 1994). Designers have modified the overhead ladder to make it more challenging for skillful users by adding dynamic elements and changing the spacing on the bars (Frost, 1992).

Making an overhead ladder accessible and safer for younger children is also important for increasing use. Frost (1990) recommends: "A general, practical guideline for height of horizontal ladders should be slightly above the reaching height of 95 percentile users" (pp. 39-40). Beckwith (1988) suggests that surfacing below the overhead ladder also may promote more active play because children playing over safe surfacing "are generally more expansive and relaxed in their movements" (p. 225).

In order to promote safe use of overhead equipment for younger children, Frost and Kim (2000) modified an overhead ladder in order to reduce risk of injury. They placed the ladder at a height of 60 inches over 12 inches of sand. An important special feature was added that allowed 3- and 4-year-old children to reach the bars from a standing position. The steel steps for accessing the ladder were replaced with special, resilient, balloon-type (ATV) tires mounted in the ground. The modified design allowed preschool-age children safer access to the equipment. Resilient, elevated platforms for accessing overhead apparatus avoids a number of common hazards, such as falling onto ladders or hard decks, or inability to reach the overhead elements. Because of the risk of falling onto the take-off elements, some manufacturers have deleted decks and bars from their products, creating additional potential hazards and reducing play value.

### Social Scaffolding

Although free unstructured play is important for children's development, social scaffolding also has an effect on children's use of overhead equipment. The idea of social scaffolding was first proposed by Vygotsky (1978), who suggested that learning occurs in a zone of proximal development (ZPD). The ZPD is the range of ability that a child can demonstrate when supported by more capable persons. Social scaffolding can come from many different sources, including encouragement, observation of others, and direct instruction. According to Gober and Franks (1988), the motives and skills of athletes are related to experiences in early childhood when parents and older siblings challenged and encouraged physical development. Children also learn through observation of others and from guided movement instruction (Bennet, 1980).

As encouragement is an important part of children's development of skills on overhead ladders, adults and peers can scaffold children by encouraging them to challenge themselves. Frost and Kim (2000) describe such scaffolding in a situation wherein a teacher and a group of children encouraged a child to cross an overhead ladder:

> *Brian stood up on the tire and moved up to the second bar. When he stopped on the second bar the teacher encouraged, "Go, Brian! Go!" He still hesitated and could not proceed. The teacher then said to the children waiting in line, "Let's cheer him up!" All the children in line and the teacher started to shout at him, "Go! Brian, Go! Go! Brian, Go!" While they clapped their hands, Brian crossed to the 4th bar and fell to the sand with a big smile on his face.* (p. 5)

Social scaffolding also can have negative consequences, however, as capable school-age children "lead children who are less physically developed to challenges they cannot handle" (Frost, Wortham, & Reifel, 2001, p. 219).

Direct instruction and positive interactions with adults also help children learn to use overhead equipment (Sawyers, 1994). One adult worked with a 4-year-old to develop competence on the overhead ladder by "support[ing] her waist as she mastered the skills necessary to grasp the bars and support[ing] her weight as she crossed the bars" (p. 33). Adults and other more capable peers can support the use of overhead equipment by offering children direct instruction, encouragement, and modeling.

## BENEFITS OF OVERHEAD EQUIPMENT

American children appear to be in an era of decreasing fitness. Today's children are at greater risk than previous generations for Type II diabetes, osteoporosis, heart disease, stress, and anxiety (Perry, 2001). Children are more sedentary as they pursue such activities as television viewing and computer use, which have been linked to greater obesity (Durant, Baranowski, Johnson, & Thompson, 1994). Children also eat a diet higher in fat than did previous generations (Frost, Wortham, & Reifel, 2001). Furthermore, children in some cases are being given fewer opportunities for physical education and free play at school (O'Brien, 1987). Children's physical fitness, in terms of upper body strength and total body weight, influences their ability to use overhead equipment. In addition, experience with overhead equipment increases children's skill, strength, and ability to use overhead equipment.

American children generally have very poor upper body strength (Gallahue, 1982). The National Children and Youth Fitness Study II (Ross & Pate, 1987), in tests of upper body strength, found that 25-30 percent of boys and 60 percent of girls could not do a single pull-up, and that 10 percent of girls scored zero on the flexed arm hang (Pate, Ross, Baumgartner, & Sparks, 1987; Ross, Dotson, Gilbert, & Katz, 1985). The low scores in completing the flexed arm hang and the chin-up are a result of poor upper body strength and excessive body weight. Low scores from national testing (the 1985 NCYFS II) led researchers to switch to the modified pull-up and therefore increase the sensitivity of the test. The modified pull-up allows children to support their body weight as they do the pull-up, yielding a more accurate measure of upper body strength (Pate et al., 1987).

Given these trends, the growing number of playground injuries reported by the CPSC during the past quarter century may well be the result of, at least in significant proportion, the declining fitness levels of children. Such a conclusion regarding the relationships between playground safety and children's skill levels is discussed in depth in Frost and

Henniger's (1979) article, "Making Playgrounds Safe for Children and Children Safe for Playgrounds."

## DEVELOPMENT OF UPPER BODY SKILLS

*Very young children do not have the necessary upper body strength or coordination necessary to handle a horizontal ladder 84 inches high and 10 feet long. However, at the age of five they don't develop these skills overnight; they must be developed gradually.* (Hendy, 1997, p. 104)

As Hendy indicates, children's physical skills generally follow developmental milestones. Traditionally, such developmental milestones have been considered the result of inviolable genetic programming. More recently, however, a theory combining the importance of such factors as social expectations, lifestyle, nutrition, and experience to those of heredity has been put forward as a model for children's growth and development. In effect, children's success on overhead apparatus is based on their experience with overhead apparatus, their perception of success on overhead equipment, and their general fitness level in tandem with their inherited abilities (Gallahue, 1989).

Applying Gallahue's lifespan model to overhead equipment, children need to have reached a point of physical growth and development that allows them to successfully navigate overhead equipment. In order for children to use overhead equipment, they need to reach a point in their growth where they can support their weight when hanging by their hands. This includes the development of grip strength and upper body strength, and can be affected by body weight. In addition, they need to develop such skills as lateral weight shift, eye-hand coordination, and visual perception of distance.

Most children develop sufficient grip and upper body strength to support their body weight by at least 3 years of age (Frost & Kim, 2000), and perhaps as early as 2 years (Gabbard & Patterson, 1980). However, a child with normal grip strength and upper body strength may not be able to use an overhead ladder if s/he is overweight. The effect of body weight on successful overhead apparatus use was demonstrated when the only two members of a group of 3- and 4-year-olds who could not complete an overhead ladder task were overweight children (Frost & Kim, 2000).

Lateral weight shift develops in children as they learn to walk. In order to walk, children must be able to shift their weight to one side of their body, so that the other side is free to move (Nelson, 1988). For upper body movement, children must be able to perform a similar task. They must support their body weight on one arm while moving the other to grasp the next rung. Obesity is a factor here as well. Children who are obese develop unbalanced locomotor patterns to compensate for carrying extra weight on their joints and muscles (Hills, 1994).

Successful use of overhead equipment also requires skill in visual perception and coordination. Children must judge the distance from one rung to the next, and then coordinate their physical movements to reach the next rung. Generally, children's gross motor coordination improves linearly as they grow older and develop skills through their playground experience (Gallahue, 1989).

There is some disagreement as to when children combine the physical skills of grip strength, upper body strength, and supporting their body weight in order to be able to successfully use overhead ladders. Hewes and Beckwith (1975) suggest that children are not able to use overhead ladders until age 5 or 6. Staniford (1979) holds that "jungle gyms, horizontal ladders, climbing bars and balance beams challenge the rather self-centered five year old" (p. 46). Thompson (1996) suggests that overhead ladders are most appropriate for users who have reached the concrete operations period of development—around the age of 7. Frost and Kim (2000), on the other hand, found that children as young as 3 could use modified overhead ladders. In a study of grip preference for overhead ladders, Gabbard and Patterson (1980) included subjects as young as 2 years old. In a separate study, Gabbard and Patterson (1981) found that 80 percent of 4-year-olds in their study could not support their body weight.

Frost and Kim (2000) studied 3- and 4-year-olds who had been introduced to an overhead apparatus (horizontal ladder) for the first time. Initially, most of the 3-year-old children were limited to supporting their weight, unable to mentally and physically initiate a pattern allowing them to traverse the bars. With daily practice, modeling, and encouragement from peers and teachers, the children traversed, unaided, the length of the apparatus (6 bars) within a few days. The two exceptions were obese children.

Government and industry standards are not clear as to when children should use overhead equipment. The CPSC *Handbook for Public Playground Safety* (1997) does not recommend overhead rings and track rides for children ages 4 and under. On the other hand, the American Society for Testing and Material's (1998) standards for playground equipment states, "The maximum height of upper body devices for use by 2 through 5 year olds shall be no greater than 60 inches" (p. 9).

## THE DEVELOPMENT OF BRACHIATION BEHAVIORS

Scales for the development of physical and cognitive behaviors are common in the field of social sciences. One scale that has been used for the organization of physical behaviors on playgrounds is a Guttman scale. According to Fox and Tipps (1995), "A Guttman scale provides a hierarchical sequence of content-related elements in which all aspects of the first elements are incorporated into the later elements" (p. 492). The items on a Guttman scale must reflect the behaviors at a level of 90 percent. The Guttman scale for swinging behaviors developed by Fox and Tipps has eight stages: balance, observation and trial and error, adaptation, timing, demonstrating prowess, refinement, security, and experimentation.

Studies of the development of brachial behaviors on overhead equipment have focused on two areas: 1) grip preference based on how children grip the bar when using climbing and overhead equipment (Gabbard & Patterson, 1980), and 2) movement pattern based on categories of movement that children demonstrate as they move across a ladder (Gabbard & Patterson, 1981).

In a study of 282 children ages 2 through 8, Gabbard and Patterson (1980) found that children adjust their grip preference on horizontal ladders as they mature. The two conditions for grip preference were thumb over the bar (cup grip) and thumb under the bar (lock grip). They found that 2-year-old children are nearly evenly split between the two grip styles. The preference for thumb under the bar began to dominate as children matured; at age 7 the preference for thumb over the bar began to increase. The grip preference for the adults' tests reflected this declining trend toward a set preference. Frost and Kim (2000) found that the cup grip was preferred by 3- and 4-year-old children.

Although not specifically studied by Frost and Kim, the diameter of bars to be gripped may influence the type of grip. Bars one inch in diameter were used in the Frost and Kim study. Smaller diameter bars may allow children to use the lock grip at younger ages. However, Frost and Kim found that several days of regular use of overhead bars resulted in extensive blisters on children's hands. While teachers encouraged children to reduce the amount of overhead bar play, continued use of the bars resulted in blisters becoming calluses with no apparent damage to children's hands. The researchers believed that overhead bars should be between 1 inch and 1-1/8 inches in diameter. Smaller diameter bars may increase the likelihood of damaging hands through blistering.

In a study of 356 four- through nine-year-olds (Gabbard & Patterson, 1981), the children followed a five-stage developmental process when using overhead equipment. These stages were: unable to support body weight, dysrhythmic time-step, rhythmic time step, unilateral swinging, and bilateral swinging. The 4-year-old children were limited to the first two stages while all of the 9-year-olds had moved on to the last four stages. Only 10 percent of the 9-year-olds had moved on to the most advanced stage of bilateral swinging.

In a study of 3- and 4-year-olds' behaviors on overhead equipment, Frost and Kim (2000) found that the children were capable of crossing a modified overhead ladder after a few days practice. Unlike the Gabbard and Patterson (1981) study, the children in this study received informal instruction and support from teachers. This reflects the importance of environment and scaffolding for development of overhead ladder movement skills. In addition, the Frost and Kim study reflects how children search for increased novelty and challenge as their skills improved. Rather than dropping to the ground or stepping onto the elevated rubber deck, the 3- and 4-year-olds started to use the support posts of the horizontal ladder to slide down to the ground. They would wrap their legs and arms around the post since the diameter was too great to grip with the hands. Such common practice (3- and 4-year-olds hugging and sliding down poles) raises questions regarding the CPSC and ASTM recommendations regarding design specifications and age recommendations for fire poles or sliding poles.

## TYPES OF OVERHEAD EQUIPMENT

### Overhead Ladders

Overhead ladders or horizontal ladders come in a variety of types. The traditional overhead ladder has evenly spaced rungs set parallel to the ground between two support beams. Modern overhead ladders have incorporated c- and s-loops, curved bars, and rings. Overhead ladders also can be inclined in order to increase the challenge.

Overhead ladders for preschool-age children should have evenly spaced rungs no more than 12 inches apart. Overhead ladders for school-age children typically should have rungs no more than 15 inches apart (CPSC, 1997).

### Track Rides

Track rides typically involve a handle or support that runs along a track support beam. The user of the track ride is expected to hold onto the handle as it moves between the two support structures.

## Overhead Rings

Overhead rings or trapeze rings can be placed side by side on parallel support beams or along a single support beam. Overhead rings allow for more elaborate movement patterns than typically seen on overhead ladders, increasing the challenge and incorporating novel skills. The support chains for overhead rings need 8 to 12 feet of chain to accommodate the rhythmic movement of a child traversing the device.

## SAFETY AND OVERHEAD LADDERS

The injuries associated with overhead equipment generally result from falls (Waltzman, Shannon, Bowen, & Bailey, 1999). Falls tend to occur when children fail to reach a rung or lose their grip on a rung and fall to the surface, onto the access ladder, or onto another structure, or when they tire before reaching the end of the structure. Because of the number of injuries associated with falls from overhead ladders, the American Society for Testing and Materials (ASTM, 1993) recommends a maximum overhead equipment height of 60 inches for preschools and 84 inches for school-age playgrounds. To minimize the risk of failing to reach a rung, maximum distances between rungs are not recommended to exceed 14 inches. To reduce the risk of a child falling onto the access deck, it is recommended that the final handhold should be at least 8 inches from the edge of the deck (Ratté, Denham, & Johnson, 1990; Tinsworth, 1996). The *Handbook for Public Playground Safety* (CPSC, 1997) concludes that 4-year-olds are generally the youngest children capable of using upper body devices. The present authors have been unable to find research supporting this conclusion.

In a study of playground injuries resulting in litigation, Frost and Sweeney (1996) found that 14 out of 190 serious injuries (7 percent) were associated with horizontal overhead ladders. Litigation usually results from very serious injuries resulting in some degree of permanent effect on the injured child. Falls from excessive heights onto excessively hard surfaces were most frequently associated with injuries connected to use of overhead ladders. In addition, unintended use of equipment was associated with injuries. "One particularly hazardous scenario occurs when children stand or walk on top of climber rungs (e.g., horizontal ladder rungs)" (Frost & Sweeney, 1996, p. 8).

## Radial Head Subluxation (Nursemaid's elbow)

> You're taking your toddler for a walk, you're holding her hand to cross the street. As you approach the curb, in an effort to help her step up onto the sidewalk again, you give her a quick hoist upwards using her outstretched arm. Suddenly she howls, holds her elbow area and refuses to bend her arm. What have you done—you BEAST? Nothing unusual. When you gave her that arm-lift, the end of the arm-bone closest to the thumb side on that arm pulled briefly out its socket, and a ligament got trapped when the bone-end went back in place. Emergency room visit? Probably not. (www.kidsdoctor.com/cgi-bin/display.cgi?/articles?)

The above reference also explains how parents can safely "pop the ligament back into place." This is reported to be a painful but very brief and effective procedure consisting of rotating the elbow in a specified manner.

The authors include here a rather lengthy discussion of radial head subluxation, or nursemaid's elbow, because of current controversy regarding whether preschool-age children should use overhead apparatus. Those believing children should not use such equipment frequently claim that the joints of the arm would be damaged by such use. The following information helps place this issue in a medical perspective.

## Medical Research on Radial Head Subluxation

Radial head subluxation (RHS), or nursemaid's elbow, was explored on 256 sites and 17 links using the Google search engine, over 300 sites on Yahoo, in medical literature, and by interviewing medical professionals who work in emergency rooms or who treat children's injuries in other medical facilities. RHS, in medical terms, is an anterior subluxation of the radial head away from the capitellum through the annular ligament (National Center for Emergency Medicine Informatics (n.d.). Retrieved April 17, 2002, from www.ncemi.org/cse/cse0917.htm). In layman's terms it is usually referred to as a "pulled elbow." The subject was explored to determine whether and to what extent the injury occurs as a result of children using overhead apparatus on the playground.

The age at which RHS is most likely to occur is between 18 months and 3 years. All our sources were in consensus that RHS is unlikely to occur after age 5, except with some children who are prone to RHS. RHS has been reported in children as young as four months and as old as 15 years. Children who have suffered RHS are more likely to have a repeat occurrence. Females are slightly more prone to RHS than males and the left arm is slightly more prone to RHS than the right arm.

Diagnosis of RHS is made primarily by history. The patterns observed include a young child with no history of trauma who suddenly refuses to use her arm. The child may have been pulled up and over an obstacle. An arm may be forcibly pulled through the sleeve of a sweater or coat. The child may hold the arm flexed 15-20 degrees at the elbow and hold the forearm partially pronated, and may support the weight of the affected arm with the other hand. The head of the radius may be tender and the child may resist moving the forearm. Following proper treatment, no permanent injury results from this condition (Wayne Wolfram, MD, MPH, Children's Hospital of Cincinnati in www.emedicine.com/emerg/topic392.htm).

The epidemiology of RHS is based on the nature of bone and ligament development. In very young children, "the ligament is somewhat lax and the bone still fairly pliable" (Doctor George.com, 2004), and is due to the "peculiar anatomic shape of the radial head, and the weakness of the annular ligament at this age (1 to 3), that allows the radial head to be pulled out" (Orthoseek, 2004). According to Wheeless' Textbook of Orthopedics (1996), the radial head does not ossify until around age 4, thus making the elbow joint more susceptible to RHS.

Medical professionals may take an x-ray to rule out any bone injuries, although RHS itself does not yield any abnormal radiological findings. The doctor reduces the radial head subluxation by holding the arm securely, and supinating the forearm fully. The radial head reduces with a palpable or audible click, following which the child gets complete relief and almost immediately starts using his arm again. If treatment is delayed by more than 12 hours, the child may take a little longer to resume use of the arm. In these cases, the arm may be rested in a splint or sling for 24 hours.

Most references concluded that RHS could result from a number of causes:

- A sudden jerk or pull on the child's straightened arm, such as when an older child, nursemaid, or adult yanks a child by the arm to make him or her behave
- Pulling or jerking a child out of danger
- Lifting a child by one hand
- Lifting a child by one or both arms and swinging him, dropping all his weight onto an outstretched arm or arms
- Deliberate violent jerking by an adult, as in child abuse.

One medical professional suggested that an important precipitating factor was the normal recalcitrance of the 1- to 3-year-old age group, resulting in adults pulling, jerking, or dragging the child. Another source (Adler, 2002) referred to the condition as "K-Mart Elbow," perhaps referring to harried parents pulling their children too vigorously in K-Mart. Others referred to parents becoming too aggressive in play activities, particularly swinging games in which the parent firmly grasps the child by the hands, wrists, or forearms and jerks or swings the child aggressively. A professor at the University of Texas in Brownsville stated that she had heard of subluxated elbow injuries related to merry-go-rounds but offered no concrete evidence. It seems reasonable that such an injury could result from the sudden, forceful pressure exerted when a child grabs a rapidly spinning merry-go-round while standing in a stable position, as well as when a child jumps from a height and grabs a bar with one hand as she falls.

Two references cite RHS as being caused when a child hangs from a climber on a playground (Gonzalez, 1999) or during play (DoctorGeorge.com, 2004). However no specific information was presented. In a follow-up with the registered nurse who wrote of RHS as being caused when a child hangs from a climber on a playground or during play, the nurse explained that the child fell or jumped from a geodesic dome. After that incident, the child's elbow was again subluxed when the child pulled away from the teacher and when he fell out of his chair.

No additional information was available on this case, but it appears likely that the child exerted an unusual amount of pressure on his elbow when falling or jumping from the top of the climber and snapping his elbow, rather than using overhead apparatus in the usual manner. The most common use of such apparatus is hanging from the bottom of the device, employing grasping strength for support.

A registered nurse with 13 years of experience—10 years in emergency rooms—related that most of the RHS cases he had seen resulted from the child being held by the hand or hands and swung in a circle while playing. This RN believed that a child could not hang onto overhead apparatus with enough grip to create sufficient pressure to dislocate the joints. Dr. Carl Gabbard of Texas A&M University supported this conclusion and proposed that while the child can hold his/her own body weight, that strength is limited and most likely not enough to cause injury. This conclusion is consistent with our observations of 3- and 4-year-old children and with accounts of teachers who supervise children playing extensively on overhead apparatus that are designed at proper heights and protected with proper surfacing.

We recommend that overhead apparatus for 3- to 5-year-olds be no more than 60 inches above the protective surfacing, maintained at more than a 12-inch depth. We also recommend that take-off decks at each end be installed that allow children to reach the overhead apparatus, and that these decks be constructed of resilient, pliable material such as vertically mounted, soft airplane tires or equivalent material. There should be no metal bars at the ends of overhead apparatus that would allow children to climb on top of the overhead bars. Metal ladder-type bars at the ends of overhead apparatus pose the risk of children striking their heads when falling.

Perhaps equally important as proper design and use of playground equipment in preventing RHS is ensuring that adults who supervise playgrounds be trained to identify conditions and actions that could trigger the injury and be trained in appropriate emergency procedure. Our research consistently has shown that children of all ages use virtually all components of play equipment as climbers, commonly in unintended ways. They will climb, attempt to support their weight, fall (especially during early stages), jump from equipment component to equipment component, and swing from bars not intended for climbing or overhead play. An element of risk for injuries such as RHS exists on any challenging playground designed for very young children.

We acknowledge that additional medical literature may be found that could result in modifying the above report and we welcome additional information about RHS, young children, and playgrounds from our colleagues interested in child safety on playgrounds.

## INTENDED AND UNINTENDED
## USES OF OVERHEAD APPARATUS

Intended use of playground equipment is a concept that does not apply to how children actually use playground equipment. According to Thompson (1988), "The idea that children can misuse equipment during play is a concept which seems absurd to many persons . . . the problem is the design of the equipment and not the play of the children who use it" (p. 73). As children master equipment, they look for more challenging ways of using playground equipment, some of which may be unintended (Frost, Sutterby, Therrell, Brown, & Thornton, 2001; Sawyers, 1994). Designers or manufacturers may assume that children will use overhead ladders by crossing from one side to the other on the rungs using alternating hands. Movement specialists also recommend using overhead equipment to hang by the knees, pull up the legs through the arms to do a flip (Gallahue, 1982), chin up on the bars, and swing side to side from the bars (Noble, 1983).

Unintended use of playground equipment is common. Risk-taking is a natural part of children's use of playground equipment as children challenge themselves to perform more physically demanding feats. In addition, overhead ladders intended for older children may be used by younger children. Younger children "do not have the skills necessary to safely imitate the activities they see older children performing" (Sawyers, 1994, p. 32). Overhead ladders are likely to be included in typical playground activities like rough and tumble play, chase games, or competitions (Frost, Wortham, & Reifel, 2001). Activities during which children interact closely with each other may result in falls when they push or collide with each other (Tinsworth, 1996). For overhead ladders specifically, other unintended use includes walking across the top of the ladder on the rungs and along the sides, and sitting on top of the overhead ladder (Friedlander & Lohmeyer, 1988; Hewes & Beckwith, 1975).

In conclusion, falling is the primary risk for children using overhead equipment. The chance of falling is increased for children under 5 years of age trying to use equipment designed for older school-age children (Frost & Kim, 2000). Like all playground equipment, overhead ladders will be used in unintended ways, thereby increasing the risk for injury. The experience of the present authors and their discussions with experts in playground safety confirm that the dual hazards of excessively high equipment and hard surfaces account for most serious injuries to children using overhead apparatus.

We have observed many parents and other adults lift preschool children (even toddlers) up to overhead apparatus designed for school-age children (7-8 feet high) and then walk away, seemingly unaware of the extreme risk they have created. Parents, teachers, and other supervisors routinely allow preschool children to use excessively high overhead apparatus and they do not routinely examine the surface material under the apparatus.

## PURPOSE

The purposes of this study were to create a developmental progression of children's skills on overhead apparatus, and to examine the use patterns of overhead equipment by children of different ages.

## QUESTIONS

In order to describe the developmental progression of children's use of overhead apparatus, the researchers investigated the following questions:

1. What characteristics of children's physical movements are associated with their beginning use of overhead equipment?
2. What characteristics of children's physical movements are associated with their development of mastery on overhead equipment?
3. What characteristics of children's physical movements are associated with their mastery of overhead equipment?

Playground experts from such fields as playground safety, design, litigation, and manufacturing were asked the following questions:

1. Are you aware of research or published opinion concluding that suspending from overhead apparatus can injure arms and/or shoulders of 2-, 3-, and 4-year-olds?
2. What is the appropriate general beginning age for using overhead apparatus? Do you agree with the ASTM/CPSC recommendations? What modifications should be made?
3. Are you aware of research papers on children's use of overhead apparatus?

## METHODS

Four doctoral students in early childhood education, all trained in playground research, conducted observations at St. Matthew's Preschool & Child Development Center (pseudonym). Three researchers observed 77 preschool children on the preschool and kindergarten playgrounds. A fourth researcher observed 41 third- and fifth-grade students on the school-age playground. A total of 1,637 episodes of overhead apparatus use were observed over a period of 7 months (1,348 preschool and 289 school-age). Videotapes and photographs were taken during all observations.

## PRESCHOOL OBSERVATIONS

The preschoolers ranged in age from 3 to 6. Each class played outdoors for 30 minutes, three times a day: in the morning, just after lunch, and in the afternoon (unless the temperature was over 103 degrees Fahrenheit). Two classes were observed: 3- to 4-year-olds and 4- to 6-year-olds. The 3s and younger 4s played exclusively on the preschool playground. The older 4-year-olds and the 5- and 6-year-olds played on both the preschool and kindergarten playgrounds. The children were observed once in the morning and once after lunch.

The preschool playground had only one piece of overhead equipment, an overhead ladder. All play equipment use zones were surfaced with 12 inches of sand. The overhead ladder was made of metal and painted blue. A large tree provided partial shade for the overhead ladder. The apparatus had 6 rungs located 60 inches from the top of the playground surfacing. In place of the usual vertical rungs for children to climb on to reach the overhead bars, playground designers buried two vertically placed balloon-type tires halfway in the sand between the vertical supports, perpendicular to the bars. As children approached the bars, they walked up one slope of the first tire. As they reached for the first bar, they were at the very top of the half-buried tire. As they released the last bar, they touched the top of the second tire with their feet and walked down its outside slope. The distance from the top of the tires to the first/last overhead bars was 50 inches. The diameter of each overhead rung was 1 inch. The diameter of the horizontal bars that connect all the overhead rungs was 2 inches.

The kindergarten playground had two pieces of overhead equipment, a slanted overhead ladder, and a set of gymnastic rings. All play equipment use zones were surfaced with 12 inches of sand. A large tree shaded both pieces of overhead equipment on this playground. The slanted overhead ladder was one component of a composite play structure. The higher end of the slanted overhead ladder extended from the composite play structure. All of the children were tall enough to grasp the first bar with their feet still on the deck, and most of the children were able to grasp the second bar before their feet left the deck. The last bar was located 60 inches above the ground. None of the children were able to touch the ground while still holding onto the last bar on the slanted overhead ladder. The six overhead rungs were 1 inch in diameter with a circumference of 4-3/8 inches, similar to the diameter of the overhead rungs on the preschool playground. The 4 posts of the slanted overhead ladder were wood. One of the 4 vertical posts also served as part of the structure for the gymnastics rings.

The gymnastic rings were located near the end of the slanted overhead ladder. The children were required to begin the ring activity from a tire half-buried in the sand and located at the end and to the side of the slanted overhead ladder. The fourth vertical post, which was shared by the overhead ladder and the ring set, was located to the right of the tire from which the children access the rings. The portion of the ring that the children grasped was oblong-shaped (taller than it is deep), about 4-3/16 inches around, and about 1 inch in diameter. Most of the time, only one ring was used while the other ring was placed out of reach by the teachers. The use zone of the rings was surfaced with 12 inches of sand.

## SCHOOL-AGE OBSERVATIONS

Twenty-three 3rd-graders and eighteen 5th-graders were observed and individually tracked almost daily over the course of two weeks during separate 20-minute recess periods at midday. The average age of the 3rd-graders was 8.5 years, and the 5th-graders averaged 10.5 years. Because a child's reach is often an essential factor in traversing overhead equipment, this was measured for each age group. The reach from the middle of each palm while arms were stretched out to the sides at a ninety-degree angle averaged 48 inches for the 3rd-graders and 50 inches for the 5th-graders.

The school-age playground included four types of overhead equipment: an overhead ladder, a chain balance component, rings suspended by eight inches of chain (ring trek), and a track ride. The overhead ladder had 6 bars, the horizontal supports for the chain balance component were 63 inches apart and 8 feet in length, the rings were aligned in 3 columns of 4 across, and the track ride was 8 feet long. The equipment use zones were surfaced with 2.5 to 6 inches of sand. All decks were padded with rubber material.

Most typical or repeating patterns of overhead usage emerged during the first two days of observations. Observations, recorded anecdotally, by digital pictures, and via video recordings, were concluded after three days of observing no new type of usage.

## DATA COLLECTION

Data were collected over a period of 7 months. Observations lasted between 20 and 90 minutes each. Videotape and digital pictures taken during all observations were used during coding to ensure accuracy.

### Coding Instrument

The coding instrument was developed over a period of 2 weeks (see Appendix). It includes 11 categories: participant number, performance, body size, reach to bar, hand hold, travel, direction, body, legs, arm-to-leg relation, and exit. Specifically, each category was coded as follows:

- Participant numbers were assigned in order to protect the identity of subjects. Participants' age and gender were noted on a separate list.
- Performance was determined to be either *individual* or *assisted*. Individual performance was defined as no help from the teacher. Assisted performance was defined as any help from the teacher.
- Body size was determined in two ways: height and build. Children were described as *short*, *average*, or *tall* in height in comparison with the other children in their class. They were also described as *small*, *medium*, or *large* in build, also in relation to the other children in their class.
- Reach to bar was described as either *1-handed* or *2-handed*, with either the *right* or *left hand leading* (reaching first). *Reaching* and *jumping* to the overhead rungs also was described in this section.
- Hand hold described the way each hand was positioned on the overhead rungs, and was noted separately for each hand. If the thumb went under the bar while the fingers went over, the position was noted as *lock grip*. If the thumb and fingers went over the bar, the position was noted as *cup grip*. If the thumb was extended out 90 degrees from the fingers (at a right angle from the fingers) with the fingers wrapping over the bar, the position was noted as *half-grip*. If the hands were facing each other either on the same or different bars, they were noted as *oppositional*.

- Travel across the bars was described as *hand-to-hand*, *hand-over-hand*, or *skipping bars*. *Hand-to-hand* travel was defined as grasping a rung with both hands before moving to the next, one hand at a time. *Hand-over-hand* travel was defined as grasping each bar with only one hand. The actual number of bars skipped was noted when appropriate. Observers also noted whether the *right*, *left*, or *alternating hands* led during travel.
- Direction was described as either *forwards* or *backwards*.
- Body motion was described as *front/back*, *side/side*, or *both*.
- Leg motion was described to be either *pedaling* (slower movement) or *running* (faster movement). If no leg motion was indicated, then children were not actively moving their legs.
- Arm-to-leg relation was noted as either *same* or *opposite*. Observers noted if the same leg as arm swung forward at the same time or if the leg opposite the arm swung forward.
- Exit was described as either *controlled*, *fall*, or *teacher assisted*. The *number of bars completed* also was described.

Coding children's performances using the above categories was done by placing circles next to the appropriate descriptor on the coding sheet. An empty circle placed in a box on the coding sheet indicates that the subject performs that particular action partially, while a filled-in circle on the coding sheet indicates that the subject performs that action completely. For instance, an empty circle in the *assisted performance* box indicates that the subject was helped by the teacher only part of the time during that turn on the overhead equipment. A filled-in circle in the same box would indicate that the subject was helped by the teacher the entire time during that turn on the overhead equipment.

Inter-rater reliability with this coding instrument was >.90.

## FINDINGS FOR PRESCHOOL CHILDREN
## (3- TO 6-YEAR-OLDS)

After completing observations, the researchers coded all videotaped observations with the coding instrument described above. A total of 1,348 episodes of overhead equipment use were analyzed during the preschool observations. The researchers then were able to use the data to answer the following research questions.

1. What characteristics of preschool children's physical movements are associated with their beginning use of overhead equipment?

Children who were beginning to use the overhead equipment needed assistance throughout their overhead apparatus use. Upon first exposure to the equipment, many 3- and 4-year-olds would stand on the tire, grasp the first rung, pull their feet up and hang suspended, not knowing how to proceed. Teachers would grasp them by the waist and partially support them as they traversed the overhead ladder. This assistance frequently was accompanied by words of encouragement (scaffolding) by both the teacher and the children. Children grasped the bars with both hands cupped, and switched hands as they traveled to the opposite end of the equipment. They only moved forward on the apparatus, and used little body and leg movement because they were being held by teachers. They either fell from the equipment or needed help with their exits.

Accessing first bar and then falling from equipment.

Assisted exit.

Proceeding hand-to-hand (hands meet on same bar before going to the next).

Running/ pedaling leg motion.

Skipping bars.

Using coordinated
rhythm.

Turning around on the
bars, using the "Texas
Twister."

Jumping to the
third bar.

The researchers noted that all children who had no previous experience on the apparatus required complete assistance from their teacher when they used the overhead ladder. Most of their traversing attempts resulted in falls by the time they reached the third rung. Within one month of initial practice, most children were traversing, albeit awkwardly, the entire length (6 rungs) of the equipment.

2.  What characteristics of preschool children's physical movements are associated with their semi-skilled use of overhead equipment?

Children who already had some experience on the overhead ladder, but who had not yet mastered the apparatus, sometimes needed assistance from teachers. As the children gained experience with the overhead apparatus, they asked for assistance less and less, and some children even rejected assistance. They usually began with both hands on the starting bar, some with cupped hands, others (usually larger children) with a lock grip (thumb going under the bar).

These children progressed from unassisted hanging by the hands, to partially assisted travel across the bars, to completely unassisted travel across the bars. They usually traveled hand-to-hand; with more experience, a leading hand usually emerged.

Some children who were on the brink of mastering the overhead equipment exhibited hand-over-hand travel. Although most children at this level moved forward across the bars, some with more experience experimented with going backward. These children could travel forward across the entire apparatus; when going backward, however, they were only able to complete at most three bars.

At this skill level, children's bodies moved in all directions, and were largely uncontrolled until they gained enough experience to use body momentum in their favor. Their leg movements were also largely extraneous and uncontrolled, and they often seemed to be running or pedaling in the air.

As they gained experience on the overhead ladder, children began to move the same side arm as leg, eventually developing a swinging motion that carried them from bar to bar (this usually happened in conjunction with hand-over-hand travel). Exits at this skill level range from uncontrolled falls to controlled exits.

Children who were semi-skilled at older ages (such as 4 and 5) gained skill more quickly than younger children. Initially, one 4-year-old requested adult assistance for traveling. After only a few crossings, she began requesting assistance less and less, gradually controlled her body and leg movements, and exhibited characteristics consistent with the refining stage. This 4-year-old gained skill more quickly than the 5-year-old observed because she continually worked on her abilities and had more experiences with the overhead ladder. The 5-year-old participated in significantly fewer episodes, and subsequently remained semi-skilled for a longer period of time.

3.  What characteristics of preschool children's physical movements are associated with their skilled use of overhead equipment?

Children who developed the skill to use overhead apparatus were those who did not need any assistance on the equipment. They could either cup or lock grip the bars. They could begin with either one or two hands on the starting bar, and often jumped to the second, third, or even fourth bar of the overhead ladder. They were able to complete the entire overhead ladder, and sometimes skip bars as they traveled.

They developed a sequence and a rhythm for their equipment use. The sequence usually consisted of grabbing the starting bar with a certain hand leading, and traveling across the bars with a certain hand leading first. Rhythm could be seen in the body and leg movements as the children moved efficiently and with little extraneous movement across the bars. Children who were skillful at using the overhead apparatus moved the same side arm and leg in a controlled fashion, and they were able to exit the apparatus with control.

The children observed to be skilled at navigating overhead apparatus often were observed experimenting with various movements on the equipment. As mentioned previously, children who were very skilled at using overhead ladders would sometimes skip bars, go backwards, or jump past the first bar and grasp the second, third, or fourth bar. They would hang upside down by hooking their knees over the bars and also would attempt to travel up the slanted overhead ladder, traveling against gravity.

The 5- and 6-year-old children challenged themselves on the rings once they had developed sufficient skill on them. They increased their momentum on the rings by kicking against the posts that supported the play structure. They also twisted and turned on the rings, spinning very quickly as they swung from the rings. They could do any of the previously described activities while hanging by one hand.

## FINDINGS FOR SCHOOL-AGE CHILDREN
### (3rd- and 5th-GRADERS)

In addition to answering the research questions, information was collected on the types of behaviors that children of different ages exhibited on different types of overhead equipment. While the younger preschoolers were limited to using a simple overhead ladder, the older preschoolers (5- and 6-year-olds) had access to the slanted overhead bars as well as the gymnastics rings, and the school-age children had access to a tall overhead ladder, a track ride, and a ring trek.

A wide variety of use patterns were observed for the school-age children, especially on the overhead ladder and ring trek. Nine unintentional falls were observed from the overhead ladder and rings, but no injuries were reported. Observations, recorded anecdotally, by digital pictures, and via video recordings, were concluded after three days of observing no new type of usage.

### Overhead Ladder

Ninety-four percent of the time, school-age (3rd and 5th grade) children employed cup type grips (thumb on top with fingers). The most difficult access from the platform was accomplished by leaping from both feet to either the third (16 percent) or fourth bars (57 percent), horizontal leaps of 24 and 36 inches, respectively. Because the span from one platform to the opposite side was 5 feet, egress typically was achieved from the fourth bar (78 percent) by utilizing the momentum from the initial leap and swinging the remaining 24 inches onto the opposite platform with both feet. The simplest type of use among both age groups was hand-to-hand, occurring 4 percent of the time. Such usage was observed for only one 3rd-grader and one 5th-grader. Children in both grades also used hand-over-hand (6 percent) and skipped either one bar (7 percent) or two bars (12 percent). Most of the children used body momentum from leaping or swinging and used very little leg movement to go from bar to bar other than to swing them onto the opposite platform. The remainder of usage included traversing or hanging on the bars with palms facing, hanging on one bar, backward travel one bar at a time, or reversing direction. Fifth-graders used the bars more of the time in random or creative ways than did the 3rd-graders. Third-graders could replicate any of the patterns performed by 5th-graders, although they did not do so as often. Behavior also included climbing onto the top of the bars and sitting for various periods of time, or hanging by the legs upside down.

### Chain Balancing Component

This device included chains stretched horizontally six inches above the ground surface and overhead chains stretched horizontally overhead. Children walked (balanced) on the lower chains and supported their movement by holding onto the overhead chains with their hands. They used the chain with either a hand-to-hand sideward slide (38 percent), or a hand-over-hand forward movement (62 percent), moving a distance of from one to four feet before dropping to the surface. All gripping was of a cup type. This device was used least of the overhead apparatus on the playground.

### Ring Trek

The cup grip was used 79 percent of the time, and the lock grip 21 percent of the time. Access was most often (60 percent) from a slight crouching position with one ring already in hand, and the other hand raised to eye level, aimed at grabbing the next ring just prior to leaping from the platform. Egress was usually accomplished (92 percent) by using the momentum from swinging to reach the opposite platform. The children spent most of their time swinging their legs in tandem to develop momentum for accessing the next ring. The more advanced swingers could achieve a sideways hip pivot of almost 90 degrees between their legs and torso. Due to the configuration of the rings in three rows, they often crossed over to an adjacent row, using the set of 12 rings in a random order. As with the overhead ladder, 5th-graders engaged in such random or creative swinging more often than 3rd-graders. Fifth-graders used the ring trek almost twice as frequently as did 3rd-graders.

### Track Ride

Among the four types of overhead equipment, the school-age children used a lock grip most frequently on the track or zip ride (38 percent of the time). Basic access and egress were accomplished using both feet to push off of and land on the platforms. Advanced access was accomplished by leaping a short distance to the u-shaped gripping device. Advanced riders could use one or both legs to push off the padded end-supports at the opposite platform sufficiently hard to traverse back to the starting platform, doing such a back-and-forth ride up to three or four times in one turn. Other advanced uses (although not intended by design) included a forward hand-over-hand movement along the top of the ring trek's horizontal support bar for a foot or two before dropping to the surface. Because of the large size of the support bar, the only possible grip was the cup type.

### All School-age Overhead Equipment

Not including the zip ride with the smaller handle (slightly under 1" in diameter), over 85 percent of the 3rd- and 5th-grader grips were of the cup type. Advanced access to the equipment typically was accomplished by leaping from both feet. Basic access was accomplished simply by reaching up to the equipment. Egress, both advanced and basic, was done by swinging onto the opposite deck or platform with both feet.

Overall, the 3rd- and 5th-graders' basic and advanced abilities to use overhead equipment were remarkably similar. Advanced 3rd-graders could replicate any of the specific actions or patterns performed by advanced 5th-graders. It was somewhat surprising to observe one 5th-grader using a hand-to-hand type of movement along the monkey bars. The only difference appeared in the degree of usage between the two age groups. Advanced 5th-graders used the monkey bars and swinging rings more of the time in random or creative ways than did the advanced 3rd-graders. Fifth-graders used the swinging rings almost twice as much as the 3rd-graders.

Preliminary findings indicate that these children were bored or under-challenged with the current equipment. Their usage was typically brief (5 to 45 seconds) and uninspired before choosing to engage elsewhere on the playground, whether on other equipment, in games, or in socializing. In informal interviews with the 5th-graders, the children who had been playing on this equipment for two to three years indicated that the equipment had become either "old" or "not very hard" and asked when new equipment might be installed. Some of the advanced 3rd-graders echoed such comments, even though their usage period had been a year or less. Despite such comments, these school-age children displayed a broad range of usage on the given overhead equipment from basic to advanced types. Also, these four pieces of overhead equipment were used almost as much as the nearby bays of swings, approximately the same amount of time as the climbing equipment, and considerably more than the linked slides, tubes, and bridges that composed the remainder of the playscape.

## THE DEVELOPMENTAL STAGES OF
## OVERHEAD LADDER USE:  AGES 3 -11

From analysis of the 1,637 coded observations, the researchers created a developmental progression for a horizontal overhead ladder. Four skill levels are described: fundamental, practice, refining, and mastery. A chart depicting the various characteristics for each stage is provided on page 113.

### Fundamental Stage

Children in the *fundamental* stage are just beginning to use overhead equipment. Children in this stage are uncertain about the apparatus or what to do with their bodies in order to traverse the overhead ladder. Full adult assistance is required during this time. Children in this stage are typically 3 years old or younger, and they frequently will not be tall enough to reach the first bar (depending on the design of the overhead ladder). In such an instance, they may need to be lifted to reach the bar.

WARNING! We believe that children should not be lifted to bars more than a few inches above the height of the take-off device, or about 12 to 16 inches above the resilient surfacing, because children will fall often during the fundamental stage. The surfacing material must be properly installed and maintained and the take-off device must be sufficiently resilient to indent slightly when the child is standing on it (e.g., a vertical tire).

Children in the fundamental stage will reach for the first bar with two hands, grabbing the bar with both hands in a cupped grip (thumbs wrapped over the top of the bar). These children will hang on the first bar and swing their bodies independent of adult assistance if the overhead ladder is included as a play structure component that provides easy access to the first rung. However, they need adult support as they attempt to travel forward, and they typically move with unsteady, unpredictable movements. For the most part, these children will attempt to travel hand-to-hand across the bars, although some may attempt hand-over-hand travel. They exhibit a distinct absence of a consistent leading hand, reaching for the next bar with either hand.

Because there is total adult assistance during crossing, little leg and body movement is present during the fundamental stage. Generally, adults support the children's body weight, essentially carrying them from rung to rung. As a result, the children do not need to create momentum with their bodies to traverse the bars. Occasionally, children may pump their legs, but this is largely unconscious, extraneous movement. Generally, their arms and legs move in the same relation to each other (right with right, left with left) because of the adults' positioning of their bodies. Full adult assistance is also needed when exiting the apparatus. Falls are more common than full crossings, especially in the initial experiences.

## Practice Stage

Children in the *practice* stage have progressed past their first experiences on overhead equipment and are beginning to be more independent in their overhead ladder use. They have had time to learn the fundamentals of navigating overhead ladders, and are ready to begin practicing those skills. Adult assistance is not required to the degree previously needed, but it is recommended that adults remain close by children during this stage; the children may request assistance, particularly if they are afraid of falling. Children in this stage are typically older 3-year-olds and 4-year-olds, and are generally tall enough to reach the first bar (again, depending on the design of the overhead ladder). Some may still need to be lifted to reach the bar, while others prefer to jump up to it.

While approaching the first bar of the overhead ladder, children in the practice stage will reach with two hands, grabbing the bar with both hands in a cupped hold (thumbs wrapped over the top of the bar). When they have grasped the first bar with both hands, they typically do one of two things: hang or travel. Those children just entering the practice stage will frequently just hang on the first bar. After they have practiced hanging and are comfortable with it, they will attempt to travel. Generally, these children will attempt to travel hand-to-hand across the bars. Just as in the fundamental stage, there is a distinct absence of a consistent leading hand; they will reach for the next bar with either hand. Complete crossings are not common during this stage.

Children in the practice stage characteristically exhibit a great deal of leg and body movement as they begin experiencing and experimenting with the effects of momentum. Early in the stage, when children are mostly hanging on the first bar, they will practice swinging their bodies forwards and backwards. They also do a great deal of pedaling and running with their legs. When hanging progresses into traveling, children's movements are so erratic that they sometimes hinder travel across the bars. As a result, children's arms and legs may move in opposition to each other (right with left, left with right) because of their inability to control the momentum and movement of their bodies.

Exiting the apparatus during this stage can be either controlled or accidental. For those children who hang on the first bar, independently controlled exits are possible. Some know that they can simply lower their feet back to the access step. For those who attempt travel, falls are more common than full crossings. This is largely because they are still developing the upper body strength necessary to support their body weight with one arm as they attempt to reach the next rung. Arms and hands become fatigued; thus, falls occur.

## Refining Stage

The *refining* stage of skill development is usually reached when children have had much experience and practice with overhead ladders. This usually occurs with children around the age of 4 to 6 years, depending on the amount of exposure to and experience with overhead ladders. At this skill level, children do not need assistance and can reach the overhead bars by themselves.

They usually begin traveling with both hands on the starting bar (not necessarily the first bar), with both hands cupped over the bar. Some children show signs of a lock grip at this point. When children at this skill level traverse the overhead bars, they usually travel hand-to-hand; that is, they place both hands on the same rung before moving, one hand at a time, to the next rung. Some children have developed the ability to move hand-over-hand on the bars at this point (only one hand grabs each bar), but they are usually on the cusp of moving into the mastery stage of overhead ladder use.

Children in the refining stage usually travel forward across the bars, but some can traverse the bars backwards for a few rungs. At this point in the developmental progression, their bodies are still moving quite considerably in front/back, side/side, or diagonal motion. Compared to the previous skill levels, however, children in the refining skill level have more controlled and rhythmic movement, which helps them move their bodies toward the opposite side of the overhead ladder. Minor pedaling of the legs still occurs, but the legs are largely used in conjunction with body movements (front/back, side/side, diagonal). In essence, the legs work with the rhythmic movement of the torso. Children are learning to swing from one bar to the next, leading with the same side arm and leg for more efficient movement than using opposite arm and leg. Children at the refining stage usually perform controlled exits from overhead equipment.

## Mastery Stage

The *mastery* stage of overhead apparatus use is usually reached when children have had extensive experience and practice with overhead ladders. This usually occurs with children approximately between the ages of 6 to 9 years, depending on exposure to and experience with overhead ladders. (There are, of course, wide individual differences in the age at which children achieve stages of use or levels of skill.) At the mastery skill level, children do not need assistance on the overhead ladder.

They can begin travel with either one or both hands on the starting bar (not necessarily the first bar). Most children use a lock grip at this point, but some smaller children who have mastered the overhead ladder are not able to use a lock grip because of their small hand size, and therefore use a cup grip. When children at this skill level move across the overhead bars, they travel hand-over-hand and often experiment with direction, skipping bars, and traversing the side bar.

Children in the mastery stage demonstrate an economy of motion, displaying little to no extraneous movement. Their bodies and legs move rhythmically and efficiently.

Children at this stage have developed the ability to swing from one bar to the next, leading with same side arm as leg for the most effective movement. Children at the mastery stage of overhead ladder usually almost always exit the equipment with control, unless they are experimenting with the overhead apparatus and happen to fall.

These findings are consistent with Gabbard and Patterson's (1981) conclusion that the ability to support body weight increases with age. They are also consistent with Hendy's (1997) assertion that skill levels increase with experience.

## INTERVIEWS WITH PLAYGROUND EXPERTS

Interviews with playground experts were conducted by two doctoral students by phone and E-mail. All answers were compiled, summarized, and member-checked. The questions were:

- Are you aware of research or published opinion concluding that suspending from overhead apparatus can injure arms and/or shoulders of 2-, 3-, and 4-year-olds?
- What should be the general beginning age for using overhead apparatus? Do you agree with the ASTM/CPSC recommendations about overhead equipment use for pre-school-age children? What modifications should be made?
- Are you aware of research papers on children's use of overhead apparatus?

One expert, Carl Gabbard from Texas A&M University in College Station, Texas, recommended 5 as the age at which many children should be allowed to use overhead apparatus. He explains that 40 percent of 5-year-old children can cross an overhead ladder without falling. Most children younger than 5 (i.e., 80 percent of 4-year-olds), Gabbard explains, are not able to support their body weight with one arm while reaching for the next rung. This finding resulted from an overhead usage study conducted by Gabbard and Patterson in 1981. In personal conversation with one of the present writers, Gabbard expressed his belief that preschool children would benefit developmentally from using overhead apparatus.

Tom Bowler, an expert who deals in playground litigation, believes that young children lack the upper body strength to use overhead equipment; therefore, he believes, "many 4-year-olds are physically not capable of holding onto the second rung before dropping." He agrees with CPSC recommendations and Gabbard's (1981) research about children's grip and support of weight, and thus he believes that height of overhead equipment should be consistent with ASTM recommendations.

A contradicting opinion expressed by other experts is that chronological age is an inadequate indicator of readiness. David Gallahue, Associate Dean in the School of Health, Physical Education, and Recreation at Indiana University, stated that he prefers to consider the developmental levels of individual children to evaluate physical readiness for overhead playground equipment. "Some children may be ready at age 2 or 3, others not until age 5 or 6. It all depends on where the child is developmentally. Furthermore, the nature of the task, the biology of the individual, and the conditions of the learning environment all interact to determine when each individual is ready for any activity."

Hesitation to allow young children access to overhead equipment stems largely from the fear of injuries caused by falls from the apparatus. Bowler believes that "the overhead

## Developmental Progression Chart

This chart summarizes the four stages of skill development on overhead ladders.

| | Fundamental (approx. 2-3 years) | Practice (approx. 3-4 years) | Refining (approx. 4-6 years) | Mastery (approx. 6-11 years) |
|---|---|---|---|---|
| **Assistance** | full assistance throughout episode | some still requested, but generally less than before | none needed | none |
| **Reach to Bar** | 2 hands, assisted, may need to be lifted to reach bar | reaches, may jump depending on height | reaches with two hands | one hand (preferred hand leads consistently); may jump to 3$^{rd}$ - 4$^{th}$ bar with both hands to start episode |
| **Hand Hold** | both hands cupped | both hands cupped | one or both hands cupped—some emergence of lock grip, usually on preferred leading hand | usually cup grip, depending on hand size and bar size; lock grip emerging |
| **Travel** | hanging, hand-to-hand, assisted, inconsistent leading hand | hanging, may travel hand-to-hand for a few bars, inconsistent leading hand | hand-to-hand, leading hand preference emerges (some hand over hand) | hand over hand; capable of skipping bars (depending on arm length); experiment with different ways of traveling |
| **Direction** | forward only | forward only | forwards, some backwards travel with more experience | forward and backward; also sideways on sidebar |
| **Body** | little movement because held by adult | all directions (front, back, side, diagonal) | all directions as before, but more controlled; developing rhythmic movement | little extraneous movement, efficient body movement; consistent rhythm |
| **Legs** | little movement because held by adult (some inconsistent leg movement) | pedaling and running motions | minor pedaling, legs used in conjunction with body momentum | leg motion is extension of torso movement |
| **Arm-to-Leg Relation** | teacher-assisted | same and opposite | same | same |
| **Exit** | teacher-assisted exits and falls (teacher catches child) | controlled exit when hanging, falls when attempting to travel | largely controlled exits after successful episode, some falls still occur | controlled exit, all bars completed |

height of 60 inches for 2- to 5-year-olds (ASTM) is really too high for many children. Overhead equipment for 2- to 5-year-olds should have special warnings for parents indicating the concern of falls, signage for spotting/helping their children, and obviously, enough resilient surfacing material for potential falls." He recommends that this equipment not be provided for 2- to 5-year-olds in unsupervised situations.

Peter Heseltine, Vice President of the International Play Association and the England representative for The Royal Society for the Prevention of Accidents, provided a statement (2001). The Society concluded that accidents (i.e., falls) linked with overhead bars result from children's limited upper body strength, from challenge levels of apparatus that exceed children's upper body capabilities, and from occasional mistakes or errors of judgment that naturally occur during the developmental process of play. The Royal Society's statement does not cite inadequate surfacing as a cause of accidents, explaining that "the result of these falls is often a broken arm or wrist regardless of the type of energy absorbing surface provided. An awkward fall caused by the swinging nature of use and the likelihood of a backwards fall can result in a break even though the surfacing meets all the [safety] recommendations."

This shift of blame away from inadequate surfacing is echoed by Susan Hudson, a representative of the National Program for Playground Safety. She believes that part of teaching children how to traverse across an overhead ladder should be a tutorial on how to fall safely. Falling naturally occurs as children progress through the developmental stages of overhead equipment use, and thus should be anticipated. Teaching children how to fall in safer ways reduces the risk of such injury as broken arms, hands, or wrists. Hudson acknowledges the contention that injuries may occur regardless of the quality of surfacing.

Still other experts suggest alternatives to overhead play equipment, namely toys for building upper body strength without forcing children to support their entire body weight with their arms, wrists, and hands. Rusty Keeler, a playground designer and installer, proposes that providing loose parts for upper body development may be more important than providing overhead apparatus in building children's upper body strength.

Experts expressed concerns about preschool children's upper body strength and their ability to use overhead equipment. However, it is unclear whether these concerns stem from preschool children's inherent lack of upper body strength, or from their lack of opportunities to use and experience with overhead equipment. Some agreement appears to exist among some of the playground experts interviewed that preschoolers may use overhead equipment safely and successfully when supervised by adults, when height is properly regulated, and when adequate resilient surfacing is provided. Safe, successful use also depends on children having sufficient experience with overhead equipment to develop the skills, strength, and perceptual abilities important for accident prevention.

## CONCLUSION

The general purposes of overhead ladders and other overhead play equipment are to support the development of perceptual abilities, motor abilities, upper body strength, and body coordination. Unintended and unsafe use occurs when children seek novelty and create new challenges for themselves on the equipment, such as walking across the top of the rungs and jumping from the top of the rungs. Most injuries involving overhead apparatus result from young children using excessively high equipment and falling onto excessively hard ground surfaces. Such conditions result from improper installation, allowing children to use excessively tall equipment, and from inadequate maintenance and supervision.

Overhead ladders are being eliminated from preschool playgrounds because of CPSC *statements* that are widely interpreted as *prohibitions*. The CPSC (1997) *Guidelines* state, "Four-year-olds are generally the youngest children capable of using upper body devices such as these (horizontal ladders and overhead rings)" (p. 21). The CPSC *Guidelines* also state that overhead rings and track rides are not recommended for preschool-age children (2 through 5 years). The rationale in the CPSC *Guidelines* is that "very young children have not yet developed some of the physical skills necessary for certain climbing activities (including balance, coordination, and upper body strength)" (p. 20). A question arising from such reservations and from the results of the present study is: How can children develop such skills and abilities in the absence of equipment and opportunities to explore and practice them?

The ASTM standards are inconsistent with the CPSC guidelines. The ASTM standards (1993) state: "The maximum height of upper body devices for use by 2 through 5-year-olds shall be no greater than 60 inches" (p. 9). The ASTM standards and particularly the CPSC guidelines are interpreted conservatively by many manufacturers and consumers, resulting in the reduction or exclusion of overhead equipment on an alarming number of preschool and school-age playgrounds throughout the United States.

This conservative approach or "dumbing down" of preschool playgrounds may well result in developmental delays for children already deprived of extensive motor activity because of loss of recess and increased time spent pursuing such sedentary activities as television and computer games. It is interesting to note that neither CPSC nor ASTM prohibit or recommend against overhead ladders on preschool playgrounds, yet popular interpretation includes such prohibition. Concerns about possible litigation resulting from injuries undoubtedly influence this conservative or cautious approach. Restricting overhead apparatus to specific age groups commonly results in absence of such apparatus at preschool centers, which typically enroll children 2 to 5 years of age.

Professor David Gallahue (identified above) from Indiana University and the National Institute for Fitness and Sport, and one of the country's leading experts in developmental physical education, writes specifically about 3- to 8-year-old children:

*Deprivation of experiences hinders learning, especially during the early formative years. Therefore, a well-planned developmentally based physical education program that incorporates a variety of movement activities provides many of the experiences that help children develop perceptual-motor and cognitive concept learning. As educators we need to continue to devise additional opportunities for movement experiences that are often absent from the lives of children.* (Gallahue, 1996, p. 82)

The issue of whether use of overhead apparatus by 3- and 4-year-old children damages hands, arms, and shoulders naturally arises in this context. The researchers engaged in extensive interviews with experts and extensive searches for data on this subject and were unable to find any medical research warning against 3- and 4-year-old children supporting their weight with their arms while using overhead equipment.

Bone growth during the 3- to 5-year-old period is dynamic and the skeletal system is vulnerable to malnutrition, illness, and fatigue (Gallahue, 1996, p. 18). The bones are hardening (ossifying) during this period and myelination (development of a fatty substance around the neurons permitting the transmission of nerve impulses) is progressing rapidly. Consequently, adults should be alert to ensure that children do not repeat motor activities to the point of exhaustion.

The researchers involved in the present study have observed many preschool children develop the physical skills and upper body strength needed to master the overhead ladder as they were exposed to overhead apparatus and provided teacher guidance (scaffolding) and supervision. Furthermore, when overhead ladders are placed at appropriate heights for preschool children's use and installed over sufficient resilient surfacing, the hazards involved with using overhead ladders are dramatically reduced.

Disagreement exists in regard to the age at which children develop the skills or physiology to use overhead ladders. While chronological age is a good general predictor of ability, individual skills vary widely across chronological ages. The best predictors only can be determined by observing the skills and abilities of children of a given age or grade level using the equipment. Even within a given age or skills group, adults will need to use discretion about the type and design of equipment that children are allowed or helped to use. For example, the ability to use an overhead ladder is greatly influenced by body weight. The overweight or obese children in the present study had great difficulty using overhead equipment.

Children's physical skills develop along milestones that are considered combinations of inherited factors, experience, and lifestyle. The use of overhead ladders requires physical development of upper body strength, along with coordination, lateral movement, and visual perception. The 3- to 11-year-old children in this study followed a pattern of *developmental progression*, summarized in four stages: *fundamental stage*, requiring assistance and including most 3-year-olds; *practice stage*, 3- and 4-year-olds, requiring some assistance; *refining stage*, accomplished by age 4 to 6 and requiring little or no assistance; and *mastery stage*, requiring no assistance and marked by skillful, novel actions.

This research demonstrates that children as young as 3 years of age can benefit from experience with appropriately installed and supervised overhead ladders. Children as young as 4 can reach the refining stage of overhead apparatus use, and children as young as 5 can achieve the mastery stage. The results of this study indicate that opportunities to use safely installed and supervised overhead ladders will ensure that most preschoolers develop the upper body strength and other skills needed to successfully navigate the equipment.

Preschool children have only limited awareness of hazards and have relatively immature motor and cognitive skills, compared to school-age children. Consequently, adults (designers, manufacturers, parents, teachers, and supervisors) must exercise special caution in ensuring safe designs, ongoing instruction, maintenance of facilities, and appropriate matching of age/skill levels to types and scales of playground equipment.

## RECOMMENDATIONS

The following recommendations reflect the data reviewed for this report and should not be used to circumvent current CPSC/ASTM guidelines and standards. The research reviewed and conducted for this study lead to the following recommendations:

- Children can successfully use properly designed, installed, and supervised (per CPSC and ASTM) overhead apparatus as early as age 3. Such opportunities should be widely available. Stage of development, not chronological age, should be the major factor in determining when children are ready to use overhead apparatus.

- Children as early as age 3 benefit physically and cognitively from using overhead apparatus. They should be given regular opportunities to play on such apparatus. During the early stages, adults should closely supervise and assist (scaffold) children in learning how to use overhead apparatus and how to safely exit the apparatus.

- Adults who design, manufacture, install, and supervise children's playgrounds and playground equipment hold special responsibilities for ensuring children's safety and healthy development. Educational programs should be expanded to help adults learn to analyze playground safety and understand the developmental values of play.

- Allowing children to use excessively high overhead apparatus over improperly installed or maintained resilient surfacing (ASTM, CPSC) is hazardous for all children and irresponsible for preschool children who are learning to use the equipment. During the initial period of development, children fall repeatedly and are at risk for serious injury if using improperly designed apparatus or inadequate surfacing. Responsible adults should ensure that preschool children not use overhead equipment designed (CPSC and ASTM) for school-age children. The writers believe that loose, non-compacted, well-maintained surfacing is safer under overhead equipment than manufactured mats or composite surfacing materials and likely to result in reduced potential for limb (arm and leg) fractures.

- Given the wide variation within chronological age groups, adults should observe children carefully to match abilities of children with complexity of equipment. For example, some beginning school-age children should continue to use equipment designed for preschoolers until appropriate skill levels are reached.

- Playground equipment should be designed for flexibility to accommodate the wide range of skill levels present among any chronological age level or grade level.

- Adults should carefully supervise children's beginning efforts to use overhead equipment. They should be alert to fatigue resulting from children's excessive use of overhead apparatus.

- Overhead rings should be 1 to 1-1/8" diameter to minimize blistering from heavy use. Plastic coating may reduce blistering.

- Overhead rings should be attached to 8" to 12" of chain to allow the swinging motions needed to successfully navigate the structure. The rhythm of motion is especially important in swinging from ring to ring.

- All overhead apparatus should have "take-off" decks, platforms, or devices constructed from very resilient material to reduce the likelihood of injury in falls. In the absence of take-off devices, children kick out loose surfacing in their efforts to gain momentum, especially on track rides. They also tie ropes and wires to track handles and stack rocks or other hazardous materials in fall zones to allow them to reach the devices.

- The take-off devices for overhead apparatus should be constructed to protect the head and other parts of the body in falls. Virtually all preschoolers in the original studies reported here fell many times during their initial efforts to use overhead apparatus. The take-off devices used were all terrain vehicle (ATV) tires of the soft, balloon type, heavily worn to reduce exposed treads (not all ATV tires have these characteristics). The tops of these devices were 12 inches above the sand surface, allowing virtually all 4-year-olds to reach the overhead bars without jumping. Some of the 3s stood on toes or jumped to reach the bars. These devices supported the weight of the children but would easily press inward with impact from falls, resulting in no injuries in head-first, face-first, or falls across stomach or back. Such resilient devices are badly needed to substitute for the steel bars, wood decks, and metal decks commonly provided as take-off devices.

- Preventing mismatch between equipment and children's skills is perhaps the most crucial factor in preventing injuries to preschool children using overhead equipment. Children quickly seek novel and more complex challenges on playgrounds, frequently extending their activities to equipment designed for older and more skillful children. Adults, even parents and teachers, commonly support and encourage such mismatches. Manufacturers should carefully consider providing educational material appropriate for training programs for purchasers and users of their equipment. This material should include multi-media and focus on both safety and child development.

# Appendix: Sample Coding Sheet

| Participant # | | | | | | | | | |
|---|---|---|---|---|---|---|---|---|---|
| **Performance:** | | | | | | | | | |
| individual | | | | | | | | | |
| assisted | | | | | | | | | |
| **Body Size:** | | | | | | | | | |
| short | | | | | | | | | |
| average | | | | | | | | | |
| tall | | | | | | | | | |
| small build | | | | | | | | | |
| medium build | | | | | | | | | |
| large build | | | | | | | | | |
| **Reach to Bar:** | | | | | | | | | |
| 1 hand | | | | | | | | | |
| 2 hands | | | | | | | | | |
| reaches bar | | | | | | | | | |
| jumps to bar | | | | | | | | | |
| R leading | | | | | | | | | |
| L leading | | | | | | | | | |
| **Hand Hold:** | | | | | | | | | |
| R hand grip | | | | | | | | | |
| R hand cup | | | | | | | | | |
| R hand 1/2 grip | | | | | | | | | |
| L hand grip | | | | | | | | | |
| L hand cup | | | | | | | | | |
| L hand 1/2 grip | | | | | | | | | |
| oppositional | | | | | | | | | |
| **Travel:** | | | | | | | | | |
| hand to hand | | | | | | | | | |
| hand over hand | | | | | | | | | |
| skipping bars (#) | | | | | | | | | |
| R hand leads | | | | | | | | | |
| L hand leads | | | | | | | | | |
| alternating lead hand | | | | | | | | | |
| **Direction:** | | | | | | | | | |
| forwards | | | | | | | | | |
| backwards | | | | | | | | | |
| **Body:** | | | | | | | | | |
| front/back | | | | | | | | | |
| side/side | | | | | | | | | |
| **Legs:** | | | | | | | | | |
| pedaling (slower) | | | | | | | | | |
| running (faster) | | | | | | | | | |
| **Arm-to-Leg Relation:** | | | | | | | | | |
| same | | | | | | | | | |
| opposite | | | | | | | | | |
| **Exit:** | | | | | | | | | |
| fall | | | | | | | | | |
| controlled | | | | | | | | | |
| teacher assisted | | | | | | | | | |
| # of bars completed | | | | | | | | | |

## References

*Active youth: Ideas for implementing CDC physical activity promotion guidelines.* (1998). Champaign, IL: Human Kinetics.

Adler, E. (2002, April 2). Parents need to be mindful of swinging children by their arms. *Kansas City Star.* www.kansascity.com/mld/kansascity/living/health/2978199.html

American Society for Testing and Materials. (1993). *Standard consumer safety performance specification for playground equipment and public use.* West Conshohocken, PA: Author.

Barbour, A. (1999). The impact of playground design on the play behaviors of children with differing levels of physical competence. *Early Childhood Research Quarterly, 14*(1), 75-98.

Beckwith, J. (1988). Negligence: Safety from falls overlooked. In L. Bruya & S. Langendorfer (Eds.), *Where our children play: Elementary school playground equipment* (pp. 223-226). Reston, VA: American Alliance for Health, Physical Education, Recreation and Dance.

Bennet, C. (1980). Planning for activity during the important preschool years. *Journal of Education and Recreation, 51*(8), 30-32.

Bowers, L., & Bruya, L. (1988). Results of the survey. In L. Bruya & S. Langendorfer (Eds.), *Where our children play: Elementary school playground equipment* (pp. 31-44). Reston, VA: American Alliance for Health, Physical Education, Recreation and Dance.

Brett, A., Moore, R., & Provenzo, E. (1993). *The complete playground book.* Syracuse, NY: Syracuse University Press.

Consumer Product Safety Commission. (1981, 1997). *Handbook for public playground safety.* Washington, DC: Author.

DoctorGeorge.com (2004). Nursemaids elbow. Retrieved June 19, 2004, from www.doctorgeorge.com/article.php?sid=313

Durant, R., Baranowski, T., Johnson, M., & Thompson, W. (1994). The relationship among television watching, physical activity, and body composition of young children. *Pediatrics, 94,* 449-455.

Fox, J., & Tipps, R. (1995). Young children's development of swinging behaviors. *Early Childhood Research Quarterly, 10,* 491-504.

Friedberg, P. (1975). *Handcrafted playgrounds: Designs you can build yourself.* New York: Vintage Books.

Friedberg, P., & Berkeley, E. (1970). *Play and interplay.* London: The Macmillan Company.

Friedlander, R., & Lohmeyer, R. (1988). A place to start: Games and sports tasks for young children. *Journal of Physical Education, Recreation and Dance, 59*(8), 70-72.

Frost, J. (1990). Young children and playground safety. In J. Frost & S. Wortham (Eds.), *Playgrounds for young children: National survey and perspectives* (pp. 29-48). Reston, VA: American Alliance for Health, Physical Education, Recreation and Dance.

Frost, J. (1992). *Play and playscapes.* Albany, NY: Delmar.

Frost, J. (2001). *Children and injuries.* Tucson, AZ: Lawyers and Judges Publishing Co.

Frost, J., & Henniger, M. (1979). Making playgrounds safe for children and children safe for playgrounds. *Young Children, 34*(5), 23-30.

Frost, J., & Kim, S. (2000). *Developmental progress in preschool-age children's using an overhead bar.* Unpublished manuscript.

Frost, J., Sutterby, J., Therrell, J., Brown, P., & Thornton, C. (2001). *The relevance of height for child development and playground safety.* Unpublished study commissioned by GameTime, a PlayCore, Inc., Company, Fort Payne, AL, U.S.A.

Frost, J., & Sweeney, T. (1996). *Cause and prevention of playground injuries and litigation: Case studies.*

Olney, MD: Association for Childhood Education International.

Frost, J., Wortham, S., & Reifel, S. (2001). *Play and child development*. Columbus, OH: Prentice-Hall/Merrill.

Gabbard, C. (1979). *Playground apparatus experience and muscular endurance among children 4-6.* Unpublished technical report. ERIC/EDRS, #228-190.

Gabbard, C. (1983). Muscular endurance and experience with playground apparatus. *Perceptual and Motor Skills, 56,* 538.

Gabbard, C., & Patterson, P. (1980). Grip preferences of children on ladder apparatus. *Perceptual and Motor Skills, 50,* 1168-1170.

Gabbard, C., & Patterson, P. (1981). Movement pattern analysis on the horizontal ladder among children 4 to 9 years. *Perceptual and Motor Skills, 52,* 937-938.

Gallahue, D. (1982). *Developmental movement experiences for children.* New York: John Wiley and Sons.

Gallahue, D. (1989). *Understanding motor development: Infants, children, adolescents* (2nd ed.). Indianapolis, IN: Benchmark Press.

Gallahue, D. (1996). *Developmental physical education for today's children.* Dubuque, IA: Brown & Benchmark.

Gober, B., & Franks, D. (1988). Physical and fitness education of young children. *Journal of Physical education, recreation and dance, 59*(8), 43-46.

Gonzalez, G. (1999). Nursemaid's elbow: It's the toddler's elbow not the nursemaids. *Child Care Health Connections, 12, 4,* 5. Retrieved April 1, 2002, from http://ericps.ed.uiuc.edu/cchp/nl1999/1999index.html

Hendy, T. (1997). The national playground safety institute: The most commonly asked questions, answered. *Parks and Recreation, 23*(4), 102-105.

Hewes, J., & Beckwith, J. (1975). *Build your own playground.* Boston: San Francisco Book Company.

Hills, A. (1994). Locomotor characteristics of obese children. In A. Hills & M. Wahlqvist (Eds.), *Exercise and obesity* (pp. 141-150). London: Smith-Gordon, Nishimura.

Mero, E. (1908). *American playgrounds: Their construction, equipment, maintenance and utility.* Boston: American Gymnasia.

Nelson, C. (1988). Infant movement: Normal and abnormal development. *Journal of Physical Education, Recreation and Dance, 59*(8), 43-46.

Noble, D. (1983). *Gymnastics for kids ages 3-7.* New York: Leisure Press.

Orthoseek.com. (2004). Radial head subluxation. Retrieved June 19, 2004, from www.orthoseek.com/articles/radialhs.html

Pate, R., Ross, J., Baumgartner, T., & Sparks, R. (1987). The modified pull-up test. *Journal of Physical Education, Recreation and Dance, 58*(9), 71-73.

Perry, P. (2001). Sick kids. *American Way, 4,* 64-65.

O'Brien, S. (1987). Childhood fitness: A growing concern. *Childhood Education, 64,* 110-112.

Ratté, D., Denham, S., & Johnson, D. (1990). *Development of human factors criteria for playground equipment safety.* Silver Spring, MD: Comsis Corporation.

Ross, J., & Gilbert, G. (1985). A summary of findings. *Journal of Physical Education, Recreation and Dance, 56*(1), 45-50.

Ross, J., Dotson, C., Gilbert, G., & Katz, S. (1985). New standards for fitness measurement. *Journal of Physical Education, Recreation and Dance, 56*(1), 62-66.

Ross, J. & Pate, R. (1987). The national children and youth fitness study II: A summary of findings. *Journal of Physical Education, Recreation and Dance, 58-59,* 51-56.

Sawyers, J. (1994). The preschool playground: Developing skills through outdoor play. *Journal of Physical Education, Recreation and Dance, 66*(9), 31-33.

Staniford, D. (1979). Natural movement for children: Guidelines on play and physical activity for young children. *Journal of Physical Education and Recreation, 50*(9), 44-47.

Tinsworth, D. (1996). Public playground equipment-related injuries and deaths. In M. Christianson & H. Vogelsong (Eds.), *Play it safe: An anthology of playground safety* (2nd ed., pp. 45-50). Arlington, VA: National Recreation and Park Association.

Thompson, D. (1988). Slides, swings and climbing equipment. In L. Bruya & S. Langendorfer (Eds.), *Where our children play: Elementary school playground equipment* (pp. 67-106). Reston, VA: American Alliance for Health, Physical Education, Recreation and Dance.

Vygotsky, L. (1978). *Mind in society.* Cambridge, MA: Harvard University Press.

Waltzman, M., Shannon, M., Bowen, A., & Bailey, M. (1999). Monkeybar injuries: Complications of play. *Pediatrics, 103*(5), e58.

Wheeless, C. (1996). Wheeless' textbook of orthopaedics. Retrieved June 19, 2004, from www.wheelessonline.com/index.htm

Wortham, M. (1990). Advances in playground equipment for young children. In J. Frost & S. Wortham (Eds.), *Playgrounds for young children: National survey and perspectives* (pp. 89-102). Reston, VA: American Alliance for Health, Physical Education, Recreation and Dance.

# CHAPTER 5
# The Nature and Benefits of Children's Climbing Behaviors

*We can take our children with us to the land. We can be there with them as they climb on rocks, play in streams and waves, dig in the rich soil of woods and gardens, putter and learn.* (Stephen Trimble in Nabhan & Trimble, 1994, p. 31)

Climbing equipment with many forms and functions can be found on most playgrounds. Climbers are functional, in that they provide access to such play events as slides or decks. Additionally, they provide children with the opportunity to climb just for the sake of climbing. This chapter examines history of playground climbing equipment, motivations for climbing, use of climbing equipment, the development of climbing skills, and safety issues. Used here, "climber" can refer to either a person who climbs or a piece of climbing equipment, depending on the context.

## HISTORY OF CLIMBING EQUIPMENT

*Tree houses. They have the same rightness. All those rickety board nests children lash and nail onto tree trunks up high where parents would not go except in their secret hearts. I would live in a treehouse if I could.* (Fulgham, 1990, p. 35)

*No matter where you lived, there always seemed to be a tree house nearby. . . . They could be in a shade tree in a backyard or in a huge oak tree on a hillside. Tree houses were places of great pride to be shown to friends who came to play, to be club houses, or simply to serve as hideouts for getting away and reflection. . . . Now, tree houses are prohibited by zoning laws in many urban areas.* (Frost, Wortham, & Reifel, 2001)

*Our new nature inspired TreeScape play systems bring the excitement of outdoor themed play back to the modern playground. Featuring unique tapered "Trees," with custom designed canopy roofs and an exclusive internal climber, children can experience the challenge and excitement of tree climbing in a modern compliant play environment.* (www.gametime.com)

### Playground Development
Climbing equipment has changed greatly over the last century. Prior to the development of apparatus specific to climbing, children used natural elements

for climbing. During the playground movement of the early 1900s in Europe and the United States, climbing became an integral part of playground development. Early playground climbers during this era tended to be large metal structures designed to encourage fitness and to be used in gymnastics routines. Play as an activity in itself was rarely encouraged with these early climbing structures. Friedrich Jahn developed outdoor gymnasia in order to instill heroic qualities in young people through exercise and physical discipline. In the 1820s, disciples of Jahn brought outdoor gymnasia to the United States. This outdoor equipment was designed to emphasize children's moral and physical development (Cavallo, 1980).

## Eras of Playground Development

*Manufactured Apparatus Era.* The Manufactured Apparatus Era, from about 1900-1950, represents the early playground movement in the United States. Playgrounds in this era were designed to keep children out of trouble and off the increasingly busy streets of towns and cities (Cavallo, 1980; Frost, 1992). Playgrounds at this time tended to have large play structures made of iron, steel, and wood. The climbing apparatus contained a number of hazards including excessive heights, and in the case of jungle gyms, the risk of falling inside the play equipment onto bars below (Frost, 1992; Thompson, 1988). Climbers in this era included pole climbers, rope climbers, and a variety of ladders (Mero, 1908).

*Novelty Era.* The Novelty Era, from about 1950-1970, represents a time of increasing innovation in the development of playgrounds. Playground equipment was designed to appeal to the imagination, and climbers often took the shape of rockets and other fantasy elements. The play structures continued to be made mostly of iron and steel. The general types of climbers did not change significantly during this era, as playgrounds continued to feature metal ladders (Frost, 1992). Excessive heights and other hazards continued to be common.

*Modular Equipment Era.*

> *A playground should present a variety of challenges, ranging from simple things that toddlers can master to ones that challenge older and more experienced children. There should be continuity, so that each child always has the dual experience of having mastered some aspects of his environment while knowing there are other aspects that he may still aspire to master.* (Dattner, 1969, p. 47)

The period from the 1970s through the 1990s saw great changes in the development of playground equipment. Equipment companies developed standardized equipment based on modular designs. Linked play equipment became more common as decks sprouted a number of connected slides and climbers. The development of plastic led to its increased use on playgrounds. In addition, some designers stressed the use of natural elements on the playground. Heseltine and Holborn (1987) suggested that climbing equipment be made from boulders and debarked trees. The number and types of climbers changed significantly as designers made climbers out of chains, tires, and other materials. Designers from this era encouraged the idea that playgrounds include a variety of climbers that provide graduated challenges, allowing children of differing climbing abilities to find challenges suitable for their levels of ability on the same playground (Dattner, 1969). Safety also became an important element of playgrounds as the Consumer Product Safety Commission (CPSC) began to study playground safety and developed guidelines for playground equipment (Frost, 1992; Frost, Wortham, & Reifel, 2001).

*Standardization Era.* The current era of playground development represents a growing standardization of play equipment as playground manufacturers attempt to develop playgrounds that satisfy the CPSC guidelines and American Society for Testing and Materials (ASTM) standards for manufacturing playground equipment (Frost, Wortham, & Reifel, 2001). In addition, introduction of the Final Rule of the U.S. Access Board for the accessibility standards for playgrounds, based on the Americans With Disabilities Act, changed designs of playground equipment and rules for surfacing. Playground equipment for large structures now must include transfer platforms, ramps, and/or climbers to allow access by children with disabilities (Hendy, 2001).

Manufacturers continue to develop a number of climbers, with variety of type and challenge important elements in design. Major manufacturers offer many different options of playground climbers: Little Tikes (2000) offers 20 climber types, Landscape Structures (2002) offers 28 types, and GameTime (2002) offers 50 types. In addition, manufacturers recognizing the increasing interest in the physical benefits of rock climbing have developed a variety of climbers that simulate rock climbing (MacDonald, 2001; McNamee & Steffen, 2001).

## MOTIVATIONS FOR CLIMBING

*Climbing trees is my private pleasure, that's all. But I'm not sure why. It's more something to be done than talked about. Must be a primitive kind of thing—a comfort to the most ancient yearnings in my DNA. Ancestors spent several hundred thousand years up in trees. Which is why a comfortable seat in the crotch of an elderly elm feels so much like home. A rightness. A belonging.* (Fulgham, 1990, pp. 34-35).

*Mary Lou Retton, the 1984 Olympic all-around gymnastics champion, says she "was always climbing on the jungle gym" as a girl growing up in Fairmont, West Virginia. "Those things built upper body strength and coordination," she says. "But even more than that was the challenge. I still remember my sense of triumph when I first made it to the top."* (McCallum & O'Brien, 1996, p. 18)

Climbing, primarily a locomotor activity, occurs for many reasons. As suggested above, people are motivated by the climbing itself as well as the desire to accomplish a goal. Also, climbing is an activity that both adults and children can engage in regularly. Fulgham (1990) describes an unexplained delight achieved through climbing. He is a member of Tree Climbers International, an organization that promotes and encourages tree climbing by adults. Tree Climbers International's Web site states, "Put simply, Tree Climbers International Inc. (TCI) is an organization for people who enjoy climbing trees. We love the challenge of reaching the top, the beauty we see as we ascend, the views from the treetops, and the peace we find once there" (www.treeclimbing.com).

Climbing is frequently associated with a sense of accomplishment, as described in Retton's recollection of her early climbing experiences. Climbing to reach the top of some object provides a concrete objective. Morrison (2002) describes the tree climbing success of 60-year-old Toshiko Hikosaka, who overcame partial paralysis to become an active tree climber and eventually reached her goal to climb a 243-foot sequoia. Morrison describes part of Hikosaka's motivation to climb as the desire to be in a unique position. Normally, "people look down on her when she's in her wheelchair. High in a tree, she says, she can look down on them" (Morrison, 2002, p. 58). Hikosaka's motivation also derives from her determination to overcome the limitations of her paralysis.

The ultimate level of climbing is mountain and rock climbing. Mountain climbing has been a sport since at least the Victorian Age, when people began to combine scientific investigation with a desire to enjoy an active physical challenge. According to Houston (1967), men climb for four reasons: for pleasure, for knowledge, for an answer to a challenge, and for gain. Climbing, especially high-risk mountain climbing, is not always enjoyable in itself, yet the individual is motivated by rewards not associated with the activity itself (Houston, 1967).

Children also climb a great deal and they also climb for a variety of reasons. A number of possible motivations have been identified for children's climbing: most children find climbing generally fun or pleasurable; children climb in order to observe from a height, explore, access play events like slides and decks, play chase, and engage in make believe; and children climb in response to peer pressure or encouragement from adults (see Chapter 3).

Readdick and Park (1998) suggest that children's climbing is a very understudied element of development. They identify many reasons for children to climb. For example, children climb because the object to be climbed, such as a ladder or hill, suggests climbing. Children climb to reach a toy or other desired object. Children climb for the pure pleasure of climbing. Children also climb to increase their visual field so that they can observe from a height (Williams, 1994).

Exploration is an important motivation for climbing. Children's play is related to stimulus seeking; children explore a novel object like a climber until they become bored with it, and then seek to approach the object in novel ways (Ellis, 1973). Children generally approach a new piece of playground equipment by climbing to the highest accessible height. Climbing of this type is more like exploration than play (Frost, Sutterby, Therrell, Brown, & Thornton, 2001).

Children also climb for the purpose of reaching a particular play event such as a deck or slide (Frost, Sutterby, et al., 2001). Climbing of this type is a means to an end in that children may not be focused on the climbing but rather on the object to be reached. Heseltine and Holborn (1987) suggest putting bells to be rung at the end of climbing equipment so that children will have a clear goal for their climbing. They also suggest making this climbing competitive by having two bells side by side for races.

Children climb to engage in play experiences. Children engage in dramatic play and chase games on play structures (Gutteridge, 1939). Play structures often promote dramatic play activities like role play. The event of climbing becomes part of the role play in which the children are engaged. The play structure often suggests particular uses; for instance, a row of bars suggests a castle or jail for children to include in their play experiences (Armitage, 2001).

Children climb as part of chase games. According to Clarke (1999), chase games are found in all cultures, and they develop and change in predictable patterns as children mature. Active outdoor chase games move from theme- or fantasy-related to more rule-governed games as children move from the preschool to the elementary years. Playground equipment can be used as a base for capture, or as a way of escaping from other children by accessing slides or fire poles as possible escape routes (Frost, Sutterby, et al., 2001).

Climbing also can be associated with peer or adult pressure. Some children are encouraged to engage in dangerous and high-risk climbing activities in order to satisfy adult desires for accomplishments. Merrick Johnston trained rigorously to become, at age 12, the youngest person to climb Mount McKinley. Her mother admits, "I put her through hell to make sure she was ready" (Henry, 1996, p. 21).

Motivation to climb is an important factor in the development of climbing ability and skills. The natural desire to climb encourages children to engage with play equipment and to challenge it by finding novel and unique ways of climbing. This natural desire to achieve a goal can be taken to extremes as adults use their own desires to encourage children to climb, and thereby lead children into dangerous situations. Nevertheless, climbing can be a part of a healthy lifestyle as children learn climbing patterns and continue to love climbing as they develop into adults.

## USE OF CLIMBING EQUIPMENT

*Climbing provides an ideal activity for children to discover their individual movement potential, build self-confidence, problem solve, and, of course, improve upon physical traits such as balance, strength and flexibility.* (MacDonald, 2001, p. 73)

Climbing as an activity challenges the child across several developmental domains. Depending on the challenge level of the climb, the child must draw on a combination of cognitive skills and such affective factors as self-confidence and physical skills.

### Cognitive Requirements

A number of studies focus on the requirements of climbing that are implicated in the children's cognitive development. These include memory, problem solving, and imagery/visualization. Memory is important in climbing in that a person who climbs has a memory of the grips and holds required to access a climber. When rock climbing, the person engages in a process called "route finding," which is the act of perceiving "possible climbing actions to find a good path to climb" (Boshker, Bakker, & Michaels, 2002, p. 25). According to these researchers, experienced people who climb "chunk" complex patterns of possible hand and foot holds on a climbing structure together to form long-term visual perceptual memories. This chunking allows them to have a more sophisticated recall of the climbing structure, and allows them to more accurately recall hand-holds and how they relate to the next hand-hold of the climb.

Memory is also important in recalling motor sequences associated with climbing for children. In a study of memory related to movement sequences, older children had a better memory of gymnastics sequences than younger children. The more experienced children had a better memory of gymnastics sequences than less experienced children. Older children and more experienced children have more sophisticated memory strategies of movement sequences, which improve performance (Ilie & Cadopi, 1999).

Cognition is an important aspect of climbing because children work to problem solve as they climb. They need to memorize climbing movement patterns as well as aspects of the structure to be climbed. In addition, as children experience climbing, they learn to adapt to additional types of climbing structures.

## Affective Requirements

*Do you remember the excitement of that first climb to the top of the monkey bars, your first successful two-wheeler ride, or your first swim all the way across the pool? We can all remember how good it felt as children to succeed and can probably remember a time or two when we did not. Those childhood successes and failures may seem remote and meaningless to us now, but they once were important events in our lives that had an influence on what and who we are today.* (Gallahue, 1990, p. 349)

The affective domain is important for children's climbing. How a child feels directly affects her desire to participate in climbing activities (Gallahue, 1990). Three areas of affective development have been explored through research: motivation, stress/relaxation, and fear.

Children who use motivational imagery of themselves as successful climbers have better climbing performances and reduced stress when approaching a climbing task (Jones, Bray, Mace, MacRae, & Stockbridge, 2002). Children who have positive images of themselves as climbers are more successful and those who have an image of themselves failing at a climbing event are more likely to experience stress and failure.

Stress can impede performance during climbing. Relaxation training given to people who are about to climb can improve their climbing performance by reducing stress. The relaxation training may allow these climbers to focus more on the success of their climb rather than worrying about possible failure (Fraser, Steffen, Elfessi, & Curtis, 2001).

Fear is also a key affective element of climbing. The development of the fear response is an important part of children's development. Children naturally develop a fear of heights as they begin to perceive depth and become more mobile. This perception usually appears when a child is about 2 months old. Children between the ages of 2 and 6 months who are placed on a visual cliff demonstrate their perception of depth by their decreased heart rates. An actual fear of heights does not appear until about 6 months. This fear of heights generally is associated with the development of locomotion (Bertenthal, Campos, & Caplovitz, 1983). Children who have experiences with falling may climb less due to a psychological fear of falling (Kingma & Ten Duis, 2000; Tinetti & Speechley, 1989).

Affective or emotional elements of climbing influence scope and success in climbing. Children who are afraid to climb will miss out on important physical and cognitive benefits of climbing. On the other hand, children who are highly motivated to climb will continue to increase their abilities as they practice climbing behaviors.

## Physical Requirements

*Human young, like the young in other species, from cats to chimpanzees, are able to climb because their bodies are built for it, with particular physical structures, such as arms that rotate up and over the head, which allows them to climb.* (Readdick & Park, 1998, pp. 14-15)

Gallahue (1990) describes climbing as a fundamental movement similar to creeping in children. Climbing, however, requires that the climber use limbs in opposition to the force of gravity. Climbing can be done with the arms only, the legs only, or in combination. The motor requirements vary for climbing depending on the object being climbed (Gallahue, 1990). Several motor skills involved in climbing include perceptual motor skills such as body, spatial, and directional awareness. In addition, abilities associated with fitness, such as power, agility, speed, balance, and coordination, are also important for climbing. Finally, visual perceptual skills are required as climbers coordinate movements based on visual information.

## Perceptual Motor

Perceptual motor skills are learned abilities that are dependent on the motor activity. According to Gallahue (1990), regular and remedial physical education programs enhance these skills. Body awareness is the ability of the child to discriminate among body parts. This awareness consists of an awareness of what the parts of the body can do and a recognition of the different parts or components of a movement act. Children develop efficiency of movement as they develop awareness of how their body parts move (Gallahue, 1990).

Spatial awareness is the awareness of how much space the body occupies and the ability to project the body into space. For very young children, spatial awareness is based on location. As children get older, they develop the ability to use objects as a frame of reference. Spatial awareness develops as children experience moving in space and "learn to first orient themselves subjectively in space and then proceed carefully to venture out into unfamiliar surroundings" (Gallahue, 1990, p. 333).

Directional awareness is the concept of left-right, up-down, top-bottom, in-out, and front-back. These skills also develop through experiences with movement where direction is important. The directional awareness skills consist of laterality and directionality. Laterality is an internal awareness or "feel" for movement of the different parts of the body, based on direction and location. Directionality is the direction or movement into space (Gallahue, 1990).

Body, spatial, and directional awareness have been related to school subjects like reading, and programs have been developed to improve academic skills through motor training. However, Kavale and Mattson (1983) found that such programs were generally ineffective for developing academic skills. On the other hand, children do learn movement skills through experiences with movement. As Gallahue (1990) writes, "Children learn by doing" (p. 343). Although research has not demonstrated a specific academic benefit from motor training, children do develop motor skills from motor training and experience.

## Motor Fitness

Motor fitness, the combination of such skills as agility, speed, power, balance, and coordination, is directly related to climbing ability in many ways. Agility is an important aspect of climbing in that it is the ability to move from one point to the other as fast as possible. Children with high agility should be able to move quickly across a climbing structure. Speed is also important in that it is the ability to cover a distance in a short period of time. Power is the ability to make a maximum effort in a short time period. Power is related to climbing in that the climber needs to coordinate strength in order to reach a new level. Speed, power, and agility improve as children get older; these abilities level off around age 13 (Gallahue, 1990).

Motor fitness is essential to children's success in climbing and affects their interaction with different types of playground equipment. Children who lack motor fitness are limited in the levels of play structures they can access (Barbour, 1999). Playgrounds with graduated challenges allow children with lower levels of motor fitness to participate in more social activities on the playground.

Children need good balance skills to support their weight on one part of their bodies as they move another part of their bodies. Balance is the ability to maintain equilibrium while the body is in various positions. This skill is influenced by a number of factors, including visual, tactile kinesthetic, and vestibular stimulation (Gallahue, 1990). (The vestibular system is located in the inner ear. Vestibular stimulation through movement such as swinging, climbing, etc., plays an important role in balance, posture, coordination, agility, and vision.)

Coordination is the ability to develop efficient patterns of movement, and is character-ized by the integration of visual information with the movement of the limbs. Climbing is related to coordination in that the climbing child needs to coordinate many movements of the hands and feet, based on visual information (Gallahue, 1990).

## Visual Perception

Differences in motor skill can be attributed to differences in visual perception (Boschker et al., 2002). The importance of visual perception in climbing is linked to an important skill—perceiving affordances. Affordances are the foot and hand holds that the person who is climbing uses to support the body while climbing. The person who is climbing adapts to the affordances available, based on that person's perception of their support for the different limbs. People who climb adjust their perception of affordances depending on the relation-ship between climbing task and body size. In other words, the person who is climbing must accurately perceive the most efficient affordances for his or her body size (Warren, 1984).

Perception of affordances changes as a person matures and gains increased levels of locomotor skills. Infants can discriminate between easier and more difficult climbing tasks, depending on their locomotor abilities. Crawling children will select a smaller set of affordances, while walking infants will select a larger set of affordances (Ulrich, Thelen, & Niles, 1990). According to Ulrich et al. (1990), the development of the perception of affordances may be the result of a number of factors, including leg strength, limb lengths, locomotor abilities, and experiences in climbing. Each person who climbs adjusts his or her perception, depending on the development of each of these abilities.

The development of the perceptual skills required to perceive affordances also comes through experiences with climbing. Novice climbers underestimate their reaching capacity while expert climbers are able to accurately judge the maximum distance they can reach. The more experience a child has with climbing, the better the child will be at perceiving distances and reaching capacities (Pijpers & Bakker, 1993).

## Combination of Components of Climbing

As the physical, affective, and cognitive components of climbing interact and climbers gain experience, perceptual skills and memory of affordances are improved. As the child matures, increased body size, strength, and coordination allow the child to reach farther and hold affordances longer. Although it is possible to examine these elements individually, looking at the entire process or combination of elements provides a clearer picture of the climbing process.

## Problems With Climbing

Children can have difficulty climbing because of problems with cognition, affective factors, and physical factors.

*Fitness.* American children generally have very poor upper body strength (Gallahue, 1982). They are in a period of declining fitness and increasing incidence of obesity, diabetes, and other health- and fitness-related problems (Sutterby & Frost, 2002). Given these trends, the growing number of playground injuries reported by the CPSC during the past quarter century may well be the result of, at least in significant proportion, children's declining fitness levels. Such a conclusion regarding the relationship between playground safety and children's skill levels is discussed in depth in Frost and Henniger's (1979) paper, "Making Playgrounds Safe for Children and Children Safe for Playgrounds."

*Obesity.* Obesity affects climbing in that children who are obese are less physically active and so they are not developing the skills and coordination required to become proficient climbers. Because of their declining fitness, American children are at greater risk than previous generations for Type 2 diabetes, osteoporosis, heart disease, stress, and anxiety (Perry, 2001). Today's children are more involved in such sedentary activities as television viewing and computer activities, which have been linked to greater obesity (Durant, Baranowski, Johnson, & Thompson, 1994), and they eat a diet higher in fat than did previous generations (Frost, Wortham, & Reifel, 2001). Furthermore, a growing number of children have fewer opportunities for physical education and free play at school. The reduction of recess is affecting children's abilities to function and concentrate in school (Jarret et al., 1998) and contributing to obesity and declining physical fitness (Frost, Wortham, & Reifel, 2001).

*Disabilities.* Children with disabilities develop climbing skills in relation to their particular disability. Those with motor impairments are particularly affected in outdoor play and participation in climbing, and they may require ramps or transfer stations in order to engage in climbing. Children also may require assistive devices in order to engage in climbing, including wheelchairs, walkers, and positioning equipment (Frost, Wortham, & Reifel, 2001).

## DEVELOPMENT OF CLIMBING

*Each individual has his or her own unique timetable for the development and acquisition of movement abilities. Although our biological clock is rather specific when it comes to the sequence of acquisition of abilities, the rate and extent of development are individually determined.* (Gallahue, 1990, p. 7)

Traditional theories of children's development suggested that norms of development are inalterably determined by genetic programming, but contemporary views reject these theories. Gallahue's (1990) theory of life span development holds that most motor development patterns are the result of interaction between heredity and environment. Heredity, or a child's basic genetic structure, is altered by the social and physical opportunities children have for engaging in an activity.

### Environment

The child's environment consists of two primary factors: the social environment and the physical environment. The social environment consists of the people who engage with the child, both peers and adults. The physical environment is the actual physical structures. These factors interact to influence the amount and quality of climbing experience the child gains over time.

Playground equipment encourages particular involvement by children. For example, linking equipment encourages social interaction on the playground and higher levels of social and cognitive play (Frost, 1992). The physical environment is important for the development of climbing behaviors in that children who have few opportunities to climb will not develop the required skills and coordination in order to climb.

The type of playground has an influence on children's development of physical skills. In a comparison of traditional and contemporary playgrounds, Barbour (1999) found that traditional playgrounds, featuring fixed climbing and swinging equipment, encouraged gross motor skills and favored children with high levels of physical competence; children with lower levels of physical competence are constrained by this type of playground. The contemporary playground that she studied provided materials for a wider range of play, including sand, water, and loose parts, in addition to large fixed equipment. Thus, children of both high and low levels of physical competence were able to interact with each other. Since no two playgrounds are identical, readers of playground research should use caution in generalizing research results from one playground to another.

The apparatus available to children on the playground has an effect on their endurance or ability to engage in sustained gross-motor activity. Provision of upper body equipment offers children opportunities to engage in activities that improve upper body strength (Gabbard, 1979, 1983). According to Gabbard (1983), "Young children in a free-play condition with the opportunity to utilize specific apparatus, would engage in sufficient activity to increase significantly their level of upper body muscular endurance" (p. 538). Opportunities for upper body exercise increased children's endurance on a fixed arm hang test, demonstrating that the activity enhanced their upper body strength.

The type of object to be climbed has an effect on how well children are able to climb the object. Children are able to climb steps with low risers before they are able to climb steps with adult level or higher risers (Gesell & Ilg, 1946). People who climb automatically adjust their preference for the height of the riser to their body size, and infants will prefer lower risers until their skill level is able to accommodate larger risers, at which point they will begin to show a preference for higher risers (Ulrich, Thelen, & Niles, 1990).

### Social Support

Vygotsky stressed that children's development occurs within a social context (Bedrova & Leong, 1996). Development occurs within a zone of proximal development (ZPD), in which a child is able to accomplish more complex tasks with the support, or scaffolding, of adults or more capable peers. Social scaffolding can take many different forms, including encouragement, observation of others, and direct instruction. Encouragement of children by peers and adults is important for the development of physical skills. Gober and Franks (1988) discuss how athletes' motivation and skill are related to experiences in early childhood when they were encouraged by parents and older siblings. Children also learn physical skills through observation and through movement instruction (Bennet, 1980).

Encouragement is critical to children's development of skills on overhead ladders. Adults and peers can encourage children to challenge themselves. This type of encouragement is described by Frost and Kim (2000) in a situation in which a teacher and a group of children encouraged a child to cross an overhead ladder.

> *Brian stood up on the tire and moved up to the second bar. When he stopped on the second bar the teacher encouraged, "Go, Brian! Go!" He still hesitated and could not proceed. The teacher then said to the children waiting in line, "Let's cheer him up!" All the children in line and the teacher started to shout at him, "Go! Brian, Go! Go! Brian, Go!" While they clapped their hands, Brian crossed to the 4th bar and dropped to the sand with a big smile on his face.* (p. 5)

Social scaffolding also can have negative consequences, as capable school-age children "lead children who are less physically developed to challenges they cannot handle" (Frost, Wortham, & Reifel, 2001, p. 219). Social scaffolding of climbing also can occur through observation. Peers observe peers performing physical tasks, which offers them the opportunity to learn through the experience of others. Although it has been found that actual physical practice at a motor task is superior to observation, a combined condition of physical practice along with observation has been found to be the most effective in helping a child to master a motor task (Shea, Wulf, Whitacre, & Wright, 2000). Children on playgrounds frequently engage in this type of combined condition as they observe other children climbing or sliding and then engage in the task themselves.

## Stages of Climbing Development

A number of researchers of climbing development have created scales for climbing. Stages for climbing development are important in that they provide a way of comparing movement behaviors between children and across ages. Table 1 illustrates different perspectives on proficiency stages of climbing.

The different stages of climbing are based on changes in proficiency and on typical developmental behaviors that appear in a particular sequence. The child typically moves from less mature climbing to more mature climbing patterns. Such development, however, depends on the complexity of the climbing task (Gutteridge, 1939). People who climb will regress to less mature forms of climbing when presented with a more complex climbing task. Adding to the complexity of climbing tasks is whether the task is ascending or descending, increasing the height of the task, and the number of affordances provided by the task.

As children master climbing, their interest in climbing for its own sake decreases. According to Crum and Eckert (1985), the simple motor activities associated with most pieces of climbing equipment begin to lose their attraction for children when they reach

## Table 1: Stages of Climbing—Multiple Perspectives

| Gutteridge: *A Study of Motor Achievements of Young Children*, 1939 | Gabbard: *Lifelong Motor Development*, 1992 | Readdick & Park: "The Climbing Child" in *Young Children*, 1998 | Gabbard, LeBlanc & Lowy: *Physical Education for Children*, 1994 | Gallahue: *Understanding Motor Development*, 1990 | Eckert: *Motor Development*, 1987 |
|---|---|---|---|---|---|
| Refusal to Climb | Marking Time Stage<br>Child steps up or down with the same foot each time. The trailing foot then follows. | Clambering<br>The child's first attempts at ascent. The child holds the object and swings a leg over the object. Arm strength is used primarily. | Unilateral (Marking Time)<br>Same side leg and then arm movement, opposite leg and then arm follow. | Initial<br>Leans body weight forward. Begins action with feet, uses a follow step and a follow grip. | Stair Climbing<br>Mark time without support. |
| Habit in Process of Formation<br>Ranges from needing help to showing ineptness to using unnecessary movements. | CrossLateral Stage<br>Rather than placing both feet at the same level, the child alternates sides and places only one foot on each level. | Initial Stage<br>Child holds onto a level with both hands, pulls up with one foot or knee. Then pulls up trailing foot. Climber is tentative. | Simultaneous Unilateral<br>Movement from same side leg and arm, simultaneously followed by opposite side movements to same level. | Elementary<br>Tends to lead with same foot and hand. Supports body weight with good balance. Begins action with preferred foot. Uses homo-lateral arm and leg action. | Alternate Feet With Support |
| Basic Movements Achieved<br>Demonstrates proficiency in climbing. | | Transitional Stage<br>Child holds level and brings feet up in a mixed pattern. Hand-foot placement varies from same side to opposite side. | Cross-Pattern<br>One side leg moves, then opposite side arm, alternative sides. | Mature Stage<br>Good balance and body control. Can lead off with either hand or leg. Smooth, fluid, rapid motion. Uses a contralateral arm leg action. | Alternate Feet Without Support |
| Skillful Executions with Variations in Use<br>Child exhibits grace, assurance, and poise. Child adds difficulties to climbing activity. | | Elementary Stage<br>The climber holds level with both hands and brings one foot up to the next level. Uses opposing hand to grasp for next level. | Simultaneous Cross-Pattern<br>One side leg and opposite arm move simultaneously, alternating sides. | | |
| | | Mature Stage<br>The climber fluidly and consistently alternates feet and hands. | | | |

approximately the age of 8, when children move from smaller, less-organized groups to more organized games. The increase in skill associated with older children often leads them to seek more challenging ways of engaging with climbing equipment (Gutteridge, 1939; Thompson, 1988).

## TYPES OF CLIMBERS

*I was not a rope climber. After the first few feet my upper body would give out. . . . I can still hear her (the gym teacher): "Just loop the rope around your feet and make an 'S.'" Meanwhile my hands were burning and three feet of height was about all I could handle. How I wished I could shinny up those ropes like my classmates!* (Kendall, 1998, p. 9)

Climbers are the most common piece of equipment on playgrounds, including chinning bars, overhead ladders, fireman poles, monkey bars, parallel bars, geodesic domes, rings, chain nets, vertical ladders, tunnels, suspension bridges, and balance beams (Thompson, 1988). In addition to traditional playground equipment, a number of schools and recreational facilities are including rock climbing equipment to encourage lifetime fitness activity. Improvements in plastic molding are advancing the ways that climbers can be shaped, allowing playground companies to produce climbers that emulate rocks and boulders.

Climbers on playgrounds generally can be placed in two categories: 1) fixed climbers are made from solid steel or wood and can be formed into a variety of shapes and forms, and 2) flexible climbers, like tire, chain, and rope climbers, may present a greater difficulty level than fixed climbers, for they require a higher level of coordination due to the unstable means of support. Because of their difficulty level, CPSC (1997) does not recommend that some climbers (fixed arch climbers and flexible climbers) be the sole means of access on equipment for children ages 2 to 5.

Ropes traditionally have been part of playground equipment. Mero (1908) describes rope climbing as "one of the best exercises, not only for strengthening the muscles of the arms and legs, but for increasing the healthiness of the heart and lungs" (p. 137). Rope climbing is also common in many physical education programs. Gabbard, LeBlanc, and Lowy (1994) offer a number of exercises with climbing ropes, such as pulling up, hanging, and swinging, to develop upper body strength and endurance. The CPSC (1997) guidelines require that all ropes be secured at both ends to prevent formation of a noose.

In addition to traditional climbers, other playground equipment can stimulate climbing. Although many climbers are designed specifically to encourage climbing, the idea that children will use pieces of equipment only in predefined and anticipated ways is an adult concept and unrealistic for children's play. Children use playground equipment in many unique and exploratory ways during play. According to Thompson (1988), "The idea that children can misuse equipment is a concept which seems absurd to many persons" (p. 73). Frost, Sutterby, et al. (2001) found that children used all parts of playground equipment, including the outside of play structures, slides, retaining walls, and panels, as climbing apparatus.

Rock climbing and rock climbing equipment are increasing in importance for school and recreational playgrounds. Participants in rock climbing can develop their movement awareness and ability, as well as gain a sense of achievement (MacDonald, 2001). In addition, rock climbing can develop a sense of balance, movement, and kinesthetic awareness (McNamee & Steffen, 2001). Rock climbing walls are made from a variety of materials, including plastic and molded concrete. These walls offer a variety of graduated challenges in the same space because novice climbers can use all of the holds while advanced climbers select only certain holds (www.boldr.com).

## CLIMBING AND SAFETY

*Being up in a tree is worth all the trouble, though. It's falling down out of a tree that is a loser. Especially if you bruise your brain. When I landed I saw double for a while, which was interesting. Then I threw up which is never interesting at all. Take the worst hangover feeling you ever had and double it—that's a concussion.* (Fulghum, 1990, p. 35)

Climbing is associated with a number of injuries. About 70 percent of all playground injuries and about 90 percent of all serious injuries are the result of falls. Eighty-six percent of injuries on climbers are associated with falls either to the surface or onto other parts of the equipment, such as rungs, decks, or support poles. Over 50 percent of injuries on public playgrounds are associated with climbers; according to NEISS recording procedures, however, such equipment as overhead ladders and track rings is included in the category of climbers. On home equipment, climbers were associated with 12 percent of injuries (Tinsworth & McDonald, 2001). Climbers are also the most common source of entrapment injuries (Beckwith, 1988).

The height of the climbing equipment and the surfacing below the equipment often are associated with the increased risk of injury from falls. According to Thompson (1988), climbing equipment is associated with 19 percent of all injuries from falls to the surface. By including falls associated with climbing equipment not intended for climbing (e.g., slides), the number increases to around 30 percent of all injuries. These injuries usually occur from loss of grip, slipping, and loss of balance. In a study of playground injuries resulting in litigation, climbing equipment was associated with 34 percent of the injuries (Frost & Sweeney, 1996).

## CONCLUSION

Climbing is an important human behavior performed by both adults and children. Children develop climbing skills through climbing opportunities. The development of climbing skills tends to occur in predictable patterns, as children move from less complex to more complex behaviors. The development of climbing skills can be negatively affected by low fitness levels, obesity, and motor impairments. In order to help children develop climbing skills, playground equipment is designed to promote climbing. This climbing equipment ranges from basic ramps, steps, and ladders, to more complex rock climbing equipment.

Climbing is associated with a high number of injuries on playgrounds, as children often climb to a height and fall to a hard surface below. The design of climbers is also a factor in injuries. Climbers featuring fixed narrow bars on which children slip while climbing and fall onto underlying bars are common injury sites.

# METHODOLOGY

## Overview

The Merriam-Webster dictionary (1998) defines "climb" as meaning, "to rise to a higher point; to go up or down by use of hands or feet." This study systematically investigates the manners in which children between the ages of 5 and 9 years rise or climb to a higher point with their hands and feet. Fifty-seven kindergarten, 1st-, and 3rd-grade children enrolled in a summer school program were observed during the month of June 2002. This study examined the developmental progression of children's skills based on observations and analysis of participants on 13 different pieces of climbing equipment on an outdoor playground. The researchers utilized both quantitative and qualitative data collection methods. Early elementary (K-3) students were purposefully recruited from a summer education program at a local private school to voluntarily participate in this project.

## Participants

The participants for this study included 57 early elementary (K-3) students enrolled in the summer education program at a local private school. The following is a grade and gender breakdown of the study participants:

> Kindergarten – 13 Girls, 10 Boys
> First Grade – 10 Girls, 8 Boys
> Third Grade – 9 Girls, 7 Boys

These students were purposefully chosen for three reasons: 1) the researchers had worked with this particular school in the past and thus had an established rapport with the administration; 2) due to the relatively short time line, the study needed to be conducted during the summer months and this school was holding summer classes; 3) a sufficient number of children in the target age groups were available for observation.

The classes observed were composed of predominantly white, English-speaking, middle- to upper-middle income children. Inclusion in the study was based on current enrollment in the summer program; no exclusions were based upon race, gender, background, health, age, or any other variable. All students were in good health, did not have any known mobility impairments, and only one was obviously obese.

The majority of the students observed had spent a minimum of one year together during the prior academic school year. Those who did not regularly attend school at the observation site nevertheless had been together from the beginning of summer school to the onset of observations—approximately two weeks. Therefore, the children were accustomed to playing together. They were also familiar with the playground equipment, having approximately two weeks of experience on the equipment installed for the purposes of this study.

Upon receiving permission from a university human subjects committee to begin participant recruitment, the summer school teachers were addressed as a group. The researchers explained the aim of the study and asked the teachers to distribute consent letters to the students' parents. Each potential participant's parent(s) received information regarding participation expectations and the nature of the study. Informed consent letters were sent home one week prior to the first formal observation session. The return rate for the consent letters was 100 percent.

Banister Rails

Cargo Net

Chain Link

Chain Net

Climbing Pole

Corkscrew

Fat Pipe

Internal Trunk

Log Roll

Megarock

Swivel Meister

Trunk Climber

Wave Climber

# DATA COLLECTION

This study sought to answer the following questions:

1. What is the developmental progression pattern on climbing apparatus?
2. How do children's climbing behaviors differ across types of climbing equipment?
3. What is the difficulty level of each type of climbing equipment?
4. Which climbing equipment is most beneficial?

In order to answer these questions, a research perspective known as pragmatism was followed. Within this perspective, researchers view the question(s) to be more important than the method (Tashakkori & Teddlie, 1998). This is an option available for empirical studies to use any methodological tool available or, in other words, using "what works" (Cherryholmes, 1992; Howe, 1988). In non-pragmatic studies, methodology is limited to qualitatively or quantitatively pure data collection. This study, however, was able to use a mixture of qualitative and quantitative tools to collect data related to the above-listed research questions.

## Methodological Tools

Three methods of data collection were used: anecdotal notation, digital photography, and videotape recording. Anecdotal notes are quickly written notes of things observed in any given context—in this case, climbing behaviors on a playground. They are meant to be short and without much detail. The main purpose of anecdotal notes is to serve as a memory jogger for future discussion or documentation (Nilsen, 1997). Digital photography and video recording, on the other hand, are meant to capture all details of behavior. An advantage of these sorts of documentation is that most children are accustomed to being photographed in this way and are generally comfortable during the recording.

After informed consent letters were collected, every observation session was documented with both video and photo media. Prior to consent confirmation, anecdotal notes were used to establish preliminary thoughts and climbing patterns on various climbers. Anecdotal notes were also made of behaviors observed after data collection had ended and the video recordings were being analyzed. The video recordings provided the primary source of data. In compliance with the regulations dictated by the human subjects review committee, all videotapes were destroyed at the conclusion of the coding process. The data recorded via anecdotal notation and digital photography are meant to be used only in conjunction with the purposes of this study.

## Setting

Outdoor play sessions were observed at a private school located in the north central area of Austin, Texas, over a period of one month. The kindergarten through 3rd-grade participants enrolled in the summer education program at the school were observed during each play time, or recess. Each recess period lasted approximately 30-45 minutes. Kindergarten and 1st-grade children were observed twice a day: once in the morning and again after lunch. Third-grade children were observed once a day during the afternoon. Typically, the children were supervised by non-certified teachers who were working as summer school employees. Most of these teachers were undergraduate education students at a local private university. The teachers typically interacted with the children only to correct inappropriate or unsafe behavior, and to remind children of the playground rules.

The playground was home to a recently installed large play structure that contains 13 elements designed for climbing: Banister Rails, Cargo Net Wall, Chain Link, Chain Net, Climbing Pole, Corkscrew, Fat Pipe Climber, Internal Treescape Climber, Log Roll, Megarock, Swivel Meister, Trunk Climber, and Wave Climber. Appendix A provides a diagram of the play structures on the playground. In addition to the climbers, the play structure contained a Double Trapeze Ring overhead ladder, a Rain Wheel Panel and Talk Tube, a Wild Slide, and a Treescape Deck with Funnel Enclosure. The ground under the play structure was covered with approximately 12" of engineered wood fibers (shredded wood prepared specifically for use on playgrounds). Pictures of each climber (plus children) are included on page 138. The purpose of the photos is to provide the reader with visuals to accompany the text.

Other play equipment available to children on the playground included swings, a tire swing, play houses, above-ground tube crawls, sandbox and sand loose parts, and wheeled vehicles. A large open space for organized games was also available for play, as were various loose parts such as jump ropes and balls.

## Materials

The materials required for the completion of the study were those necessary for data collection. Two researchers collected data with personal digital and video cameras.

## DATA ANALYSIS

Researchers conducted deliberate and systematic analysis throughout the data collection process. This was a process of formative analysis, or analysis that is done "in the moment." These moments came at three points: 1) during each observation session, 2) during the time interval between observations within one week, and 3) during the time interval between data collection weeks. Summative analysis, or analysis that is done on the collected data, was completed after all the observation sessions had been completed.

## Formative Analysis During Each Observation Session

Each observation session (post-consent) was conducted with the same methods: participants were photographed and videorecorded by researchers who walked around the play structure. However, decisions during the observation regarding specific recordings were based upon in-the-moment flow of the children's play. For example, during times of high volume use of the equipment, multiple children were observed climbing up the Megarock. Instead of continuing to record that climber, the researcher could decide to follow a particular child from the Megarock to another climber because of the potential valuable data the child could provide.

## Formative Analysis During the Time Interval
## Between Observations Within One Week

Observations were conducted Monday through Friday mornings (kindergarten and 1st grade) and early afternoons (3rd grade), generally between the hours of 9:30 a.m. and 3:00 p.m., for four weeks. During the "down" time between observations, the researchers discussed the data and used it to guide their thinking before the next day's observations.

Decisions regarding methodology and logistics were made at this time. For example, during one observation a kindergarten girl was observed placing her feet on the Chain Link climber rungs in a way that previously had not been seen. Based on this observation, it was decided to dedicate more time the next day watching this girl to see if this foot pattern was unique to this particular climber or if she used it consistently. It was also decided to watch the Chain Link climber to see if any other children were using this sort of foot pattern.

## Formative Analysis During the Interval Between Data Collection Weeks

Much like the formative analysis during the observations within one week, formative analysis between data collection weeks was conducted by the researchers for the purpose of logistical decision-making. On weekends, the two researchers discussed the data collected during the previous week. Comparisons and reflections on data were the focus of conversation, and plans based on those conversations were made for the upcoming data collection week.

## Summative Analysis

Once all the data had been collected and the contents of the videotapes coded, summative analysis began. Summative analysis is the stage of data analysis for the purpose of presentation and interpretation. The results of this analysis, presented in the Findings section, were used to answer the research questions.

During this phase of data analysis, the data collected on videotapes made during observations were collapsed into a single unit, rather than disjointed components (i.e., anecdotal notes, photos, and videos). Approximately 30 hours of video were watched and coded and approximately 450 digital photos logged. The researchers generated a data coding sheet based upon preliminary observation analysis of the video recordings. Appendix B contains a sample blank coding sheet, which includes the following elements:

- Hand Pattern: how hands are placed when climbing equipment
- Foot Pattern: how feet are placed when climbing equipment
- Hand/Foot Relationship: how the child moves the active hand in relation to the active foot
- Other Parts of Body Used for Climbing: any body part other than hands or feet used in navigating equipment (e.g., knees, elbows, etc.)
- Speed: the rate at which the child climbed
- Body to Equipment Relationship: directionality (up, down, lateral) and positioning (facing equipment, facing away from equipment)
- Visual Focus: where the child was looking while climbing
- Estimated Level of Expertise: assessment of performance based on the coding of above-mentioned elements (beginner, intermediate, or advanced).

Observers coded data recorded on video and then translated it into meaningful findings through measures of frequency, comparative examination, and emerging patterns. Measures of frequency were made by counting the total number of times each piece of equipment was used. The purpose of this type of analysis is to allow the data to show levels of preference among the 13 pieces of climbing equipmenters. Comparative examination and emerging patterns work together to reveal areas that may serve as answers to the research questions. Specifically, by comparing the hand and foot patterns documented in the coding sheets, it becomes clear that the Trunk Climber poses more of a challenge for smaller children than for larger children. This finding contributes to the emerging pattern suggesting that climbing equipment inclined less than 90 degrees may be more challenging than vertical equipment, as it requires greater balance skills.

## VALIDITY & RELIABILITY

Validity of an empirical work is the extent to which the findings permit one to draw appropriate, meaningful, and useful inferences (Crowl, 1996). Reliability is the extent to which a measuring instrument measures something consistently. Both criteria (validity and reliability) are essential in order to trust the findings. Trustworthiness of a study is achieved through deliberate actions to ensure that the research process is carried out systematically. It is established through credibility, transferability, dependability, and confirmability, as well as authenticity (Erlandson, Harris, Skipper, & Allen, 1993; Manning, 1997). Actions to achieve these elements were woven into this study's methodology for data collection, data analysis, and final narrative presentation.

### Validity

Researchers established validity through techniques of triangulation, prolonged engagement, and peer debriefing. Triangulation means to examine a single social phenomenon from more than one perspective (Schwandt, 1997) or data collection method. This study incorporated multiple methods of data collection into the research design: anecdotal notation, digital photography, and video recordings. The presence of two researchers engaging in the three methods of data collection also functioned to establish validity through triangulation.

Prolonged engagement with the participants throughout the one-month-long study added to validity. Prolonged engagement is an authenticity strategy that involves lengthy and intensive contact with the participants in order to assess possible sources of distortion and variations in their beliefs. By closely observing the participants for an average of 3 hours every day for one month, it is believed that the requirements for declaring prolonged engagement as a strategy to establish authenticity were met.

Peer debriefing also was used as a method to reach validity standards and ensure trustworthiness of the results. This method involved the two data collection researchers holding daily conversations (Monday through Friday) about the data being accumulated. Elements of surprise, interest, and consistency were the topics of these conversations. In addition, these researchers regularly discussed their ideas with the lead researcher, Joe L. Frost, who then would offer suggestions for further observation.

### Reliability

Reliability refers to the consistency of measurement. For example, if a reliable test was administered to 100 people and then their memory of the test was erased, the same people should make the exact same scores on the test if it was administered to them again under precisely the same conditions. Because this study did not involve this type of data collection method, inter-rater reliability (Crowl, 1996) was utilized. Measures that involve observations and/or interpretation on the part of the evaluator are checked for objectivity by comparing the ratings assigned by two or more raters.

The use of multiple investigators participating in field observations required that inter-rater reliability be established before coding began. To do this, the two researchers simultaneously coded the children's interactions with the playground climbing equipment. Coding was compared between the investigators and discussed. The process was repeated until consistent coding was achieved over 95 percent of the time.

## FINDINGS

This study was designed to answer the following questions:

1. What is the developmental progression pattern on climbing apparatus?
2. How do children's climbing behaviors differ across types of climbing equipment?
3. What is the difficulty level of each type of climbing equipment?
4. Which climbing equipment is most beneficial?

Findings related to each question, derived from the data collected and coded as described in the previous section, are described below:

### Q1: What Is the Developmental Progression Pattern on Climbing Apparatus?

For each observed episode of climbing, an evaluation of proficiency was made. The children were labeled beginner, intermediate, or advanced in their climbing skills, based upon what was seen in their climb. These labels were assigned on a "between group" basis, meaning that the climbing patterns of kindergarten children were compared to the climbing patterns of 1st- and 3rd-graders, the climbing patterns of 1st-graders were compared to that of kindergartners and 3rd-graders, and the climbing patterns of 3rd-graders were compared to that of kindergartners and 1st-graders. This type of comparison provides a framework for a detailed examination and dissection of what beginning climbers do versus what advanced climbers do across age groups. A kindergarten child may be able to do things on the corkscrew climber that is advanced for a kindergartner, but is not able to do things that are advanced for a 3rd-grader. By comparing between groups (kindergarten to 3rd grade) rather than within groups (kindergarten to kindergarten), a more detailed developmental progression for climbing can be generated. This sort of categorization is not meant to be used as an age gradient—age and ability are not being correlated in this comparison, although the results suggest that characteristics of age may be associated with characteristics of physical ability that contribute to children's climbing abilities.

The developmental categories and characteristics derived from the data collected are presented in Table 2. The categories in the first column are the elements that the researchers believed to be pertinent to the development of climbing patterns. The labels on the top row pertain to the skill development level, or level of climbing proficiency (beginner, intermediate, advanced). These categories of climbing proficiency are consistent with stages of climbing described by other researchers (see Table 1 on p. 134). The level of proficiency designated as "Beginner" shares characteristics with Gutteridge's (1939) "Habit in Process

## Table 2: Developmental Progression Pattern on Climbing Apparatus

| | Beginner | Intermediate | Advanced |
|---|---|---|---|
| **Hand Pattern** | hand to hand pattern | hand to hand, hand over hand, or alternating pattern; may skip 1 handhold | hand over hand pattern; may skip more than 1 handhold |
| **Foot Pattern** | foot to foot pattern | foot to foot, foot over foot, or alternating pattern; may skip 1 rung (step) and jump from second step or rung from bottom to ground | foot over foot pattern; may skip more than 1 rung (step) or jump from anywhere on equipment to ground |
| **Hand/Foot Relationship** | move hand and foot one at a time | same hand to foot relationship, or one at a time when practicing hand over hand or foot over foot pattern | opposite hand to foot relationship |
| **Body Assistance** | other parts of body used for support during climbing | other parts of body used occasionally, usually when practicing new movement patterns | will use other parts of body on equipment when exploring new ways to play on a piece of equipment |
| **Speed** | cautious, slow speed | confident on already acquired skills, cautious on newly developing skills | confidently quick, only slowing down when playing socially or "hanging out" on equipment |
| **Body/Equipment Relationship** | can climb up, but not down; face equipment | can climb up confidently but more cautious climbing down; will explore laterally if possible; will usually face equipment both up and down, and face away from equipment climbing down on occasion | can go up, down, or laterally with ease; can face equipment or face away from equipment when climbing |
| **Visual Focus** | focus on hands and feet | visual focus is usually on destination, but can be on hands and feet when practicing new climbing skills and patterns | visual focus is usually on destination or other playmates |
| **Physical Characteristics** | short limbs, less able to comfortably reach elements of climbers | more able to comfortably reach climbing elements | longer limbs, able to span most distances on climbers |

of Formation"; Gabbard's (1992) "Marking Time Stage"; Readdick and Park's (1998) "Initial Stage"; Gabbard, LeBlanc, and Lowy's (1994) "Unilateral"; Gallahue's (1990) "Initial"; and Eckert's (1987) "Stair Climbing" categories. The level of proficiency designated as "Intermediate" shares characteristics with Gutteridge's (1939) "Basic Movements"; Gabbard's (1992) "Cross Lateral Stage"; Readdick and Park's (1998) "Transitional" and "Elementary" stages; Gabbard, LeBlanc, and Lowy's (1994) "Simultaneous Unilateral" and "Cross-Pattern"; Gallahue's (1990) "Elementary"; and Eckert's (1987) "Alternate Feet with Support" categories. The level of proficiency designated as "Advanced" shares characteristics with Gutteridge's (1939) "Skillful Executions"; Gabbard's (1992) "Cross Lateral Stage"; Readdick and Park's (1998) "Mature Stage"; Gabbard, LeBlanc, and Lowy's (1994) "Simultaneous Cross-Pattern"; Gallahue's (1990) "Mature Stage"; and Eckert's (1987) "Alternate Feet Without Support" categories.

### Q 2: How Do Children's Climbing Behaviors Differ Across Types of Climbers?

Findings suggest that certain types of playground climbers encourage children to engage in certain types of climbing behaviors. The types of behaviors that were observed were: use of hands and feet, use of feet and lower body, use of hands and upper body, use of equipment in multiple ways, and balancing the body on moving equipment.

*Equipment That Required Use of Both Hands and Feet.* Some climbers required children to use both their hands and feet for access. Children playing on the Trunk Climber, Corkscrew Climber, Internal Treescape Climber, Cargo Net Wall, and Chain Link Climber were always observed using their hands and feet to interact with the climbers. This may be because of each of these climbers was tall (up to 56 inches) and quite steep (with inclines between 60 to 90 degrees as measured from the ground).

Measured Incline of Climbing Equipment

|  | Incline (in degrees) |
| --- | --- |
| Banister Rails | 35 |
| Climbing Pole | 90 |
| Trunk Climber | 55 |
| Internal Treescape Climber | 90 |
| Corkscrew Climber | 90 |
| Chain Link Climber | 90 |
| Chain Net | 60 |
| Cargo Net Wall | 90 |
| Megarock | 45 |
| Wave Climber | 45 |
| Fat Pipe Climber | 35 |

Furthermore, the Cargo Net Wall had flexible components, which made balancing difficult. Additionally, the surface areas on which the children placed their hands and feet were quite small and sometimes rounded in shape, thereby possibly requiring children to increase the total surface area to balance on by using all limbs available to them. By using hands and feet rather than only hands or only feet, children could double the surface area on which they could balance their bodies, as well as provide more points of support and grip for their bodies. Furthermore, these children might have lacked the strength or balance to use only their hands or only their feet to access these climbers.

*Equipment That Required the Use of Feet and Lower Body Strength.* Some climbers required the use of children's feet and lower body during play. The Fat Pipe Climber, Wave Climber, Megarock, and Chain Net Climber all required that children use at least their feet for access. Some children used both their hands and feet to climb these climbers, but many children were observed to use only their feet and lower body strength to climb up and down these pieces of equipment. Most of these climbers have large surface areas on which children can balance without the use of their hands. The Chain Net Climber was short and inclined at 60 degrees, which made it easy for children to access it using only their feet.

*Equipment That Requires the Use of Arms.* Some pieces of climbing equipment require the use of arms and upper body strength for access. The Banister Rails required that children use their arms while playing, even if the children chose to use their legs as well. Kindergartners through 3rd-graders were observed playing with the Banister Rails in the following ways:

- Hanging onto the rails from the underside, either facing towards or away from the equipment, and inching their hands alternately up or down the rails
- Hanging onto the rails from the underside and raising their legs to the rails so that the undersides of their knees were perched on top of the rails
- Grasping the rails from the top and facing away from the equipment, resting the undersides of their thighs over the tops of the rails, and inching their way down the rails
- Approaching the rails from the ground, placing their hands and feet on top of the rails, and walking with hands and feet up the rails facing towards the equipment
- Hanging from the rails as they jump off the platform.

The Banister Rails was the only climber that children accessed using just their hands. Because children have more opportunities to develop their lower body strength than they have to develop their upper body strength, it is not surprising that they use only their feet and lower body strength on more climbers.

*Equipment That Promoted Multiple Uses.* Children used equipment, such as the Banister Rails, Cargo Net Wall, Trunk Climber, Internal Treescape Climber, Megarock, Corkscrew Climber, and Wave Climber, in multiple ways. These climbers may have promoted diverse types of climbing behaviors because of certain characteristics. For instance, Banister Rails' simple design allows children to play in different ways, such as hanging, sliding, hand-walking, and balancing, as opposed to the Log Roll, a more complex piece of equipment that the children were observed using in only two ways (running on and seated on). The Cargo Net Wall, Trunk Climber, and Megarock were all wide enough to allow children to move laterally for significant distances and to accommodate multiple children at the same time. Each was large enough to allow children to explore different ways of using the climber. Furthermore, the Trunk Climber and the Megarock were located in high-traffic areas (in the very center of the playground next to the organized game area), thus increasing the total frequency of use. With more frequent use, children become more experienced and more willing to attempt more challenging types of climbing behaviors.

The Corkscrew Climber and the Internal Treescape Climber were round in shape. Although children often accessed the exterior of the Corkscrew Climber and the interior of the Internal Treescape Climber, they did attempt to climb up the less obvious or accessible side of each climber. Some children climbed into the center of the Corkscrew Climber and found different ways of climbing up, down, and exiting the climber. Other children climbed up the exterior of the Internal Treescape Climber and sat on the large green arms of the "tree" or climbed onto the underside of the Trunk Climber without touching the ground. Others liked climbing back and forth through the rungs of each of these climbers.

The Wave Climber served as both staircase and slide for children. They found ways to access it with their feet and hands, feet only, seats, and sides. Sometimes they rolled loose parts, such as playground balls, down the climber.

*Equipment With Moving Elements.* Climbing equipment with moving elements elicited certain balancing behaviors from the children. Children usually accessed the Log Roll and the Swivel Meister with hands on rails and feet on log or swing. No child was able to roll the log smoothly because of the uneven distribution of the sand inside—the movement during play with this piece of equipment was at best choppy, even for the most-coordinated children. Some children were able to balance and swing on one leg on the Swivel Meister, and would swing to jump off. The Cargo Net Wall and the smaller Chain Net Climber also contained moving or flexible elements. The height and width of the Cargo Net Wall provided ample opportunities for children to access it with all hands and feet, thereby providing them with a balance activity that was quite different than what they experienced with the other pieces of climbing equipment on the playground. The Chain Net Climber, being much shorter and sloped, allowed children to balance using only their feet, some of them being able to run up the climber with no hands, others starting at the top and jumping down after taking a step or two with no hands.

*Equipment on Which Children Used Parts of the Body Other Than Hands and Feet.* Eight climbers offered situations in which children were able to use parts of their bodies in addition to their hands and feet. These climbers include: Banister Rails, Internal Treescape Climber, Trunk Climber, Megarock, Log Roll, Cargo Net Climber, Wave Climber, and Corkscrew Climber. Children commonly used thighs, knees, and elbows for weight support as they worked their way up or down the Banister Rails. Downward climbs on the Megarock, Wave Climber, Internal Treescape Climber, and Trunk Climber often were done using bottoms—sitting on the equipment provided a way for less-skilled children to interact with the apparatus. A few children used their knee joints for assistance to access the Cargo Net Climber as a foot substitute—while the opposite foot was being raised to the first rung, the knee helped maintain balance. Regarding the Corkscrew Climber, when children climbed up or down the inside of the corkscrew, they used their knees and bottoms to support their bodies as they moved their feet or hands to the next hand/foot hold.

## Q3. What Is the Difficulty Level of Each Type of Climbing Equipment?

To answer this question, the researchers looked at children's patterns of use on different climbers. Some children displayed intermediate to advanced proficiency skills on such equipment as the Fat Pipe Climber or the Megarock, but would revert to more beginner-level climbing behaviors when they approached such equipment as the Trunk Climber, Banister Rails, or Cargo Net Wall.

Based upon the findings of this study, the most difficult climber was the Trunk Climber. Reasons for this appear to be due to the following:

- Small, round area on which to place feet
- Large vertical spaces between rungs
- Height of equipment
- Steep incline (55 degrees).

As discussed earlier in this section (i.e., Question 1), the climbing skills for children rated as "Beginner" largely are the result of short limbs, more cautious movements, and one-at-a-time hand and foot placements. These children can climb up, but are less comfortable climbing down and need to face the equipment they are using. The Trunk Climber presents a high level of difficulty because the height and incline create visual intimidation, evoking an initial fear response (e.g., reluctance, frowning). Once on the equipment, the large spaces between the rungs are challenging for shorter legs. In addition, because "Beginner" and "Intermediate" children lack confidence in climbing down, the steep incline (55 degrees) and height of the Trunk Climber sometimes discourages them from attempting the advanced type of climbing required by this equipment.

Other climbers also considered to be difficult were the Climbing Pole, Banister Rails, the Log Roll, and the Cargo Net Wall. The Climbing Pole and Banister Rails were ranked as difficult because of the level of upper body strength required to successfully use the climber, as observed by the investigators. The Log Roll posed a challenge because some children found it difficult to simultaneously balance and roll the log. For example, some children could not make the log roll, some fell off, and a few were able to successfully balance and roll the log as intended by the designer. It is noted here that this finding may not be generalizable because the difficulty was the result of an uneven weight distribution inside the log. The Log Roll was filled with sand that tended to pack into one side of the device, making rolling uneven and difficult. Finally, the Cargo Net Wall was challenging not in terms of the climbing element, but rather when a child attempted to cross over one side of the net to the other by climbing over the top support bar.

Data indicated that the easiest climber was the Swivel Meister. This device may more accurately be identified as a type of swing, yet it resembles a climber in that it requires skill in balancing, coordination, and strength. It is believed to be the easiest because it is very close to the ground; has a large, flat surface on which to step; and provides vertical hand rails that are readily available for children of widely differing heights. Children of all ages who approached this piece of equipment were successful in using it.

## Q4. Which Climbers Are Most Beneficial?

Considering all the evidence presented in this document, and after much deliberation and study about the most beneficial climbers, three criteria were found for "most beneficial" climbers. The most beneficial in one sense may not the most beneficial in another sense. The three criteria are: 1) open-endedness, 2) levels of challenge, and 3) frequency of use.

*Open-ended Climbers.* Open-endedness is the provision for freedom from limitations, independent thinking, creativity, and living/working/playing outside of preset expectations. Sculpting clay, wet sand, and a box of art supplies are open-ended materials with which children (and adults) can play. The things that can be created with these items are limitless and, as a result, a user's interest, motivation, and enjoyment are high. In contrast, closed-endedness is the presence of a determined outcome, a right answer, a restriction on individual differences. Puzzles and connect-the-dots are examples of closed-ended play events. Boredom generally sets in quickly when children are asked to participate in such events.

Playground equipment also possesses open- and closed-ended characteristics. Equipment, in this case climbing equipment, that allows for children's creativity can be considered open-ended. Just as children become intensely engaged in hands-on, independently driven play, such as painting, they become intensely engaged in outdoor play that is independently driven. In this study, several climbers offered opportunity for open-ended play because their components allowed for various methods and levels of climbing. Such climbers are believed to be more beneficial than those that allow less variety of use.

While all pieces of climbing equipment that were observed for the purposes of this study were designed with intended uses in mind, open-ended characteristics are more present in some climbers than others. Potential for multiple use may be determined by space, location, or function. The Trunk Climber, Megarock, and Cargo Net Wall Climber provide an element of space freedom. All are wide enough to accommodate multiple children and lateral movements. Location allows for open-ended play as well. The Trunk Climber and Megarock were in places that allowed them to be included in chase games, not just serving as isolated climbers. The Wave Climber provided an opportunity for individual creativity in that children experimented with ways to interact with it. They found ways to access it with their hands, feet only, seats, and sides. Sometimes they rolled loose parts such as playground balls down the climber. The Banister Rails also allowed for variations in use because children could climb with just their hands, with their hands and feet, or with their hands and knees, and they could climb over, under, across, and through it.

Anecdotal notes also provided examples of the multiple creative ways that children found to use certain pieces of equipment. For example, the children often sat on the yellow and green support structures (not intended for climbing) that were located around the Internal Treescape Climber. The large green pipes look like large branches on a tree, and form little nooks where children liked to lounge.

Children would sit in this area alone or congregate and talk with others on these "tree branches." Sometimes, they would walk around the Internal Treescape Climber by stepping on the horizontal pieces that extend from the "branches" to the climber.

One 1st-grade boy was able to access the Trunk Climber from the Internal Treescape Climber without ever touching the ground. He would climb up or down the Internal Climber, climb between the third and fourth rungs from the bottom, sit on a green "branch," grab onto the underside of the Trunk Climber, swing his body and step on the Trunk Climber several times, and then swing back onto the Internal Climber or climb onto the topside of the Trunk Climber. As suggested by Frost, Sutterby, et al. (2001), all parts of the playground should be considered as possibly climbable by children who have advanced climbing ability.

Children also engaged each other socially in pretend play, chase, and while lounging on some climbing components. The top of the Banister Rails served as a hang-out for Pokemon characters, and the underside of the Megarock served as a jail and doctor's office. As suggested by Gutteridge (1939) and Armitage (2001), the shape and form of equipment often suggests dramatic play uses for the equipment. Similar to Clarke's (1999) findings, the Megarock, Trunk Climber, and Corkscrew Climber were often used during chase games. Children lounged on the rungs of the Trunk Climber, Internal Treescape Climber, Corkscrew Climber, and top rail of the Cargo Net Wall. While lounging, they would either engage other children in conversation or watch other children on the playground.

*Levels of Challenge.* Climbers that promote progression from less-skilled climbing to more-skilled climbing are beneficial in terms of children's physical development. This study established three categories of skill: Beginner, Intermediate, and Advanced. Children at the beginner level exhibit climbing behaviors that are slow and cautious, such as using a hand to hand and foot to foot pattern, and moving limbs one at a time. Over time and with practice, they are able to begin incorporating some hand over hand and foot over foot movements into their climbing. They also demonstrate confidence in their willingness to jump to the ground from a higher place and to look at where they are going rather than at their hands and feet. From this intermediate stage, children continue to advance in their climbing skills until they ultimately reach the point at which they consistently move with hand over hand and foot over foot patterns, with an opposite hand to foot relationship. They can skip rungs with hands and feet with ease, and their movements are quick and fluid. The hallmark of advanced climbing skill is the ability to climb up, down, or laterally with equal ease, and to face away from equipment when climbing down.

The most beneficial climbers with regard to challenge are those that allow for progression and extended development of skill. The Trunk Climber is a good example of this type of equipment. The small, round area on which feet are placed and the large, vertical spaces between the rungs make this a difficult piece of equipment for children at the beginner level to climb—they spend a lot of time thinking about what they are doing with their hands and feet. Intermediate level climbers are challenged in their abilities to climb down or to climb facing away from the equipment. Their longer limbs are helping them progress in movement patterns: hand to hand starts becoming hand over hand. Finally, advanced level children are challenged in that they can experiment with more difficult climbing strategies, such as feet only, climbing up or down with their bodies facing sideways to the equipment, or climbing down facing away from the climber. Climbing up and down while facing away from equipment requires advanced balancing skills on the more difficult climbers. In addition, advanced climbers can increase the challenge level by climbing parts of the play equipment that are not intended for climbing.

Other climbers that are beneficial for children's physical development are the Climbing Pole, Banister Rails, and Cargo Net Wall. These climbers are beneficial because they require children to use upper body strength. As stated previously, children have more opportunities to develop lower body strength than upper body strength, so providing activities that require children to use upper body strength challenges them and helps them develop and maintain upper body strength (Frost, Brown, Thornton, Sutterby, & Therrell, 2001).

*Frequency of Use.* Obviously, a climber is not beneficial for children if it is not used. The 13 climbers involved in this study were accessed 608 times over the course of the observation:

- kindergarten total use: 241
- 1st-grade total use: 281
- 3rd-grade total use: 86

The large difference between kindergarten and 1st grade, compared to 3rd grade, frequency of use can be attributed to two factors. First, 3rd-graders were observed on the playground only half as many times as the other two grades because 3rd-graders were only assigned one outdoor play session per day, whereas the younger children were allowed to play outdoors two to three times per day. Second, 3rd-grade outdoor play took place during the heat of the late afternoon, whereas the kindergartners and 1st-graders played in the morning and after lunch, when the heat was less intense. Thus, 3rd-graders tended to stay in the shady areas of the playground and tended not to play on the unshaded composite play structure.

The climbing equipment most frequently used by the children overall was the Megarock (110). The Megarock was also the equipment used most frequently by kindergartners and 1st-graders; the Trunk Climber was the climber used most frequently by the 3rd-graders. Other popular climbers for kindergartners and 1st-graders were the Cargo Net Wall and the Corkscrew Climber. The other popular climbers for 3rd-graders were the Megarock and Internal Treescape Climber.

| Most Frequently Used | | |
|---|---|---|
| Kindergarten | First | Third |
| • Megarock (33) | • Megarock (54) | • Trunk Climber (33) |
| • Cargo Net Wall (31) | • Cargo Net Wall (37) | • Megarock (23) |
| • Corkscrew Climber (27) | • Corkscrew Climber (34) | • Internal Climber (7) |

The climbing equipment used least frequently by the children overall was the Climbing Pole. Other climbers used less frequently were the Swivel Meister, Log Roll, and Chain Link Climber. Climbers used least by the 3rd-graders were the Log Roll, Swivel Meister, Fat Pipe Climber, and Cargo Net Wall.

| Least Frequently Used | | |
|---|---|---|
| Kindergarten | First | Third |
| • Climbing Pole (5) | • Climbing Pole (4) | • Climbing Pole (1) |
| • Swivel Meister (5) | • Chain Link Climber (5) | • Log Roll (1) |
| • Chain Link Climber (6) | • Log Roll (9) | • Swivel Meister (1) |
| | | • Fat Pipe Climber (1) |
| | | • Cargo Net Wall (1) |

The frequency of use findings are represented in the bar graphs on pages 152-153. Age groups are represented in separate graphs (i.e., graph 1 = kindergarten; graph 2 = 1st grade;

## Kindergarten Climber Usage

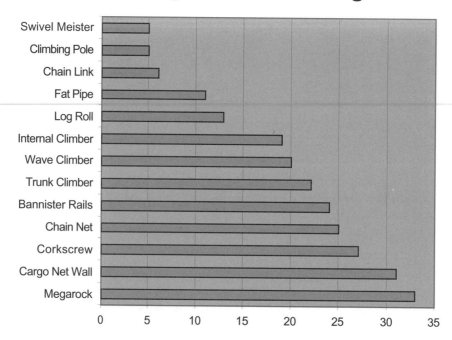

## First Grade Climber Usage

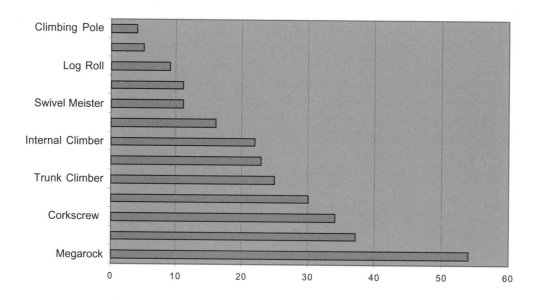

## Third Grade Climber Usage

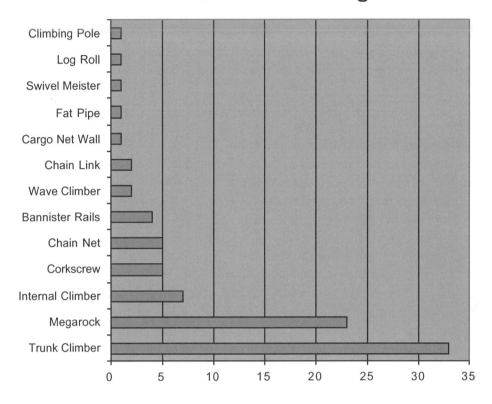

## Total Climber Usage (K - 3)

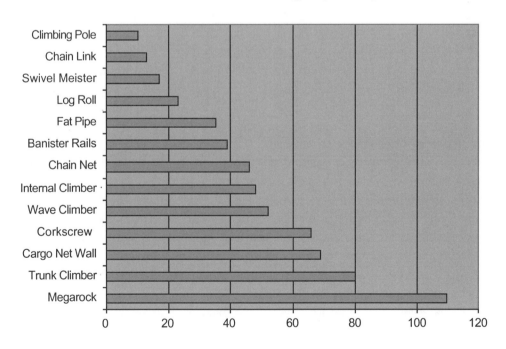

graph 3 = 3rd grade); all 13 climbers are included in each graph. The climbers are represented in a most- to least-used sequence. The fourth graph depicts the total usage overall with the same type of sequencing.

We can conclude, therefore, that the most beneficial climbers are open-ended, fostering creativity in children's play; are challenging to children of different ages; and can maintain children's interests over a long period of time and across different age groups.

## ADDITIONAL DATA GATHERED

### Affective Factors in Climbing

The two affective factors most noted by the researchers during field observations were fear and motivation. Fear appeared to come into play most on the Trunk Climber, which was determined to be the most difficult climber, and when climbing over the top of the Cargo Net Wall. Children responded by hesitating before attempting the climb and by reverting to a more immature level of climbing. Frost, Sutterby, et al. (2001) observed toddlers climbing to the top deck of 12-foot-high slides, then becoming frightened and having to be rescued by adults. No cases were observed of children having to be rescued by adults in the present study, probably because the children in the present study were older and the climbing structures offered a variety of ways to get down from the equipment. One kindergarten boy followed a group of peers up the Cargo Net Climber. As he reached the top and raised a leg to go over, however, he immediately put his foot back onto the climber rung. He went down the same way he went up, then ran around the climber to join the rest of the pack.

Direct observations of children at play led to the conclusion that the two most frequent sources of motivation for climbing were to participate in social chase games and to participate in dramatic play. This indicates that the primary motivation for climbing on this playground was social in nature. The children used the climbing structure as a prop for their games. Gutteridge (1939) suggested that climbing is often part of dramatic play, as children play "as if" games. Star Wars and other dramatic themes were common on the playground. A few children were motivated to perform for the observers, and some children climbed as a solitary activity. Climbing for these children seemed to be more goal-oriented, as suggested by Readdick and Park (1998), as the children climbed because the object was there to be climbed and its shape and form suggested climbing.

### Unintended Use of Equipment

Children also climbed on equipment that was not intended by the designers or manufacturers for climbing. This equipment included the green arm-like supports around the Internal Climber, the Crunch Bar located by the Fat Pipe Climber, the Wild Slide, and the seats and support poles located under the Rain Wheel Panel and by the Corkscrew Climber.

As mentioned previously, the green arm-like supports around the Internal Climber were favorite lounging spots for children, especially kindergartners and 1st-graders. The children also liked to walk around the Internal Climber on these supports, and swing out to other areas of the composite structure (such as the Trunk Climber) from these supports.

First-grade children would access the Crunch Bar from the Fat Pipe Climber, place their feet on the bottom rails of the protective barrier just above the platform at the top of the Fat Pipe Climber on either side of the Crunch Bar, face the bar and hold it so that their arms were extended to their thighs, and lean back into a backbend so that their upper bodies formed an arch away from the equipment and their heads hung back. None of the children were observed using the Crunch Bar as intended.

Children of all ages observed often would use the Wild Slide as a climber as well as a slide. Some children possessed enough strength and skill to stop in the middle of a descent, turn around, and climb back up. Some children would use the slide for pretend play, chase, or social interactions, gathering in the middle or at the bottom of the slide to discuss their plans until they were told by teachers to exit the slide. Some children liked to slide down in groups so that they landed one behind the other at the bottom of the slide.

Children also liked to climb the round seats under the panel by the Corkscrew Climber and reach up onto the platforms above. Some older children were able to stand on a seat, grab the platform above, and simultaneously use their arm strength and lower body strength (sometimes jumping, sometimes shimmying up a support pole) to pull themselves up onto the platform above. Older children would also use this same route to descend to the ground, using the seats as a stepping stool to the ground. This was observed more frequently at the seats by the Corkscrew Climber, where children used the support pole as "base" during chase games.

### Interview and Anecdotal Data

Researchers talked to children and teachers during the observation periods on the playgrounds. The following summary captures the main points that children and teachers made about the intended and unintended climbing equipment, as well as observations researchers were unable to code using the equipment use coding sheet.

*Interviews With Children:*

Kindergartners:
- Would give the panel a spin as they ran by—liked the sound of it.
- Called the Trunk Climber a "fairy ladder" during pretend.
- Loved the Wild Slide, Megarock, and Toadstools, as evidenced by their enthusiasm and use.
- Called the toadstools "stepping stones" because they had just been on a field trip to the Nature Center and saw stepping stones that went across a brook.
- "I like the rock and the inside of the tree."
- "I really like the log roll!"

1st-graders:
- "The rock is my favorite part. There's a Velociraptor on the other side!"
- "I like the rock but not those things [Banister Rails]. They rub my legs when I have shorts on." (When questioned about their preference for the Banister Rails when they had long pants on, children said that they liked it because they could use it in multiple ways without their skin sticking to it.)
- Liked the O-Rings.
- Liked the "bumpy slide [Wave Climber] because it's easy to climb up."
- Liked the "green sitting bars" around the Internal Climbers.
- "I like the slide best. I don't like the parallel bars [Banister Rails] or the log roll."

- "I like the phones but not the log roll."
- "I think the slide is too slow."
- "I don't like the corkscrew because you have to go down the inside and then it's hard to get out the bottom."
- Didn't like the Rain Wheel Panel because "it's not that exciting."
- Didn't like the seats because "there's always bird poop on them."

3rd-Graders:
- Reported favorites: Megarock, Wild Slide, hole at the top of the Internal Climber, Cargo Net Climber.
- Descended backwards down Wild Slide.
- Congregated at top of Internal Climber.
- Slid down around Corkscrew Climber (sitting on climber with both legs towards center of climber, not straddling climber).
- Swung on the Swivelmeister two at a time.

*Interviews With Teachers:*
Kindergarten teachers:
- Regarding Cargo Net Climber—"They call that their exercise!"
- "They really love the Toadstools because they remind them of the stepping stones they saw on Monday at the Nature Center."
- "I'm surprised at how much the children go up the bars [Banister Rails]."
- Regarding the composite play structure—"I love this thing. There are so many things for them to do on it."

1st-grade Teachers:
- Liked the log roll—"It lets them run off all that energy."
- Liked the Mega Rock—"The fossil is really neat."
- Didn't like the Swivel Meister—"It's kind of weird."

3rd-grade Teachers:
- Regarding children playing freeze tag around the Megarock/Corkscrew Climber area—"They have been playing that same game for 3 days now!"
- "They love that slide!"
- Regarding the play structure—"This thing is great! They like it better than the big playground!"

*Anecdotal Notes:*
- Children gained climbing skills very quickly.
- Proficiency on overhead apparatus seemed to translate to proficiency on climbing apparatus.
- Children would often enter the playground, run up the Megarock, and then spread out from there.
- Children would swing from the arches that formed the overhead protective barriers at the entryway to slides and climbers.

- Younger children modeled older children, and younger children wanted to play with older children.
- Even with 60 children on the playground, there was no crowding.
- Initially, children would form lines waiting to use the Log Roll and lots of children would go to the treehouse deck
- Fossil and space under Megarock used a lot.
- Seats were almost always in use.
- Children seemed to be "naturally" cautious—when they were in climbing situations that seemed dangerous, they behaved more cautiously.
- Banister Rails seemed to prompt the most diversity of use.
- Children climbed up the Fat Pipe Climber on the rail side of the climber (with their legs going under the rail to reach the steps).

Interview and anecdotal data generally supported observation data. Children voiced a multitude of opinions about the playground equipment. The pieces of equipment that were mentioned most enthusiastically by children were the Megarock and the Wild Slide. As previously mentioned, the Megarock was the most frequently used climber overall during the observations. Also evident in the anecdotal notes as well as the interview statements was the creativity fostered by the Megarock, Banister Rails, Trunk Climber, and the Internal Climber—the open-ended climbers.

## DISCUSSION

Data collected for the purpose of this study suggest that children's climbing behavior is a sequential process. Children progress through levels of sophistication as they age, grow, and practice climbing skills. They start out as beginners, and their continued participation in climbing activities moves them into the intermediate stage. With more experience, they enter a final transition into the advanced level. The progression through the three stages is not specifically age-determined, but rather is determined by opportunities for practice and by physical growth and ability.

Physical stature and ability are mutually dependent. One of the signs of a beginner level climber is the characteristic of short limbs. As children's bodies grow, they become physically able to move to more challenging climbing apparatus and behaviors. Without the acquired skills of climbing that only come with practice, however, longer legs and arms are not of much use. Conversely, high levels of skill are less effective without limbs that reach easily from step to step.

As mentioned above, the issue of physical stature is significant. Because of the limitations shorter limbs impose, options for climbing are limited and the type of object to be climbed determines how well children are able to climb it. Children are able to climb steps with low risers before they are able to climb steps with adult level or higher risers (Gessell & Ilg, 1946). It appears that children automatically adjust their preference for the height of the riser to their body size, and infants will prefer lower risers until their skill level allows them to climb higher risers, at which point they will begin to show a preference for the higher risers (Ulrich, Thelen, & Niles, 1990).

The validity of this "Physical Stature + Rise Height + Skill = Preference" notion was clearly demonstrated in this study:

- Kindergarten and 1st-grade participants fell exclusively within the "Beginner" and "Intermediate" categories of skill development. In fact, for almost every observation coded, kindergartners were labeled beginners and were considered short in height, 1st-graders were labeled intermediate and were either short or medium in height, and 3rd-graders were generally always rated as advanced and medium to extra-tall in height.
- Data indicated that the kindergarten and 1st-grade children engaged in climbing behaviors most often with the Megarock, a climber that had diverse rise heights and therefore could accommodate children of many different skill levels.
- Data also indicated that the 3rd-grade children, most of whom were tall when compared to the kindergartners, engaged in climbing behaviors most often with the Trunk Climber, which was the climber with the most distance between steps (rungs).

The kindergarten and 1st-grade students preferred the Megarock most because it provided variety in step heights—low rise accommodated smaller body sizes and higher rise accommodated larger body sizes. The Trunk Climber was the most preferred climber for 3rd-graders, probably because it has the largest rise out of all climbing equipment on the playground.

Physical stature and ability or skill development also help determine how certain types of playground climbers encourage children to engage in certain types of climbing behaviors. Climbing requires use of limbs in opposition to the force of gravity. Climbing can be done with the arms only, the legs only, or in combination. The motor requirements vary, depending on the object being climbed (Gallahue, 1990). In this study, participants were observed using their hands and feet, feet and lower body, hands and upper body, and balancing of the body on moving equipment.

The way in which the body was used, however, depended upon the individual's size as well as strength, the latter being dependent largely upon opportunities for and experience with climbing equipment. Children have difficulty with climbing for a combination of reasons. American children generally have very poor upper body strength (Gallahue, 1982). Climbers observed in this study that required a notable amount of upper body strength were the Climbing Pole and Banister Rails. Of the 608 coded observations generated from the videotaped data, the Climbing Pole received 10 incidents of documented use. From the play of 60 children over the period of one month, the Climbing Pole was used only 6 percent of the time. The Banister Rails were coded 39 times, accounting for 15 percent of the overall coded play. Many of the children observed did not even attempt these climbers. It seemed that only the children who were more advanced on other climbers would attempt these climbers; however, they still demonstrated lower proficiency behaviors on these climbers than they did on other climbers (climbers that did not require as much upper body strength).

The high level of difficulty and the low level of use related to these two climbers support Gallahue's (1982) assessment of children's climbing abilities as a perpetual cycle of under-development. Children do not engage with these climbers because they have poor upper body strength, but they have poor upper body strength because they do not engage with challenging climbers. This seems to be a cycle that gets worse with age. The kindergarten children account for 5 of the 10 coded observations; 4 by 1st graders; and only 1 by a 3rd-grader. This finding suggests that as children get older, they may become less interested in participating in activities that engage their upper bodies if they have not already developed considerable upper body strength. In other words, they may not see challenging climbers as fun if they are not as skilled at accessing them, and may therefore avoid these climbers.

This play site had only two elements that were intended primarily for the development of upper body strength, and the remaining 11 climbers require lower body, or leg, strength. While the Trunk Climber was the most difficult climber on the playground, it was still a frequently used piece of equipment because children had sufficient lower body strength to access it. Inclusion of overhead ladders or other similar equipment designed to increase upper body strength on playgrounds will increase strength and endurance (Gabbard, 1979, 1983).

The Swivel Meister required a minimum level of lower body exertion. It is the easiest and least challenging climber on the playground because it is very close to the ground, and it has a large, flat surface on which to step. The body is not required to move up or down, only forward and backward with a swinging hip movement. Essentially, it is a stand-up swing. The only climbing involved is stepping off the ground onto the swing surface, which, when appropriate levels of ground covering are in place, amounts to only around 2 inches. The children used the Swivel Meister in more difficult ways, however, such as swinging on one leg or creating enough momentum to jump off the swing and land a few feet away from the structure.

The nine remaining climbers, Megarock, Cargo Net Wall, Corkscrew, Wave, and Internal Climber, Chain Net, Fat Pipe, Log Roll, and Chain Link Climber, have difficulty levels that fall between the Trunk Climber and Swivel Meister. A hierarchy of difficulty levels was not developed because multiple variables create fluctuations in the difficulty scale. Providing variety in difficulty level of equipment is critical. The type of playground has an influence on children's development of physical skills. In a comparison between traditional and contemporary playgrounds, Barbour (1999) found that the traditional playgrounds in her study encourage gross motor skills and favored children with high levels of physical competence, while children with lower levels of physical competence were constrained by this type of playground. The contemporary playground in her study, on the other hand, allowed children of both high and low levels of physical competence to interact with each other and the equipment.

Vertical climbers (e.g., ladders, Cargo Net Wall) usually allow the person climbing to fall away from the structure and directly onto the underlying resilient surface. Climbers with flexible components (e.g., Cargo Net Wall) reduce the impact of falls to some degree. Climbers such as the Banister Climber have no underlying components to fall onto unless the person climbing is standing on top of the climber. Several children were observed slipping and sliding down the Megarock Climber with no indication of injury. This appeared to result from the slope of the climber coupled with the smooth rounded edges of the handholds and the relatively shock absorbent quality of the plastic from which the climber was fabricated. The quality and maintenance of protective surfacing is, of course, critical in all falls.

A second concern regarding safety of climbers arose when two very obese junior high school-age children were observed during installation of the equipment. All openings in climbers into which children may enter (e.g., Internal Climber, Corkscrew Climber) should be of sufficient size to accommodate the growing number of very obese children who may use the climber. Designers and manufacturers should pay close attention to this growing problem and avoid openings in equipment that could entrap obese children. Designers also should be aware that teenagers may enter the playground after school hours and play there.

The nature and benefits of children's climbing behavior is well summarized in this quote: "Climbing provides an ideal activity for children to discover their individual movement potential, build self-confidence, problem solve, and, of course, improve upon physical traits such as balance, strength, and flexibility" (MacDonald, 2001, p. 73).

## RECOMMENDATIONS

The following recommendations are based on three strands of evidence: 1) the findings of this study, 2) the review of literature, and 3) researchers' personal experience and observations. The audiences for these recommendations are playground supervisors or playleaders, playground designers, and playground equipment manufacturers.

- A close relationship exists between age/grade in school and climbing skill, but wide variation in individual abilities suggests that careful attention be given to matching skills of children to complexity of climbers. This requires that playground supervisors or playleaders develop skills in observing children at play in order to assess their levels of skill development.
- Playgrounds for kindergarten and primary children should allow for movement from the less complex playground (for 2- to 5-year-olds) to the more complex playground (for 5- to 12-year-olds) and vice versa, based on skill development and age rather than age or school grade alone.
- Children in the beginner and intermediate stages should develop climbing skills on the less complex equipment before advancing to the more complex equipment. Playleaders should introduce increasingly challenging equipment as children's climbing skills improve.
- Designers should ensure that playgrounds for children of all ages have a wide range of climbing equipment that provides for multiple challenges. They also should include a range of both climbing and overhead equipment on composite structures to support a range of skill development.
- Designers should address the following key ingredients for safety, challenge, fun, and skill development in climbers: height, distance between climbing components, size of climbing components, flexibility and density of climbing components, slope of climber, ease of transition to upper level, adaptability for socialization, adaptability for dramatic play, adaptability for games, and children's preferences.
- Improving skill development, playability, and safety on playground climbers depends on several factors: the training of adults who supervise children at play, the provision of a wide range of challenges, the selection of fall-free climbers, and the provision of proper surfacing under and around equipment. Manufacturers can play a crucial role in playleader training by making emerging research widely available in useable form.
- Overall, placing a range of climbers on children's playgrounds is a wise investment for countering declining levels of physical fitness and for enhancing perceptual-motor skills, balance, strength, flexibility, and socialization.

- Modular units should be designed that include various types of climbers and with a variety of difficulty levels. Types should vary depending on the type of climbing involved. Some variables include: flexibility, incline, number of users, and type of body part used.

- Climbers that require upper body strength for access should be placed in high-traffic areas of the playground to encourage children to use these pieces of equipment. This would increase their opportunities for developing upper body strength and provide challenging and varied climbing experiences.

- Ensure that children have access to an abundance of "social climbers." These are climbers that allow multiple children to climb at the same time on the same climber or on climbers placed close to each other. Children were observed not only playing chase and pretend games, and talking on climbers, but also helping each other learn or improve climbing skills. This "scaffolding" is a highly valued action, both for the scaffolder (the one helping) and the scaffolded (the one being helped).

- Manufacturers should consider eliminating a number of the vertical solid metal climbers that do not have fall-free characteristics.

- Designers and manufacturers should consider offering rope or simulated rope climbers. Rope is flexible and it offers a resilient impact surface for falling. Rope could be used to replace the chains in some climbers. Adding rope climbers would offer variety of climber type and difficulty level. Ropes, of course, must be secured at each end to prevent looping (around necks).

- Designers and manufacturers should consider adding to the widths of climbers (e.g., the Wavy Climber). A 4'- or 5'-wide version could accommodate a larger number of climbers. In addition, a taller version with a steeper incline would make a challenging climber even for older, more advanced climbers.

- A rating scale could be added to the different climbers. A "lemur" or "chimpanzee" scale would start with a 0 rating for a ramp to imply total accessibility, 1 for a simple staircase or transfer platform, and on up to a 5 or 6 for the climbing pole and the trunk climber. This would indicate to purchasers that the climbers they are purchasing offer a range of climbing challenge levels.

- Designers and manufacturers should reconsider openings in equipment that allow the growing number of obese children to become entrapped. Traditional opening sizes do not accommodate many of these children.

# APPENDIX A: PLAYGROUND STRUCTURE DIAGRAM

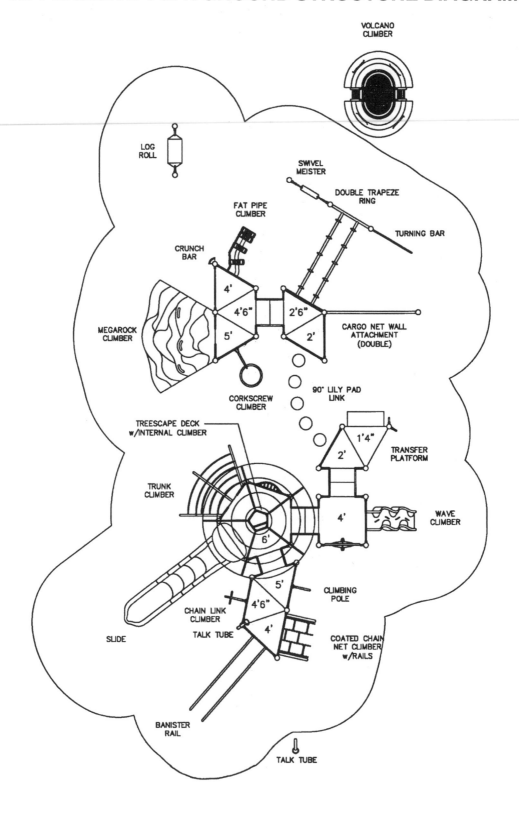

## APPENDIX B:  BLANK CODING SHEET

| Participant Characteristics | | | | | | | | | |
|---|---|---|---|---|---|---|---|---|---|
| grade level (K, 1, 2) | | | | | | | | | |
| gender (F/M) | | | | | | | | | |
| height (S/M/L) | | | | | | | | | |
| weight (S/M/L/XL) | | | | | | | | | |
| **Hand Pattern** | | | | | | | | | |
| hand to hand | | | | | | | | | |
| hand over hand | | | | | | | | | |
| alternating hth and hoh | | | | | | | | | |
| handholds skipped | | | | | | | | | |
| **Foot Pattern** | | | | | | | | | |
| foot to foot | | | | | | | | | |
| foot over foot | | | | | | | | | |
| alternating ftf and fof | | | | | | | | | |
| steps skipped | | | | | | | | | |
| **Hand/Foot Relationship** | | | | | | | | | |
| same | | | | | | | | | |
| opposite | | | | | | | | | |
| one at a time | | | | | | | | | |
| **Other Parts of Body Used for Climbing** | | | | | | | | | |
| seat | | | | | | | | | |
| knees | | | | | | | | | |
| thighs | | | | | | | | | |
| elbows | | | | | | | | | |
| **Speed** | | | | | | | | | |
| cautious | | | | | | | | | |
| confident | | | | | | | | | |
| **Body to Equipment Relationship** | | | | | | | | | |
| up | | | | | | | | | |
| down | | | | | | | | | |
| lateral | | | | | | | | | |
| facing equipment | | | | | | | | | |
| facing away from equipment | | | | | | | | | |
| **Visual Focus** | | | | | | | | | |
| hands | | | | | | | | | |
| feet | | | | | | | | | |
| destination | | | | | | | | | |
| nothing in particular | | | | | | | | | |
| cannot ascertain | | | | | | | | | |
| **Estimated Level of Expertise** | | | | | | | | | |
| Beginner | | | | | | | | | |
| Intermediate | | | | | | | | | |
| Advanced | | | | | | | | | |

## References

Armitage, M. (2001). The ins and outs of school playground play: Children's use of "play places." In J. Bishop & M. Curtis (Eds.), *Play today in the primary school playground* (pp. 37-57). Buckingham, England: Open University Press.

Barbour, A. (1999). The impact of playground design on the play behaviors of children with differing levels of physical competence. *Early Childhood Research Quarterly, 14*(1), 75-98.

Beckwith, J. (1988). Playground design: A scientific approach. In L. Bruya (Ed.), *Play spaces for children: A new beginning* (pp. 49-102). Reston, VA: American Alliance for Health, Physical Education, Recreation and Dance.

Bedrova, E., & Leong, D. (1996). *Tools of the mind: The Vygotskian approach to early childhood education.* Englewood Cliffs, NJ: Merrill.

Bennet, C. (1980). Planning for activity during the important preschool years. *Journal of Education and Recreation, 51*(8), 30-32.

Bertenthal, B. I., Campos, J. J., & Caplovitz, K. S. (1983). Self-produced locomotion: An organizer of emotional, cognitive, and social development in infancy. In R. N. Emde & R. Harmon (Eds.), *Continuities and discontinuities in development.* New York: Plenum.

Boschker, M., Bakker, F., & Michaels, C. (2002). Memory for the functional characteristics of climbing walls: Perceiving affordances. *Journal of Motor Behavior, 34*(1), 25-36.

Cavallo, D. (1980). *Muscles and morals: Organized playgrounds and urban reform, 1880-1920.* Philadelphia: University of Philadelphia Press.

Cherryholmes, C. C. (1992). Notes on pragmatism and scientific realism. *Educational Researcher, 21*, 13-17.

Clarke, L. (1999). Development reflected in chase games. In S. Reifel (Ed.), *Play and culture studies, 2* (pp. 73-82). Stamford, CT: Ablex Publishing.

Consumer Product Safety Commission. (1997). *Handbook for public playground safety.* Washington, DC: Author.

Crowl, T. K. (1996). *Fundamentals of educational research* (2nd ed.). Madison, WI: Brown & Benchmark Publishers.

Crum, J., & Eckert, H. (1985). Play patterns of primary school children. In J. Clark & J. Humphrey (Eds.), *Motor development: Current selected research* (pp. 99-114). Princeton, NJ: Princeton Book Club.

Dattner, R. (1969). *Design for play.* New York: Van Nostrand Reinhold Company.

Durant, R., Baranowski, T., Johnson, M., & Thompson, W. (1994). The relationship among television watching, physical activity, and body composition of young children. *Pediatrics, 94*, 449-455.

Eckert, H. (1987). *Motor development.* Indianapolis, IN: Benchmark Press.

Ellis, M. (1973). *Why people play.* Englewood Cliffs, NJ: Prentice Hall.

Erlandson, D. A., Harris, E. L., Skipper, B. L., & Allen, S. D. (1993). *Doing naturalistic inquiry: A guide to methods.* Thousand Oaks, CA: SAGE Publications.

Fraser, R., Steffen, J., Elfessi, A. M., & Curtis, J. (2001). The effect of relaxation training on indoor rock climbing performance. *Physical Educator, 58*(3), 134-139.

Frost, J. (1992). *Play and playscapes.* Albany, NY: Delmar.

Frost, J., Brown, P., Thornton, C., Sutterby, J., & Therrell, J. (2001). *The developmental benefits and use patterns of overhead equipment on playgrounds.* Unpublished manuscript.

Frost, J., & Henniger, M. (1979). Making playgrounds safe for children and children safe for playgrounds. *Young Children, 34*, 23-30.

Frost, J., & Kim, S. (2000). *Developmental progress in preschool-age children's using an overhead bar.* Unpublished manuscript.

Frost, J., Sutterby, J., Therrell, J., Brown, P., & Thornton, C. (2001). *The relevance of height for child development and playground safety.* Unpublished manuscript.

Frost, J., & Sweeney, T. (1996). *Cause and prevention of playground injuries and litigation: Case studies.* Olney, MD: Association for Childhood Education International.

Frost, J., Wortham, S., & Reifel, S. (2001). *Play and child development.* Upper Saddle River, NJ: Merrill.

Fulgham, R. (1990). *It was on fire when I lay down on it.* New York: Villard Books.

Gabbard, C. (1979). *Playground apparatus experience and muscular endurance among children 4-6.* Unpublished technical report. ERIC/EDRS, # 228-190.

Gabbard, C. (1983). Muscular endurance and experience with playground apparatus. *Perceptual and Motor Skills, 56,* 538.

Gabbard, C. (1992). *Lifelong motor development.* New York: Wm. C. Brown Publishers.

Gabbard, C., LeBlanc, B., & Lowy, S. (1994). *Physical education for children.* Englewood Cliffs, NJ: Prentice Hall.

Gallahue, D. L. (1982). *Understanding motor development in children.* New York: John Wiley & Sons.

Gallahue, D. (1990). *Understanding motor development: Infants, children, adolescents.* Indianapolis, IN: Benchmark Press.

GameTime. (2002). *Park and playground products catalog.* Fort Payne, AL: Author.

Gesell, A., & Ilg, F. (1946). *The child from five to ten.* New York: Harper.

Gober, B., & Franks, D. (1988). Physical and fitness education of young children. *Journal of Physical Education Recreation and Dance, 59*(8), 43-46.

Gutteridge, M. (1939). A study of motor achievements of young children. *Archives of Psychology, 224,* 1-178. 244.

Haywood, K., & Getchell, N. (2001). *Life span motor development.* Champaign, IL: Human Kinetics.

Hendy, T. (2001). The Americans With Disabilities Act insures the right of every child to play. *Parks & Recreation, 36*(4), 108-118.

Henry, S. (1996). Children at risk. *Women's Sports and Fitness, 18*(6), 21-23.

Heseltine, P., & Holborn, J. (1987). *Playgrounds: The planning, design and construction of play environments.* New York: Nichols Pub. Co.

Houston, C. (1967). Mountaineering. In R. Slovenko & J. Knight (Eds.), *Motivation in play, games and sports* (pp. 626-636). Springfield, IL: Charles C. Thomas.

Howe, K. R. (1988). Against the quantitative-qualitative incompatibility thesis or dogmas die hard. *Educational Researcher, 17,* 10-16.

Ilie, A., & Cadopi, M. (1999). Memory of movement sequences in gymnastics: Effects of age and skill level. *Journal of Motor Behavior, 31*(3), 290-300.

Jarrett, O., Maxwell, D., Dickerson, C., Hoge, P., Davies, G., & Yetley, A. (1998). Impact of recess on classroom behavior: Group effects and individual differences. *The Journal of Educational Research, 92*(2), 121-126.

Jones, M., Bray, S, Mace, R., Bray, S., MacRae, A., & Stockbridge, C. (2002). The impact of motivational imagery on the emotional state and self-efficacy levels of novice climbers. *Journal of Sport Behavior, 25*(1), 57-73.

Kavale, K., & Mattson, P. (1983). One jumped off the balance beam: Meta analysis of perceptual motor training. *Journal of Learning Disabilities, 16,* 165-173.

Kendall, N. (1998). At the end of her rope, Mom smiles and swings. *Christian Science Monitor, 90*(127), 9.

Kingma, J., & Ten Duis, J. (2000). Severity of injuries due to accidental falls across the life span: A retrospective hospital-based study. *Perceptual and Motor Skills, 90,* 62-72.

Landscape Structures. (2002). *Playplanner*. Delano, MN: Author.

Little Tykes. (2000). *Commercial play systems*. Farmington, MO: Author.

MacDonald, D. (2001). KidRock. *Parks and Rec, 36*(8), 72-79.

Manning, K. (1997). Authenticity in constructivist inquiry: Methodological considerations without prescription. *Qualitative Inquiry, 3*(1), 93-115.

McCallum, J. & O'Brien, R. (1996). Monkey barred. *Sports Illustrated, 84*(21), 18.

McNamee, J., & Steffen, J. (2001). Getting off the ground with rock climbing. *Teaching Elementary Physical Education, 12*(6), 26-30.

Mero, E. (1908). *American playgrounds*. Boston: The Dale Association.

Morrison, J. (2002). Lofty aspirations. *Smithsonian, 32*(12), 52-60.

Nabhan, G. P., & Trimble, S. (1994). *The geography of childhood: Why children need wild places.*

Nilsen, B. A. (1997). *Week by week: Plans for observing and recording young children*. Albany, NY: Delmar Publishers.

Perry, R. (2001). Sick kids. *American Way, 4*, 64-65.

Pijpers, J., & Bakker, F. (1993). Perceiving conflicting affordances. In B. Bardy, R. Bootsma, & Y. Guiard (Eds.), *Studies in perception and action III. Eighth international conference on perception and action* (pp. 145-148). Hillsdale, NJ: Erlbaum.

Readdick, C., & Park, J. (1998). Achieving great heights: The climbing child. *Young Children, 53*(6), 14-19.

Schwandt, T. A. (1997). *Qualitative inquiry: A dictionary of terms*. Thousand Oaks, CA: SAGE Publications.

Shea, C., Wulf, G., Whitacre, G., & Wright, D. (2000). Physical and observational practice afford unique learning opportunities. *Journal of Motor Behavior, 32*(1), 27-36.

Sheps, S., & Evans, G. (1987). Epidemiology of school injuries: A 2-year experience in a municipal health department. *Pediatrics, 79*(1), 69-75.

Sutterby, J., & Frost, J. (2002). Making playgrounds fit for children and making children fit on playgrounds. *Young Children, 57*(3), 36-41.

Tashakkori, A., & Teddlie, C. (1998). *Mixed methodology: Combining qualitative and quantitative approaches*. Thousand Oaks, CA: SAGE Publications.

Thompson, D. (1988). Slides, swings and climbing equipment. In L. Bruya & S. Langendorfer (Eds.), *Where our children play: Elementary school playground equipment* (pp. 67-106). Reston, VA: American Alliance for Health, Physical Education, Recreation and Dance.

Thompson, D., & Hudson, S. (2000). Monkeybar injuries. *Pediatrics, 105*(5), 1174-1175.

Tinetti, M. E., & Speechley, M. (1989). Prevention and falls among the elderly. *The New England Journal of Medicine, 20*, 1055-1059.

Tinsworth, D. K., & Kramer, J. T. (1989). *Playground equipment-related injuries involving falls to the surface*. Washington, DC: U.S. Consumer Product Safety Commission.

Tinsworth, D., & McDonald, J. (2001). *Special study: Injuries and deaths associated with children's playground equipment*. Washington, DC: Consumer Product Safety Commission.

Tsanoff, S. (1897). *Educational value of the children's playgrounds*. Philadelphia: Author.

Ulrich, B., Thelen, E., & Niles, D. (1990). Perceptual determinants of action: Stair climbing choices of infants and toddlers. In J. Clark & J. Humphry (Eds.), *Advances in motor development research, Volume 3* (pp. 1-15). New York: AMS Press.

Warren, W. (1984). Perceiving affordances: Visual guidance of stair climbing. *Developmental Psychology: Human Perception and Performance, 10*, 237-304.

Williams, G. (1994). Talk on the climbing frame. *Early Child Development and Care, 102*, 81-89.

# CHAPTER 6
# Functions and Benefits of Playground Swings

*The Swing*

*How do you like to go up in a swing,*
*Up in the air so blue?*
*Oh, I do think it is the pleasantest thing*
*Ever a child can do!*

*Up in the air and over the wall*
*Till I can see so wide,*
*Rivers and trees and cattle and all*
*Over the countryside*

*Till I look down on the garden green*
*Down on the roof so brown*
*Up in the air I go flying again,*
*Up in the air and down!*
—Robert Louis Stevenson

## HISTORY OF SWINGS

Swings are used by children of all ages. "For the youngest, swinging means feeling snug and a pleasant tickling in the stomach. Older children play together on the swing, talk, sing, and push each other" (Noren-Bjorn, 1982, p. 63). Hendricks (2001) asserts that we never grow out of our love for swinging. "Even at eighty swinging is a wonderfully stimulating experience" (p. 133).

Robert Louis Stevenson's poem suggests that swinging closely ties us to the experiences of our ancestors, to our own childhoods, and to the childhoods of our children. Swinging has been around as long as vines have hung from trees (Hogan, 1982). The development of swinging for recreation has a long history. The pendulum action of swinging and associated sensations of flying and falling have made swings one of the most popular pieces of playground equipment.

The physical structure of swings includes a horizontal support, some sort of suspended pendulum (ropes or chains), and a support for the swinger (seat). Manufacturers continue to tinker with the basic structural elements to improve swings' positioning and action. Contemporary tire swings that have the tire seat positioned in a horizontal rather than vertical position allow for a relatively safe multi-person swing. However, other designs, such as heavy metal animal swings, led to numerous serious injuries and deaths and were recalled by the Consumer Product Safety Commission. A number of special-purpose swings are available to accommodate children with disabilities, and mechanical swings have been designed for incubators to help premature infants sleep and thus promote faster growth (Cheng, Ching, Yung, & Tsu, 1997).

Swings are among the earliest pieces of equipment designed for recreation. People in Europe and Asia have used swings for centuries. Representations of the wealthy class enjoying swings can be found in paintings dating back several centuries, and written works from the 16th century describe women enjoying swings in the gardens of Versailles. These early amusements were usually reserved for the wealthy, who had time for leisure (Hendricks, 2001). People swinging also appear in early pictures and statues from Crete, Greece, pre-Columbian middle America, Asia, and post-medieval Europe. Women on swings were a popular 17th and 18th century art subject, and the swing in this art represented the element of air, idleness, and the fickleness of women (Posner, 1982).

## MOTIVATION FOR SWINGING

Swings on a playground provide children unique experiences with speed and force, which are not found on fixed equipment, such as climbers and overhead ladders (Thompson, 1988). The playground movement of the early 1900s recognized the popularity and value of swings on public playgrounds. The most popular devices on the playground are those that provided a sense of falling. According to Mero (1908), these included tilts, teeter ladders, sliding poles, coasts, swings, trapezes, and traveling rings, devices that are still on playgrounds in modified form. Mero's writing about turn-of-the-century playgrounds suggests that swings, climbing apparatus, see saws, and merry-go-rounds should be part of the available apparatus.

The movement of swings provides two different sensations that motivate children to engage in the activity. The first sensation is the rhythmic movement of the swings. When the child achieves a regular motion on the swings, it can produce a relaxing effect on the central nervous system. Rhythmic swinging also can stimulate the central nervous system, creating a sense of excitement. Children generally will be attracted to the movement that meets their current mood or needs. A child who is overexcited may approach a swing to relax, while a child who is bored or under-stimulated will be motivated to create an excited swinging motion (Welzenbach, 1996; Yisreal, 1998).

The National Survey of Elementary School Playground Equipment (Thompson, 1988) found that swings were the second most common piece of playground equipment after chinning bars. Swing sets made up 12.9 percent of the equipment available on playgrounds.

A number of concerns have been expressed about swings, yet they are very popular with children. Some critics claim that traditional swings provide very few opportunities for play, considering the amount of space required. One must consider the space required to install the swing and the extensive fall zones for resilient surfacing; the CPSC and ASTM recommend a fall zone extending twice the height of the overhead support beam in the to-fro direction and six feet from the vertical swing supports in the other direction. Some professionals question, however, whether falling from the swing supports is a relevant safety issue. In addition, swings are considered dangerous because children often walk into the path of moving swings (Hewes & Beckwith, 1975). This hazard is well-documented by injury data and led to the recall of heavy swing seats (e.g., animal seats). For the most part, heavy metal or wooden swing seats have been replaced by resilient, lightweight seats. Freidberg (1970) calls the heavy solid swings found on playgrounds in the 1960s "medieval torture contraptions" (p. 58). In some states, swings have been eliminated from playgrounds because of their association with risk of injury (Harrison, 2001). The risk factor appears to have been determined through a focus on injuries from improperly designed, installed, and supervised swings and a misunderstanding or ignorance of the developmental value of swings.

## USE OF SWINGS

Traditional swings are designed to take advantage of the pendulum action of the suspended seat, allowing for a rhythmical forward and backward motion. The motion of swinging can be described in two ways: driven oscillation and parametric pumping. Driven oscillation is when the swinger rotates the center of mass around the end of the swing's pendulum. This type of action is most common at low levels of swinging amplitude. Parametric pumping occurs when the swinger raises and lowers the center of mass along the length of the pendulum. This type of action is more common at greater amplitudes (Post, 1991).

The way swings are used does not always correspond to the designer's intent. According to the CPSC's *Handbook of Playground Safety*, children often jump from swings. Children also stand in the swings, swing on their stomachs, twist the chains of swings and twirl, and swing side to side as well as to and fro. One young inventor, Steven Olsen, was awarded a patent on an alternative method of swinging. His method involves pulling on the chains of the swing alternately in order to create a side-to-side swinging motion. His method, called "Tarzan" swinging, is designed for children who have not mastered the action of pumping their legs to create the swinging motion (Swing Theory, 2002).

Noren-Bjorn (1982) found that equipment that encouraged movement, such as swings and slides, was much more popular than fixed climbing equipment. Her study of Swedish playgrounds includes numerous references to the popularity of swings over other play equipment. She reports that girls 7-10 years old preferred "to swing, turn summersaults, and hop twist" (p. 78). Swings, along with sand pits, rated high in popularity with children on most playgrounds over all other pieces of playground equipment. Children in her study also used swings in dramatic play, placing their dolls on the toddler swings. "The child or children (often two swung together) who succeeded in getting to the swing first sang or yelled triumphantly while swinging" (p. 95).

Swings were used 5.4 percent of the total play time in Noren-Bjorn's study. Of the two conditions studied, traditional (to-fro) swings were used 10-12 percent of the time on unsupervised playgrounds but only 3-4 percent of the time on supervised playgrounds. Tire swings were used 2.8 percent of the time. Swing use on play spaces represents a fairly large percentage of the time coded. In her study of two play spaces, Moore (1992) found that swings ranked behind open areas, sand play areas, slides, and climbing superstructures as children's preferences. The tire swing and regular swings accounted for between 5 and 7 percent of the observations combined. Swings typically rank in the top 5 of all playground activities for preschoolers, with swing use accounting for 8-12 percent of playground activity (Ihn, 1998; Park, 1998; Riddell, 1992; Shin, 1994).

The preference for swings appears to be affected by the variety of equipment choices available to children. Myers (1981) compared equipment choices of children on conventional playgrounds, containing only large, fixed equipment, versus creative playgrounds, containing a wider range of fixed and portable equipment. She found that on traditional playgrounds children preferred swings, where they were the most-used equipment. The swings on the creative playground, with a larger variety of equipment choices, ranked number five in both equipment use and preference. Frost and Campbell (1985) found that children selected swings in 23.7 percent of their choices, making them their number-one choice among all equipment on a traditional playground containing only a few pieces of large, fixed equipment. On a comparative creative playground featuring a wider variety of fixed equipment as well as portable and natural materials such as sand, swings were selected by children 5.7 percent of the time, making them their eighth ranking choice. Since no two playgrounds are alike in all respects, care should be taken in generalizing results to other playgrounds.

## Age and Gender

Age and skill development are factors in the playground swinging preferences of children. In the studies cited above, the percentage of children selecting traditional swings rose from kindergarten through 1st to 2nd grade on a traditional playground. On the other hand, tire swings were selected more frequently by kindergartners than by 1st- or 2nd-graders. Naylor (1985) found that swings ranked high in preference on the three playgrounds she observed, ranging from first to third choices. Frost, Kim, Therrell, and Thornton (2000) found that swings were first in popularity for a group of preschoolers, and third in popularity for toddlers (behind wheeled toys and loose parts).

Children appear to lose interest in swinging as they grow into the higher grades. Older children begin to lose interest in swings as they take a greater interest in more organized group activities (Thompson, 1988). Older children also prefer to play in larger groups, which is difficult to accomplish on swing sets designed for a limited number of users. This may not be the case for all play environments. Lewis and Phillipsen (1998) found equal amounts of swing play between older and younger children. The extent of swing use varies with the number and type of swings available and the amount and variety of other equipment available to children. Since no two playgrounds are alike, distinctions must be made based on the overall availability of equipment and the ages and developmental skills of children. Readers should be cautious about comparing findings across studies and generalizing findings from one playground to other playgrounds.

Gender also appears to be a factor in a preference for swings. Representations of women and swinging are a common occurrence in artistic expression, while men and boys are rarely depicted so (Posner, 1982). Girls prefer to swing more than boys do (Crum & Eckert, 1985; Strickland, 1979). Boys prefer highly organized activities and group games. Also, boy groups typically average five or more members, while girls tend to play in dyads or triads (Pellegrini & Smith, 1993). Thus, swings may not satisfy boys' play preferences, as swing sets typically have only two swings per bay.

Strickland (1979) also found gender preference for swings, in that girls preferred swings more often than boys during free play. This resulted in the girls engaging in significantly more parallel play than the boys. Myers (1981) also found that girls chose swings more often than boys. Lewis and Phillipsen (1998) found, however, that swings promoted mixed-gender play. In other areas of the playground, boys and girls played in same-gender groups, with boys preferring the hard court area while the girls preferred the jungle gym and tree areas of the playground.

## BENEFITS OF SWINGING

### Physical Development

Swinging involves a number of physical motor skills. Swings and other moving equipment are conducive to "open skill" development (Gentile, 1972), activities that require constantly changing movement. These activities require constant monitoring, as the mover must pay careful attention to the environment. Open skills are thus more complex than limited movement skills and lead to the development of even more mature movement and perceptual skills.

Equipment that moves also provides children opportunities to practice swaying, running, and turning (Langendorfer, 1988). Swings promote fitness and develop skills through such actions as leg pumping, running, pushing, jumping, and landing. The pendulum action of acceleration and deceleration of swings contributes to the development of balance (Thompson, 1988), and promotes pectoral muscle development (Hewes & Beckwith, 1975). The rhythmic movement of swinging promotes development of a child's sense of rhythm and balance (Jambor, 1990).

### Social and Emotional Development

Swings also are beneficial for social and emotional development. They require cooperation and sharing because of the limited number of users they can accommodate. Infant and toddler swings require social interaction as an adult or older peer must push the child in order for the child to swing. Multi-person swings such as tire swings allow for social interaction while swinging (Noren-Bjorn, 1982).

Swinging is associated with positive feelings from the motion of the swings; the fun and enjoyment associated with swinging encourages children to continue the activity, leading to physical benefits (Thompson, 1988). Swings also can be relaxing for the user. According to Cheng et al. (1997), "Swinging can cause a phasic event that excites the semicircular canal system to produce natural wave signals which, in turn, stimulate the raphe system of the brain through the vestibular nerve and ganglion" (p. 3192). This stimulation can relax the users and help them fall asleep more easily.

### Cognitive Development

Swings benefit children's cognitive development by helping to create an element of dramatic imagination. As the swing moves, it helps the child imagine situations and events that are enhanced through the movement of the swing. Activities like swinging can act as pivots to help children create a mental representation in their minds of an object that is not physically present (Vygotsky, 1978). This encourages the child to separate the object from the meaning of the object. The swing thus allows a child to better imagine herself as a pilot or an astronaut, for example. This dramatic play is important for the development of children's problem solving and cognitive development, and is considered one of the most sophisticated levels of play (Smilansky & Shefatya, 1990).

## Sensory Stimulation

The body's sensory systems are especially affected by swinging. Sensory integration begins in the womb as children sense movement and the force of gravity on their movements (Yisreal, 1998). Sensory integration is divided into two primary areas: vestibular development and proprioceptive development. The vestibular system is located primarily in the inner ear and responds to gravity and movement. There are three semicircular canals in the inner ear that respond to movement or acceleration of the head in horizontal, vertical, and diagonal planes (Langendorfer, 1988).

The proprioceptive system draws information from the muscles and joints. The information from muscles and joints helps the body balance and represents body awareness. Proprioception is developed through the body through space as neurons signal the central nervous system, which then stimulates physical action in response to the stimuli (Nottingham, 2004). Swinging benefits a child's proprioceptive system as he moves through space and is thus required to make subtle adjustments to posture.

The vestibular system and proprioceptive system are also highly influenced by the visual system. Post, Peper, and Beek (2003) found that a swinger's coordination of swinging is reduced when the eyes are covered. They suggest that the body uses visual information to help coordinate the muscular responses of the body.

Children who have difficulty with sensory integration can have difficulty with their sense of balance. These children may lack coordination, may overreact and/or underreact to touch, and have difficulty relating to others. Children who have under-responsive vestibular systems have difficulty standing up straight and lack coordination. Children who have over-responsive vestibular systems dislike being picked up and can experience motion sickness and dizziness. Therapists who work with children with vestibular sensory integration problems have them sit in rocking chairs, swings, hammocks, and engage in other rhythmical movement activities in order to stimulate the vestibular system.

Available research and professional literature support the view that playground swings and opportunities for children to swing are very valuable for children's physical, emotional, and social development. The time-honored swing should continue to be a standard element on playgrounds.

## DEVELOPMENT OF SWINGING BEHAVIORS

The development of swinging behaviors is a function of a child's ability to operate the swing independently. As the child develops, she experiences the action of swinging in different ways. For infants, the motion can be soothing as they are propelled by adults or mechanisms. Noren-Bjorn (1982) described how swinging experiences differ for children. The youngest child gets a sense of security and pleasurable sensations from swinging, as well as enjoyment from the rhythmical motion. At around 3 years, exploratory play is typical, and children are able to swing and propel themselves, spin and twist each other, and make long jumps from swings. For children over age 5, social functions are common, and swings are used as a place to meet and socialize.

In a very comprehensive study of children's swinging development, Fox and Tipps (1995) developed a Guttman scale for swinging behaviors. A Guttman scale creates a hierarchical set of stages in which the early stages are incorporated into the later stages. In this study, children ages 3, 4, 5, and 6 were observed in a child care center playground with available swings. According to the scale created from this study, children proceed through eight stages for their development.

| Stages of Swinging Development (Fox & Tipps, 1995) | Characteristics of Stage |
|---|---|
| Stage I: Balance | Able to sit and hold chains, but require a push from another to be able to swing |
| Stage II: Observation and Trial and Error | Observation of others, able to move legs and bend trunk, but with lack of coordination |
| Stage III: Adaptation | Enter the swing by running to create motion<br>Pumping still untimed and ineffective<br>Exit by jumping from the swing |
| Stage IV: Timing | Children begin to develop coordination between arm and leg movements<br>No longer require a push<br>Exit by jumping or dragging feet |
| Stage V: Developing Prowess | Children want to demonstrate prowess to others<br>Beginning of experimentation like chain twisting and non-periodic swinging |
| Stage VI: Refinement | Increased confidence in ability to move swing<br>Able to create a large amplitude |
| Stage VII: Security | Able to swing for large periods of time and create large amplitudes while swinging |
| Stage VIII: Experimentation | Experimentation with abilities and by manipulating the swing<br>Experimenting with "bumping effect" at the top of the swing arc |

## TYPES OF SWINGS

A variety of playground swings are recommended by professionals and by the CPSC for use on public playgrounds. In addition, a number of swings not recommended by the CPSC for public playgrounds are commonly available as home playground equipment. The CPSC (1997) and ASTM (1993) publish separate standards for public playground equipment and home playground equipment. The CPSC guidelines and the ASTM standards for public playground equipment are more detailed and stricter than the ASTM standards for home equipment. Finally, there are home-made swings that do not meet either CPSC or ASTM standards for public playground or home equipment (see ASTM, 1991).

## Rope Swings

*A rope swing! Inspecting the length and take off position, I figured this one could give me a good ride clear across the Connecticut River and maybe into Vermont. Wasn't that what it was for? A swing across water and then a drop splash?* (Kendall, 1998, p. 9)

Perhaps the oldest type of swing is the rope swing. Ropes or vines hung from tree branches allow for swinging and quick entrances into rivers and ponds. A rope swing in its simplest form is a rope suspended from a tree with a knot for the swinger to grasp. These swings are most typically found in backyard play spaces where they can become gathering places for players of different age (Gwyther, 1996). Autobiographies, old photos, and other historical sources show many variations of seats for rope swings, including burlap sacks partially filled with loose materials, board seats tied to ropes at each end, and tires suspended vertically and horizontally. Rope swings lacking a heavy seat, such as a tire, however, can present a strangulation hazard, since the ropes can form a noose.

## Traditional Swings

Traditional swings have changed little over the last 100 years. The major change in traditional, manufactured swings has been a move from hard, heavy seats to lightweight, resilient seats made from rubber and plastic. The soft swing seats supported by A-frame structures, suggested in Mero (1908), are still standard staples on most playgrounds. Traditional swings are defined by the nature of the action, swinging in one (to-fro) direction and then returning in a linear path. As suggested by Eriksen (1985), such playground swings would be easily recognized by swingers of many eras.

## Tire Swings

Tire swings became popular shortly after the invention of rubber tires. They can be hung vertically from a single rope, hung horizontally from a crossbar by using multiple chains or ropes with a mechanism that allows for 360° rotation, or hung from a crossbar, using two supports to create a to-fro swing.

Heavy tractor tire swings encourage cooperation because they require more than one child to push them, as well as multiage use of the swings as younger children hold on and older children push the swings (Noren-Bjorn, 1982). Although great for socialization, the heavy mass of tractor tires can pose hazards if they hit children standing or moving nearby. Tire swings allow for multiple users and encourage group games and interactions (Freidberg, 1970). Swings should be installed near the outside of regular traffic patterns to limit the risk of people walking into their paths. The posts on the tire swing should be far enough from the motion of the swing to keep the tire from hitting the supports (Hewes & Beckwith, 1975). The CPSC specifies distances that help prevent impact of the swinger's head on support beams during swinging. Careful study is still needed to determine specific heights of overhead support beams necessary to prevent children hitting their heads while swinging. Hogan (1982) offered a modification of the tire swing called the cantilever tire swing, which is supported by a long post, set at an angle to the ground, that allows for the swing to be suspended by a single support from the top of the post. The possibility of children hitting their heads on the support beam precludes this option for most playgrounds.

## Motorized Swings

*Keep your baby happy in a swing that responds to her cries. The Smart Response Swing features a sound-activated mechanism that will automatically start the swing when your child cries.* (eToy.com's description of a Fisher Price motorized swing)

Motorized or mechanical swings are popular primarily for children from ages 0-12 months (Therrell, Brown, Sutterby, & Thornton, 2002). These swings need to be designed to support the whole child. The rocking motion of the swings is used to calm the child and, as one company suggests, "lull baby off to dreamland" (babystyle.com). Motorized swings also are used to help premature infants sleep longer in order to increase their growth (Cheng et al., 1997). Adults should be alert to the possibility of children spending too much time in such passive devices, thus depriving them of opportunities to learn basic movement skills.

## Toddler Swings

The toddler swing is an adaptation of the to-fro swing. The toddler swing includes a seat that supports the entire child. These swings require an adult to place the child in the swing and push the swing, rather than relying on the child to move the swing her/himself. Toddler or tot swings should have support that does not present a strangulation hazard and should be placed in a separate bay from traditional belt seat swings (CPSC, 1997).

## Animal Swings

Animal swings were first introduced in the 1950s to encourage fantasy play. Other novelty elements included rockets, horses, and other fanciful objects (Frost, 1992). Animal swings weighed from 30-80 pounds and were made from cast aluminum or molded plastic in the shapes of horses, zebras, pelicans, ducks, and other animals and objects. Such swings installed from 1951-1991 have been implicated in several deaths and at least 42 serious head injuries resulting from children being impacted by the swings. These swings were officially recalled in 1995 (CPSC, 1995) by manufacturers and the CPSC, and they are currently not recommended for public playgrounds, according to the CPSC *Handbook for Public Playground Safety* (1997).

## Adaptive Swings

The focus on making swings adaptive has made them accessible to children with disabilities. In addition, several types of swings designed specifically for children with disabilities are available from a number of manufacturers. Adaptations typically involve additional straps or modifications of the seat to support the child, the use of pulleys or handholds to move the swing for children unable to use their legs to create motion, or structures to hold or support an entire wheelchair. Swings that support an entire wheelchair may require a fenced area or careful supervision to keep children from walking in front of the necessarily heavy swing.

## Multiple Occupancy Swings

According to the CPSC *Handbook for Public Playground Safety*, and with the exception of tire swings of typical automobile (not truck or tractor) sizes, multiple occupancy swings are not recommended for public playgrounds because their greater mass presents a risk of impact injury. Certain types of multiple occupancy swings are currently available for home playground equipment, which is regulated by the CPSC guidelines for toys and ASTM *Standard Consumer Safety Performance Specification for Home Playground Equipment* (1991).

## HAZARDS ASSOCIATED WITH SWINGS

*Swinging is safe; the swing is unsafe. The problem is the design. A child hit by a tire suffers negligible damage, more to the psyche than to the body.* (Freidberg, 1970, p. 59)

Historically, playground designers have been aware of the hazards of swinging. In 1913, Curtis recommended that heights be limited to 8-10 feet and the swings should be placed in out-of-the-way areas of the play yard so that there will be less risk of striking a passing child. He also recommended using padding to lessen the blow if a child is struck by the swing.

The pattern of injuries associated with swings differs between public playgrounds and homes. According to Tinsworth and McDonald (2001), swings are second to climbers in the percent of injuries associated with playground equipment. According to this study, swings are associated with about 19 percent of injuries on public playgrounds. However, swings are associated with over 66 percent of all injuries related to backyard playground equipment (Tinsworth & McDonald, 2001).

The age of children injured in swinging incidents also differs between public playgrounds and home playgrounds. Older children are more likely to be involved in swing injuries on public playgrounds than are younger children. Over 50 percent of the children injured on swings are between the ages of 13 and 14 years old. On home playgrounds, children ages 5-9 are most likely to be injured on swings (58 percent) (Tinsworth & McDonald, 2001). This most likely represents different use patterns of playground equipment by older and younger children and the relative numbers of swings available on different types and locations of playgrounds.

In a study of playground injuries associated with litigation, swings ranked equally with slides as the most common equipment involved in litigation (Frost & Sweeney, 1996). This study of 190 cases involved two cases in which children were killed by the impact of moving swings and several in which children suffered serious injuries from impact with heavy swings or protruding elements on swings.

A number of swings have been recalled by manufacturers, including infant swings. For example, Little Tikes' high back swing for infants was recalled for tipping forward and dropping children to the ground. Playskool recalled the 1-2-3 swing after 50 children were injured falling out of the swing. Graco carrier swings required an attachment to keep children from falling out of the swing. Swing-n-cradle swings from Carlson Children's products were exchanged because they might present a strangulation hazard to children. In addition to heavy animal swings for which recalls affected a number of manufacturers, playground swing manufacturers have had to replace swing supports (Playworld), swing seats (Hedstrom, Miracle), chains (Rainbow), trapeze bars (Backyard Products), and multiperson swings (Miracle).

## Falling/Jumping From the Swing

For both home playgrounds and public playgrounds, about 80 percent of the injuries reported that are associated with swings involve falling to the surface or onto another part of the equipment. These injuries are frequently associated with children jumping from swings (35 percent). Deaths associated with falls usually involve a head injury. Swings, climbers, and slides are most frequently implicated in deaths involving falls (Tinsworth & McDonald, 2001).

## Impact Injuries on Swings

Impact injuries associated with swings involve between 3-6 percent of injuries on playgrounds. Frost and Sweeney (1996) report on two deaths associated with children being struck by swings in the study of playground litigation. Tinsworth and McDonald (2001) also report on two deaths (perhaps the same cases) associated with impact injuries caused by swings, although they report that deaths from swing impact are now rare.

## Strangulation and Entanglement

Strangulation is the most frequent cause of death involving playground equipment (Tinsworth & McDonald, 2001). Swings rank third behind slides and climbers in the number of deaths involving strangulation. Strangulation on swing cords is a common scenario for deaths associated with swings. Typically, the cord or rope forms a noose around the child's neck, leading to strangulation (Tinsworth & McDonald, 2001). Although cords and ropes are still found on home swings, they are becoming rare on public playground swings.

## Tip Over/Collapse of Swing Frames

Collapse of playground equipment was associated with 24 deaths between 1990 and 2000. Swing sets, especially homemade swing sets, are the most frequently reported equipment in incidents involving deaths from collapse (Tinsworth & McDonald, 2001).

## Protrusion Injuries on Playground Hardware and Open S-Hooks

Protruding bolts cause severe injuries to children, in some cases penetrating the brain cavity and resulting in permanent damage. Open S-hooks and hardware that protrudes from the equipment present clothing entanglement hazards. These factors are especially important on moving equipment such as swings. Open S-hooks and protruding bolts can entangle clothing, leading to strangulation, or can cause a protrusion injury if a child falls against or runs into the open hardware (CPSC, 1997; Frost, 1990; Thompson, Bruya, & Crawford, 1990).

## Preventing Swing Injuries and Deaths

Each type of injury associated with swings involves a different approach to injury prevention. Swing seats should be made of lightweight, resilient materials in order to reduce injuries associated with impact by the swing. Heavy wood and metal should not be used for swing seats. In addition, in order to reduce impact injuries, swings should be placed away from traffic patterns and other playground equipment. A visual barrier of tires embedded vertically around the swing structure can help cue children to be aware of moving swings. In order to reduce injuries from falls, resilient surfacing should be placed below swings and maintained properly, as swinging is likely to result in deterioration of the surfacing (Frost, 1990).

Other areas of concern on swings involve making sure all S-hooks are closed, all protrusions are avoided, and the swing set is firmly anchored in the ground. Several types of connecting links that close completely are available to replace S-hooks. Each costs a few cents more than S-hooks. The author has long held that S-hooks should not be used on playground equipment since they are frequently installed improperly (e.g., they are not closed) and special tools are needed to open and close them. Swing seats and other spaces on swings should meet the dimensions recommended by CPSC and ASTM. Chain links need to be properly maintained and hardware should be inspected frequently to make sure the motion of the swing has not severely worn the chains or supports (Thompson, Bruya, & Crawford, 1990).

The National Survey of Elementary School Playground Equipment (Bowers, 1988) found a number of safety hazards to be common on swings and surrounding areas:

- 91 percent did not have covered chains to prevent pinch points
- 26 percent had sharp corners, edges, or projections on swing seats or chains
- 1/3 of swings were in poor condition
- 51 percent of swings did not have appropriate surfacing.

Thompson (1988) recommends that swings be regularly inspected and maintained in order to reduce the risk of injury. The inspection program should be written and made available to all adults involved with the playground, and potential hazards should be promptly reported and corrected.

## METHODOLOGY

The purposes of this study were to examine how children use various playground swings. Specifically, the study determined the frequency of children's use of various swing types, the types of gross and fine motor skills that children use while swinging, the developmental progression of children's swinging skills, and children's motivations for playing on swings. This research is best described as "descriptive" because the questions of the study are "designed to produce information about what is or has been happening" (Mertens, 1998, p. 52).

### Research Questions

1. Which swings do children choose to play with most frequently?
2. What gross and fine motor skills do children use or develop when playing with swings?
3. What is the developmental progression of children's skills when playing on swings?
4. What are children's motivations for playing on swings?

Based upon these questions, the design of the study required methods of qualitative and quantitative research that identify the quantity and quality of swing play. The quantitative methodology involved coding sheets to quantify the frequency of swing use and document the children's choices of swings. The coding sheets were used to identify the type of fine and gross motor skills used on swing equipment and to document the developmental progression of skills when playing on swings. The qualitative methods used were general anecdotal observation descriptions and interview data. The observation anecdotes were used to understand the quality of swing play regarding the type of motor skills used and the progressive developmental skills for swinging. The observation notes and the interview data were used to determine the motivation for swing play.

## Participants

Approximately 65 children participated in this study. The children were divided and observed according to the following age groups:

| Age Range | Number of Children |
|---|---|
| 1.5 to 2.5 years old | 5 |
| 3 to 4 years old | 20 |
| 6 to 7 years old | 20 |
| 10 to 11 years old | 20 |

The 3- to 11-year-olds were part of a private school summer recreation program. The majority of participants were white, middle-class, and English-speaking. A few children were Hispanic. All children appeared physically healthy and typically developing. They were chosen based on age and parental consent. The children were observed during their regularly scheduled recess times, from early morning to late afternoon, generally in half-hour time allotments. If the temperature rose above 102 degrees Fahrenheit, the children did not play on the outdoor playgrounds. This occurred twice during the observation periods of this study.

The summer recreation program and facilities did not provide a program for the toddlers between 18 months and 2.5 years old. For the purpose of this study, children of this age group were recruited from another local preschool and child care center. These children were observed on a local playground with a strap swing and toddler bucket swing. They were also predominantly middle-class, white, and English-speaking. Age and parental consent also determined their participation in the study.

## Setting and Equipment

The main setting for the study took place on outdoor playgrounds at a private school during a summer recreation program during the month of June 2003. The school was selected based on a past research relationship and newly installed swinging equipment on the playgrounds. There were three playgrounds, each for a different age group: the "pre-school" playground, the "little" playground, and the "big" playground. Twelve inches of resilient surfacing, in the form of engineered wood fibers, was present under all playground equipment.

The preschool playground was used by the 3- to 4-year-old children. They had access to two strap swings, which were exposed to direct sunlight during all daytime hours. A plastic pirate ship for climbing and pretend play, sand and water, plastic and wooden houses, tricycles, plastic cars, shade trees, and a flower and caterpillar garden were also available.

The "little" playground was used by the 6- to 7-year-old children. It included two strap swings, a bucket swing, a hard flat swing for standing, and a hard plastic saucer-like tire swing. These swings were located under trees that shaded them during all daytime hours. A composite play structure, two small wooden play houses, a sand box, a water table, garden, open area, balls, picnic tables, shade trees, and a space for organized games were also available.

The "big" playground, for the 10- to 11-year-old children, had a hard plastic chair swing designed for disabled children, a strap swing, a hard standing swing, and a hard plastic saucer-like tire swing. Although these swings were located near a large shade tree, the swings remained unshaded for most of the children's outdoor playtimes. A large, complex, permanent composite play structure, trees, a small open space for organized games, and a basketball court were also available on this playground.

The 1.5-year-old to 2.5-year-old children used a strap swing and a full bucket seat swing on a local playground that also had a slide, traditional climbing bars, a merry-go-round, and a digging device with a seat. The swings were completely shaded throughout the day.

## Swing Seats and Structures

The following is a description of the different types of swing seats and structures available for the children at the time of the study:

The full bucket swing, also called the enclosed tot swing, was supported by two galvanized steel chains from an overhead bar. The seat was made from flexible but durable black plastic that formed a bucket- or bowl-shaped seat. Two openings in the front side and two in the back side allowed room through which small children placed their legs. The plastic completely wrapped around the front and back of the child's torso when seated, providing support to the child's body, front and back.

The half bucket swing, also known as the bucket seat, is similar to the full bucket except that there is no plastic belt in place for support on the front part of the swing. There are two openings in the back side of the swing. This swing is held by two galvanized chain link ropes suspended from an overhead beam.

The strap swing, or the belt swing, is made from the same black plastic material as the bucket swings; however, it is just one flexible strap of plastic held between two galvanized steel chains suspended from an overhead structure.

The solid flat standing swing, called the super seat, is also supported by two galvanized chain ropes on two sides; however, the swing is made of a thicker and harder plastic than the strap swing. Children used this swing to either sit or stand while swinging.

The tire swing was made of a durable and sturdy gray plastic. The gray saucer-shaped tire swing with a hole in the middle also featured a textured surface with raised lines to provide traction. It was supported by three galvanized chains, connected to a special swivel, and attached to a swing frame above the swing.

The chair swing, or the adaptive swing seat, was a supportive chair molded out of a hard, durable beige-colored plastic. The chair was large, with arm rests, and was attached to a swing frame by three galvanized chain ropes, one of which was attached to the back of the chair and split into two chains to form a Y and attach to the support bar of the frame.

**Full bucket swing**

**Half bucket swing**

**Strap swing**

**Solid flat standing swing**

**Tire swing**

**Chair swing**

## Data Collection

The following methods were used to collect data: videotaped and photographed observations, anecdotal records, and informal interviews with the participating children and their teachers. The videotaped observations were used for later coding of most physical movement and anecdotal records of other child behaviors.

During the month of June 2003, two early childhood researchers recorded approximately 15 hours of video recordings and took over 300 digital photos of the children using the swinging equipment. The children's swinging activities were then reviewed and coded, according to the type of movements used while swinging.

Anecdotal records, or field notes, were descriptive of the children's activities, paying special attention to details such as conversation and personal interactions. Field notes are analytical, focusing on the researchers' ideas, notation of perceived patterns, and reflection on the children's activities (Glesne, 1999). Also, these notes described the possible intentions of the children while swinging, social interactions, pretend play scenarios involving the swings, explorations with movement on the swings, such as coasting or leaning, and the quality of leg pumping and leaning while swinging. These documented behaviors were used to examine the children's frequency of swing use, the types of motor skills used while playing on the swings, and the developmental progression of swinging skills.

The teachers and children were interviewed throughout the study to better understand the preferences of play, motivation for play, and perceptions about the quality of play with the swinging equipment. The teachers were asked about their observations of the children's swing play, and about which swings were most preferred by them and by the children. The children were asked the following interview questions:

- Why did you choose to play with that swing?
- What were you playing on the swing?
- What were you thinking about/feeling when you were swinging?

## Data Analysis

A coding sheet was developed over a two-week period prior to the study by the research team (see Appendix). The coding sheet followed a similar format as previous developmental and descriptive research on playground climbing apparatus (Frost, Brown, Thornton, & Sutterby, 2002) and overhead apparatus (Frost, Brown, Thornton, Sutterby, & Therrell, 2001) and coding sheets used in swing research by Fox and Tipps (1995). The coding sheet was created after observing children's physical behavior while swinging, and revised as additional observations were made and the researchers were able to experiment with movement on the swings themselves.

The Swinging Coding Sheet included these categories: a child's physical characteristics, entry to swing, relation of body to swing, hand grip, swinging, direction of swinging, rhythm and coordination, and exit from swing. The type of swing and the duration of the swinging episode also were noted.

Each category was coded and defined as follows:
1) Physical Characteristics of a Child
   a. Height was described as short, medium, or tall in comparison with all other children in the study.

b. Weight was described as light, moderate, or heavy in comparison with all other children in the study.

2) Entry to the Swing—how a child becomes seated or standing upon the swing
   a. Assisted on: the child is either lifted or pulled onto the swing seat by an adult or another child.
   b. Wiggle on: the child sits on edge of swing seat and uses a rocking hip motion to slowly move back onto the swing seat
   c. Full lift: a child grabs the swing chains and lifts his or her body up over the seat and lowers his or her body into a sitting position
   d. Step over: the child stands behind the swing seat and lifts one leg at a time over the seat and sits down
   e. Running: the child grabs onto the chains of the swing and runs while pulling or pushing the swing. Whether beginning in front of the swing or behind, the child will run, holding the chain, then lift himself up and onto the seat.

3) Relation of Body to the Swing—description of how the child positions the body while swinging
   a. Lying on stomach: the child faces the ground; the stomach is supported by the swing seat
   b. Seated: the child sits on the swing seat
   c. Squatting: the child's feet are on the swing seat and legs are bent at the knees
   d. Standing: the child's feet are on the seat swing with legs straight
   e. Legs on both sides of swing seat: legs are facing same side of swing seat
   f. Legs straddle swing: legs are on opposite sides of swing seat
   g. Facing in or out (of tire swing): the child's legs are either facing toward the inner circle of tire swing seat or facing the outer rim of the tire
   h. Other body parts propped on swing: for example, head or feet are propped on swing seat.

4) Hand Grip—how the child is holding the chains supporting the swing
   a. Number of hands used (0, 1, 2): child is holding onto the chains with hands
   b. Both hands on same chain: child is holding one chain with both hands
   c. Hands on opposite chains: child is gripping each chain of the swing using both hands; the right hand grips the right chain and the left hand grips the left chain.

5) Swinging
   a. Number of children swinging on swing (0-3)
   b. Swing is pushed by an adult or another child: while child is on the swing, another person pushes the child's back or other body part to allow the swing to move
   c. Number of assisted pushes: how many times the child is pushed by another person
   d. Low swinging (less than 30 degrees from vertical): the height the child reaches while swinging
   e. Moderate swinging (between 30 and 60 degrees from vertical): the height child reaches while swinging
   f. High swinging ( higher than 60 degrees from vertical): the height child reaches while swinging.

6) Direction of Swinging—describes how the swing was being moved while swinging
   a. To and fro: the swing moves back and forth, forwards and backwards, in a somewhat straight line
   b. Side to side: the swing moves in a rocking motion from left to right or reversed
   c. Diagonal/circular/elliptical: the swing is moving somewhat back and forth, but loops around so as not to be in a straight motion
   d. Swiveling: the swing may be moving to and fro, but the child is rocking one side of the swing forward while the other is slightly twisted or pulled back
   e. Spinning: the child twists the chains around while sitting on the swing seat and releases, allowing the swing to spin around.

7) Rhythm and Coordination—how the child's legs and torso are used to swing and the quality of the swinging movement
   a. Legs pumping: legs held parallel; extended and bent at the knee simultaneously
   b. Legs running/pedaling: legs are moving but not in unison; one leg is extended while the other is bent at the knee
   c. Torso leaning in sync: as legs extend out from swing, the child's torso leans back and then reverses direction when legs bend in
   d. Torso leaning out of sync: the child's torso moves and leans back and forth, but not in unison with the legs pumping
   e. Quality of movement: (smooth or jerky) describes how the child executes the swinging movement with legs and whole body.

8) Exiting the Swing—how the child dismounts from the swing
   a. Assisted stop: adult or other child grabs the swing and halts the motion
   b. Assisted exit: adult or other child lifts child off or out of swing
   c. Dragged feet: slows the swing down by dragging the feet over the surface
   d. Coasting to a stop: child ends all movement and waits as swing slows down or stops moving, then exits unassisted
   e. Walked off: the swing has slowed down, but the child walks off as the swing continues motion
   f. Jumped off: the swing is still moving and the child jumps away after releasing hand grip from chains or other part of swing
   g. Fell off: child intentionally or unintentionally drops from swing while swing is moving or not.

The researchers coded each characteristic, and the frequency of the type of equipment used and the type of movements displayed were calculated.

The qualitative data collected through anecdotal records and interviews were analyzed following the general steps of qualitative data analysis described by Miles and Huberman (1994). The first set of field notes and interview transcripts were coded according to similarities, patterns, or themes, along with differences and contradictions within the data. Personal reflections of both researchers were considered. From these broad themes, smaller themed subgroups were identified. Finally, generalizations were made and examined, based on anecdotal consistency and previous playground equipment research and developmental theory. The data were used to understand the quality of the motor skills used, the developmental progression of swinging skills, and the children's motivations.

## Validity and Reliability

This study followed the guidelines established by the University of Texas' Institutional Review Board for Human Subjects and was approved by this board. Inter-rater reliability for the coding instrument, or the consistency between the two researchers in coding the swinging behaviors, was established as >.90.

Validity, or credibility of qualitative research (also known as trustworthiness), is usually assessed through the following criteria: triangulation, prolonged or persistent observation, peer review and debriefing, member-checking, and negative case analysis (Glesne, 1999; Mertens, 1998). This study addressed these issues of credibility in the design and implementation of the study.

Triangulation is the "use of multiple data-collection methods, multiple sources, multiple investigators, and/or multiple theoretical perspective" (Glesne, 1999, p. 32). In this study, the researchers used such different data collection methods as interview, coding, and anecdotal records and field notes. The multiple sources of data were collected from researcher observation, teacher response, and child response. Finally, more than one researcher observed and coded and analyzed the children's behaviors.

The researchers addressed the need for persistent observation by continuous daily observations throughout the month of June 2003 and through careful examination of the video recordings and photographs.

Peer review and debriefing occurred throughout the study. The coding instrument was created through researcher collaboration. After observations and videotaping, the researchers consulted one another at least three times weekly. At each stage of the research, the two observers also consulted with lead researcher Joe Frost regarding methodology, general impressions, and preliminary interpretation of data.

Member checking is defined as a way to verify with participants that researchers are accurately documenting and interpreting data (Glesne, 1999). Throughout the observations and taping of the swinging, researchers maintained contact with the teachers and children, informally holding conversations with the participants about the swinging experiences. Final documentation and presentation of the data interpretation was shared with the school.

Negative case analysis is a deliberate search for cases in the data that do not fit the emerging patterns in the process of interpretation and analysis of the data (Glesne, 1999). Throughout the analysis of the data and during peer debriefings, the researchers searched and documented such cases and refined their understanding of the data.

## FINDINGS

In order to answer the research questions, the researchers turned to the data coded from videotaped observations, as well as anecdotal notes taken during observations and interview data collected from the children and their teachers.

## Question 1: Which Swings Do Children Choose To Play With Most Frequently?

According to the coded data across all age groups observed, children chose to play most frequently with the strap swings. Out of a total of 317 swinging episodes, strap swings were used 115 times (36 percent of the time). The start of an episode was defined as the moment at which a child put her/his full weight on a swing for any length of time, and the end of an episode was defined as the point at which the child broke contact with the swing and moved away from it. Frequently, children would change positions on the swing, going from sitting to standing or lying on their stomachs; these position changes were considered to be part of one episode as long as the child did not actually break contact with and move away from the swing. Episodes ranged less than 1 minute long to 29 minutes long.

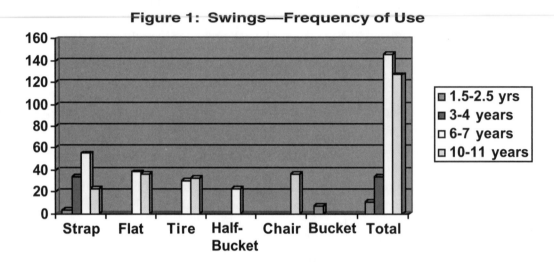

**Figure 1: Swings—Frequency of Use**

Several reasons can be identified for strap swings being used most frequently. First, the strap swings were available on all the playgrounds observed. Strap swings accounted for 1 out of 2 swings for the 1.5- to 2.5-year-olds, all of the swings available to the preschoolers, 2 out of 5 of the swings available to the 6- and 7-year olds, and 1 out of 4 swings available to the 10- and 11-year olds. Second, on the playgrounds with a variety of swings, strap swings were located in the middle of the other swings. These centrally located swings often were chosen by children who wanted to be "in line" for the other swings, or by children who wanted to interact with peers on the other swings. Third, according to interview data, some children preferred the strap swings because they were used to them.

Following the strap swing in frequency of use across all age groups was the flat swing, at 23 percent of total use, and the tire swing, at 20 percent of total use. The least frequently used swing was the bucket swing, at 2 percent of use, followed by the half-bucket swing, used only 7 percent of the time.

Looking at swing use within the four age groups yields a very different story. The 1.5- to 2.5-year-olds played most frequently with the bucket swing. The 3- and 4-year-olds played exclusively with strap swings because strap swings were the only type of swing available to them. The 6- and 7-year-olds played most frequently with the strap swings, and the 10- and 11-year-olds played most frequently with the chair swing and the flat swing (spending an equal amount of time on each). Several possible reasons are indicated for these findings. In the case of the toddlers (1.5- to 2.5-year-olds), the children were always attended by an adult, and most adults chose the bucket swing for the children.

Based upon laughs and smiles, the toddlers seemed to enjoy the bucket swings more. Based on coding of height of swinging and length of time, adults pushed the youngest children the longest and highest while the children were in the bucket swing. One toddler actually pointed to the bucket swing when asked which was his favorite. In the case of the 6- to 7-year-olds, they had access to two strap swings and only one swing of another type; of all the children observed, the 6- to 7-year-olds were allowed to play on the playground for the longest amount of time. In the case of the 10- to 11-year-olds, the novelty of the chair and flat swings may have attracted their attention.

Observation notes indicate that the children took turns to use the chair swing and used the other swings while waiting. In response to these new swings being placed on the playground, an older child commented, "I like the old (strap) swings but sometimes you need a little change." Another child replied, "Yeah, you need some excitement—something different."

### Question 2: What Gross and Fine Motor Skills Do Children Use or Develop When Playing With Swings?

Children develop a wide range of gross and fine motor skills when playing on swings. The gross motor skills addressed in the coding instrument were locomotor skills, balancing skills, and body coordination. The fine motor skills addressed in the coding instrument mainly concerned children's hands and grip. A combination of gross and fine motor skills was observed when a girl manipulated a tire swing using a combination of leg strength and foot movement.

Gross motor skills observed in this study included such locomotor skills as running and jumping onto the swing, running or walking while exiting the swing, jumping off of the swing while the swing was still in motion, and running or walking while pushing the tire swing before jumping onto it. Non-locomotor gross motor skills needed to access and exit the swings included stepping over the swing to sit on it, lifting the body onto the swing, stepping up to stand on the swing, dragging feet to slow the swing down, and standing up or stepping down from the swing. Gross motor skills also included skills needed to maintain balance while on the swing. These skills included being able to assume and maintain a sitting, standing, or stomach-down position on the swing, as well as being able to place other parts of the body (e.g., feet, legs) on the tire swing.

Other gross motor skills developed included various combinations of body movement in order to increase, maintain, and decrease swing movement and amplitude. These most often involved leaning the body back and forth, as well as pedaling or pumping of the legs. Gross motor skills were also involved in some children's explorations of alternate swinging behaviors, such as leaning the body back until it was parallel to the ground, and moving the body to create elliptical, circular, or side-to-side motions on to-fro swings.

Fine motor skills developed while swinging primarily were related to hand and finger coordination and the development of grip strength to hold onto the swings and swing chains. Researchers also observed one girl who manipulated a tire swing by herself using her foot to push against the ground, a circling motion of her ankle to rotate the tire swing, and her leg strength to actually move the entire tire swing into an elliptical motion.

### Question 3: What Is the Developmental Progression of Children's Skills When Playing on Swings?

Children followed a clear progression of developing swinging skills, although these skills overlapped at many proficiency levels. Referring to coded data collected, the researchers

## Figure 2:  Swinging Skills & Proficiency Levels

| | Beginner | Intermediate | Advanced |
|---|---|---|---|
| **Swing Entry** | Shorter children need assistance or may wiggle on; taller children may sit on or step on | Shorter children wiggle on or lift themselves on by grasping the chains; taller children sit on, step on, or step over; children also run and lift themselves or run and jump on | Children sit on, step on, step over, run and lift themselves, or run and jump on |
| **Relation of Body to Swing Seat** | Children lay on stomachs or sit on bottoms; they place both legs on the same side of the swing | Children lay on stomachs, sit on bottoms, stand or squat on feet; they place both legs on the same side of the swing or they straddle the swing; they can prop other parts of their bodies on the swings, especially on the tire swing | Children may place any part of their bodies on the swing, including their stomachs, bottoms, feet, and knees; they can prop other parts of their bodies on the swings, especially on tire swings |
| **Hand Grip** | Hands grip opposite chains | Hands grip opposite chains, same chain, or seat; children can balance using the crook of their elbows instead of gripping with their hands | Hands grip opposite chains, same chain, or seat; children can balance using crook of elbows and also without using hands or elbows |
| **Swinging** | Children must be pushed to start swinging; their peak swinging height is less than 30 degrees from the vertical; they can swing to-fro, and sometimes they unintentionally swing in erratic patterns and different directions; the quality of the swinging motion is jerky or choppy | Children do not need assistance to begin swinging; their peak swinging height can reach up to 60 degrees from the vertical; they may be able to intentionally swing in directions other than to-fro; the quality of the swinging motion may alternate between jerky and smooth | Children do not need assistance to begin swinging; their peak swinging height may be limited only by the swing structure itself; they are able to intentionally swing in any direction; the quality of the swinging motion is smooth |

## Figure 2: Swinging Skills & Proficiency Levels (cont'd)

|  | Beginner | Intermediate | Advanced |
|---|---|---|---|
| **Rhythm and Coordination** | Children sit in the swing without moving their legs and torsos, or they pedal their legs as if they were running; they do not move their legs and torsos in sync with the movement of the swing | Children may pedal or pump their legs and move their torsos; they may be able to move their legs and torsos in sync with the movement of the swing; they may not extend their legs to the apex of the forward and upward motion of the swing | Children pump their legs and extend them to the apex of the forward and upward motion of the swing; they lean their torsos in sync with the motion of the swing |
| **Exit** | Children may need assistance to exit the swing; they may also wait until the swing loses most or all of its momentum and then exit the swing by hopping to the ground, falling off the swing, or standing up and walking away from the swing | Children do not need assistance to exit the swing; they will sometimes wait until the swing loses its momentum; they may also drag their feet to stop the swing themselves; they either hop to the ground or stand up to leave the swing; some children may even attempt jumping from the swing at low heights, or they may run off the swing as their feet touch the ground | Children will often leave the swing when the swing is still in motion, walking, running, or jumping off of the swing before it loses its momentum |

developed a chart outlining children's development of swinging skills (see Figure 2).

These levels of proficiency in swinging skills bear some similarities to previous findings of swinging skill progression described by Fox and Tipps (1995). The "beginner" proficiency level described in this study shares similarities with the first three stages of the Fox and Tipps progression, which were called balance, observation and trial and error, and adaptation. The "intermediate" proficiency level described here seems to correlate somewhat with the fourth and fifth stages described by the Fox and Tipps progression, the stages titled timing and demonstrating prowess. The "advanced" proficiency level outlined above bears resemblance to the sixth and seventh stages of the Fox and Tipps progression, which are refinement and security.

However, Fox and Tipps include an eighth stage, which they call experimentation. The description of this stage seems to imply that children in the other stages do not experiment while swinging until they reach this highest of all stages. The researchers conducting the present study found that experimentation occurred in all of the stages of swinging skill development. Beginners experimented with swinging, as did intermediate swingers and advanced swingers. The difference was that advanced swingers could most often maintain the rhythm of their swinging while experimenting, intermediates sometime lost some amplitude while trying out alternative swinging patterns, and beginners lost all amplitude and would come to a standstill while experimenting with other types of swinging behavior. Additionally, because the skill level of the swingers observed in this study varied widely, and swingers of varied skill levels often would be playing together on the same playground, beginners who were swinging next to advanced swingers would attempt some of the same experimental swinging movements as the advanced swingers, although with less successful results.

## Question 4: What Are Children's Motivations for Playing on Swings?

The researchers in this study asked children the following types of questions during the playground observations in order to assess the factors that might contribute to their motivations for playing on swings:

- Why did you choose to play with that swing?
- What were you playing on the swing?
- What were you thinking about/feeling when you were swinging?

The researchers were able to review the videotaped data repeatedly to help in understanding children's unstated motivations for playing on swings.

Children often chose to play on swings for social reasons. Many children would play on swings in groups. They would choose a swing that could accommodate many children (e.g., the tire swing), or they would choose swings next to each other in the swing bays. Children would enter the swings at the same time as their friends, talk and laugh with their friends while swinging, and then leave the swings when their friends left. Children would push each other, especially on the half-bucket and chair swings, which did not allow for leaning torso movement and therefore restricted the children from achieving high swinging amplitudes without help from their friends, as well as on the tire swings, which could be pushed quite high and in circular and elliptical patterns.

Some children would choose to swing because they could ask for help from the teachers and therefore get attention and social interaction from the adults. Even children who did not need assistance with the swings would ask teachers to push them so they could interact with the teachers. Often, when one child was already swinging and another child approached a swing and asked for help from the teacher, the child already swinging would stop her/his swing and also ask the teacher for help whether or not s/he originally needed the help.

The adults or parents pushing the swings of the 1.5- to 2.5-year-old children often engaged the young children verbally or with facial expressions and smiles. The adults would face the children and talk to them while pushing. Some adults and the toddlers would wave to each other. Adults would comment on the height the child would be swinging and ask the child for requests of going higher, faster, slower, or stopping. The children would respond to the adult in some way or initiate a response from the adult by asking for "more." The social interaction with adults was most interesting with the 1.5- to 2.5-year-olds and with the 6- to 7-year-olds; once the children were pushed to an acceptable height, some adults would sit on a nearby swing and join in swinging with the child. Some faced the same direction of the child, while others faced in the opposite direction.

Some children chose to swing on particular types of swings for specific reasons. Children were only allowed to stand on the flat swing, and so they would choose that swing when they wanted to swing standing up. (However, it was noted that occasionally a child would use the flat swing by sitting on it like a strap swing.) Some children were drawn to the novel swings, and therefore chose to swing on the flat swings, the half-bucket, the chair, and the new tire swings. Other children preferred the tried-and-true strap swings, and would choose them over the new swings.

Swings prompted competition between children. Children wanted to see who could swing higher, faster, and longer. Children wanted to see who could get the highest in the shortest amount of time. Some children thought that the flat swing was the fastest climbing swing, so the children who liked to get up high fast would choose the flat swing first. They also liked to see who could push the tire swing "the best." That meant high, fast, and in interesting patterns. Often, the children would ask the teachers to push the tire swing so they could go as high as possible and touch the crossbar that supported the swing with their outstretched hands.

The swings enhanced children's pretend play in many different ways. Some children would pretend they were birds or airplanes, or other flying animals and objects. One girl would pretend to sleep and snore, and would make funny faces at her friends as she played on the swing. Sometimes, other children would join her on the neighboring swing and pretend to sleep and snore.

Swings also inspired children to create extended pretend scenarios with their friends. One pair of boys pretended to be rocket pilots for more than 20 minutes. The boys had been swinging for a few minutes, when one of the boys began to drag his feet in the sand and said, "I'm gonna slow down." The other boy exclaimed, "We have to stay this high!" Then one boy began yelling "Rocketpower!" and the other boy joined in so that they were yelling this back and forth to each other several times. Then one boy said, "Rocketpower goes so fast!" The other boy repeated this phrase. The banter continued in this vein for several minutes until one boy said, "Close your eyes." The other one responded, "You're nuts!" The first answered, "I'm going higher than you!" They began a contest for "who can swing the highest." After the battle reached the highest that either boy could swing, one boy intentionally began twisting his body so that his swing seat swiveled as it traveled to and fro. He said, "I'm slowing down."

At this point, the boys began to purposefully match each other's leg movements, and eventually their leg pumps were completely synchronized. Then one boy looked at the other and said, "We're the same," to which the other boy responded, "I'm going higher!" The first boy responded with "Now blast off to the moon!" They began to emit matching screams and exclaiming "OH!" Then one boy yelled, "I need more fuel!" The other one started yelling "Mayday!"

Running and pushing the tire swing          Jumping onto the tire swing

Squatting on flat swing          Standing on flat swing

Leaning back

Teacher helping
two children who can
already swing on their own

They made crashing sounds as they stopped themselves by dragging their feet in the sand, and they remained sitting on the swing seats. One boy said, "My wing is breaking!" They got off the swings and pretended to hammer and "fix" them. After a few minutes, they got back onto their swings and began creating an airplane scenario in which the speed of the airplane was dependent on the color of the airplane. A yellow plane was fast, a black plane was "super duper fast," and a brown plane was "faster than a sonic boom."

While using the swings, primarily the tire swing, the 6- to 7-year-old children would create games. For example, one child would gather walnuts from the school playground, push the tire swing with no one on the swing, and then try to throw the walnuts through the hole of the tire swing seat. Other children would try to throw other objects from the tire swing while swinging. One group of children devised a game in which three girls sat on the tire swing and were pushed by two boys. After pushing for some time, the boys would allow the moving tire swing to lightly bump them. The boys would pretend to have been hit hard by the swing and fall into the sand surrounding the swing. The girls would squeal and encourage the boys to continue falling by chanting the boys' names. The older children made up a game in which the child in the chair swing being pushed would put out her hands and try to slap the hand of another child standing in front of the swing and to the side.

The researchers also asked children what they were thinking or feeling as they played on the swings. Some children wanted to swing to cool off, even if the swing was not located in the shade. Other children just liked the feeling of going high: "I go higher and higher and then I go up into the sky!" Other children were vague: "I just like it." An older child commented, "It's more fun with friends. You don't feel alone or left out."

## DISCUSSION

The development of swinging skills follows a general progression similar to the development of skills on other types of playground equipment, such as climbers and overhead apparatus. Children must have certain physical characteristics and skills in order to successfully mount and dismount swings. They also must learn how to coordinate their bodies in order the manipulate swings successfully. The characteristics of the swings

A 4-year-old girl wiggling
onto a strap swing

Pushing from front and
learning to pump

themselves also contribute to the development of children's swinging skills. Most important, swinging skills are learned primarily through experience with swings and scaffolding provided by teachers and other children.

Children's physical characteristics provided some obstacles to their play on swings. All of these obstacles could be overcome, however, and most were overcome without help from teachers or other students. The shortest children usually "wiggled" onto the swings. Wiggling on did not indicate that the child was a beginner. It simply meant that the child's body was not tall enough for the child to reach the seat without extra manipulations. Other children who could not reach the swings easily would jump on, crawl on, or lift themselves up and onto the swings by grasping the chains in opposite hands. As children grew in height, they were able to sit on the swings without having to do extra work. Children's physical height made no difference once they were in the swing and ready to swing. Shorter children could reach high amplitudes of swinging, just as tall children could. Shorter children did have to coast to a stop or jump to exit the swing because they could not reach the ground in order to drag themselves to a stop. Therefore, the researchers found that the child's physical characteristics were related to how children accessed and exited the swings, but were not related to their swinging proficiency.

Besides learning to access the swings, children also needed to learn how to coordinate their bodies to make the swing move in certain ways. This was often done by scaffolding. Teachers and other students would help children learn to swing by pushing them, instructing them, or modeling swinging behaviors for them. One of the teachers at this particular site pushed the children's feet from the front instead of pushing their backs. She would tell the children to push against her hands with their feet, and when she felt the resistance, she would push their feet down and back. She felt that pushing the students in this manner helped them learn to pump their legs in sync with the motion of the swing.

The researchers did observe that children moved their legs in a pumping motion when the teacher was pushing them from the front. When the teacher finished pushing and the children were swinging on their own, the researchers did notice that some children who were previously pushed by this teacher were not extending their legs to the front apex of their swings, and thus were cutting themselves short of reaching the upper limit of their swinging. However, they were moving their legs in sync with most of the swing motion, and they were reaching a medium to high swinging amplitude. Thus, the researchers concluded that full extension of the legs to the apex of the swinging arc is necessary for reaching full swinging amplitude, although children can swing successfully without ever reaching the apex of the swinging arc. However, children were not considered to be advanced swingers until they did learn to extend their legs to the upper limit of their swinging arc.

Researchers also observed that some children produced jerky swinging movements, or smooth swinging movements with some moments of jerkiness. The researchers could not pinpoint a specific reason for the jerky movement, but were able to draw the conclusion that the jerkiness could be attributed to swingers not having the expertise or body coordination necessary to produce a smoothly swinging arc motion. One boy produced a very jerky swinging motion; on closer observation, he seemed to be pumping his legs but holding his torso rigidly upright on the strap swing seat. The rigidity in his body, the lack of torso leaning, or a combination of both could have led to the jerky movement. The boy was able to swing at a medium to high amplitude, and so the jerkiness did not seem to impede his ability to create a swinging motion. However, the jerkiness seemed to inhibit him from being able to reach the highest amplitude possible.

After observing this, the playground researchers became interested in the phenomena of torso leaning and its relationship to swinging. The researchers noticed a large amount of emphasis placed on pumping the legs in the literature as well as on the playgrounds. By testing the swings themselves, however, the researchers found that successful swinging seemed to be much more affected by the degree of torso leaning while swinging. The chair swing located on the 10- and 11-year-old playground, for example, allowed for very minimal torso leaning, and thus the swingers in the chair swing usually had to rely on another person to push them even though they were fully capable of pumping their legs in sync with the motion of the chair swing. Children in the chair swing rarely swung above medium amplitude during the observations. The researchers found that with synchronous torso leaning and leg pumping, a high amplitude of swinging could be reached on the strap and flat swings within 3 or 4 to-fro arcs.

The new tire swing garnered a great amount of attention from the children for several reasons. It was made of a harder material than the original tire swing. The new tire swing was lighter, saucer-shaped, and very aerodynamic, allowing children to reach high amplitudes quite quickly. The new tire swing was also wider than the original tire, and the hole in the middle of the new swing was much smaller than the hole in the original tire swing. This allowed children more space on which to sit and prop their legs, but it also brought the outside edge of the tire swing closer to the overhead support beam when the children were swinging.

The swivel mechanism that allowed the tire swing to rotate 360 degrees was about 6 inches long. When this mechanism was attached to the bottom of the overhead support beam, it effectively created a fulcrum 6 inches below the actual support beam. This in turn shortened the length of the new tire swing chains by several inches. Shorter chain lengths make swinging easier; therefore, the shorter chain lengths on the new tire swing allowed it to reach its maximum swinging height more easily and more quickly.

Children's swinging activities were severely limited by playground rules. Children were not allowed to stand on any swings except the flat swing. They were not allowed to swing on their stomachs. They were only allowed to swing to and fro on all swings except for the tire swing. They were required to keep both hands on the chains when swinging. They were not allowed to jump from the swings to the ground. Nevertheless, the children engaged in prohibited swinging activities. Many children swung on their stomachs and stood on the strap and tire swings. Many tried swinging without holding onto the chains, balancing themselves by hooking the crook of their elbows around the chains or holding onto the seat with their hands, or they would remove their hands for very brief periods of time and balance on their seats while swinging. If children were allowed to experiment safely with different types of swinging activities, the development of their swinging skills would greatly improve.

## RECOMMENDATIONS

Based on the findings from this study, the researchers make the following recommendations regarding children's swing play:

- Teachers should encourage torso leaning in addition to leg pumping while swinging. Torso leaning greatly enhances the motion of the swing, especially when performed in sync with legs pumping and the arc of the swing.

- Teachers should encourage children to extend their legs to the apex of the forward swinging arc in order to maximize the movement of the swing.

- The aerodynamic nature of the new tire swing in combination with the greater diameter of the new tire seat prompted the researchers to conclude that a number of factors should be considered in designing tire swings, including diameter of tire, height of suspension swivel, length of suspension chains, height of overhead beam, space between vertical support posts, and age and skill levels of children using the swing. Tire swings move differently than to-fro swings that are attached to the overhead support beam by two chains, making it possible during extreme swinging for children's heads to impact the overhead support beam. Such is most likely to occur when the tire swing has short support chains, when the swing is being violently pushed by more than one child or by an adult, or during horse-play.

- School administrators and teachers should allow children to experiment safely with swinging. The conservative limitations on the children observed in this study prevented them from exploring swinging activities and skills that could have helped them further develop their balance, coordination, and other physical skills. We believe that children with advanced motor skills, such as strength, flexibility, coordination, and balance, are more able to protect themselves in potentially hazardous conditions than are children with poorly developed skills.

- Playground designers and manufacturers should continue to develop new types of swings, and schools should provide children with a wide variety of swings. Having a variety of swings that move in different ways and accommodate different skill levels, numbers, and populations of children ensures that children of different skill and ability levels will have access to swings that challenge them and swings that they can master.

- The research herein supports the view that swings are valuable additions to playgrounds, promoting social, cognitive, and perceptual-motor development. The available injury data on serious injuries related to playground swings are misleading, because the injuries result primarily from playing on poorly designed equipment and fall surfaces, and/or improperly installed and maintained equipment, coupled with poor or absent adult supervision.

- Existing research on swings and swinging should be communicated to child care centers, schools, public parks, and other organizations sponsoring children's playgrounds. Currently, lack of objective, accurate information is leading to the removal of swings and other valuable playground equipment from many playgrounds in the United States.

## APPENDIX—Swing Coding Sheet

| Start Time | | | | | |
|---|---|---|---|---|---|
| **Child's Physical Characteristics** | | | | | |
| gender (female or male) | | | | | |
| height (short, medium, tall) | | | | | |
| weight (light, moderate, heavy) | | | | | |
| **Entry to Swing** | | | | | |
| assisted on by (adult or child?) | | | | | |
| wiggled on | | | | | |
| full lift | | | | | |
| stepped over | | | | | |
| running | | | | | |
| sat on | | | | | |
| stepped on | | | | | |
| **Relation of Body to Swing Seat** | | | | | |
| seated, lying on stomach, squatting, standing? | | | | | |
| both legs on same side of swing | | | | | |
| legs straddle swing | | | | | |
| facing in or out (tire swing) | | | | | |
| other body parts propped on swing | | | | | |
| **Hand Grip** | | | | | |
| # of hands used (0, 1, 2?) | | | | | |
| hands on opposite chains | | | | | |
| hands on same chain | | | | | |
| **Swinging** | | | | | |
| # of children on swing (0-3?) | | | | | |
| swing pushed by adult or child | | | | | |
| # of assisted pushes | | | | | |
| peak swinging--low (<30° from vertical) | | | | | |
| peak swinging--moderate (30°<x<60°) | | | | | |
| peak swinging--high (>60°) | | | | | |
| **Direction of Swinging** | | | | | |
| to-fro | | | | | |
| side-to-side | | | | | |
| diagonal/elliptical/circular | | | | | |
| swiveling | | | | | |
| spinning | | | | | |
| **Rhythm and Coordination** | | | | | |
| legs pumping | | | | | |
| legs running/pedaling | | | | | |
| torso leaning in sync | | | | | |
| torso leaning out of sync | | | | | |
| quality of movement (smooth or jerky?) | | | | | |

## APPENDIX—Swing Coding Sheet (cont'd)

| Exit | | | | | |
|---|---|---|---|---|---|
| assisted stop | | | | | |
| assisted exit | | | | | |
| dragged feet | | | | | |
| coasting to a stop | | | | | |
| walked off | | | | | |
| ran off | | | | | |
| jumped off | | | | | |
| fell off | | | | | |
| stepped off (from standing) | | | | | |
| **Stop Time** | | | | | |
| **Duration of Swinging Episode** | | | | | |

### References

American Society for Testing and Materials. (1991). *Standard consumer safety performance specification for home playground equipment.* Philadelphia: Author.

American Society for Testing and Materials. (1993). *Standard consumer safety performance specification for playground equipment for public use.* Philadelphia: Author.

Bowers, L. (1988). The national survey of elementary school playground equipment. In L. Bruya & S. Langendorfer (Eds.), *Where our children play: Elementary school playground equipment* (pp. 13-30). Reston, VA: American Alliance for Health, Physical Education, Recreation and Dance.

Cheng, H., Ching, H., Yung, J., & Tsu, F. (1997). An automatic swinging instrument for better neonatal growing development. *Revolutionary Science Instruments, 68*(8), 3192-3196.

Consumer Product Safety Commission. (1995). CPSC and manufacturers alert playgrounds to remove animal swings. *Journal of Environmental Health, 57*(10), 26.

Consumer Product Safety Commission. (1997). *Handbook for public playground safety.* Washington, DC: Author.

Crum, J., & Eckert, H. (1985). Play patterns in elementary school children. In J. Clark & J. Humphrey (Eds.), *Motor development: Current selected research* (pp. 99-114). Princeton, NJ: Princeton Book Club.

Curtis, H. (1913). *The reorganized school playground.* Washington, DC: U.S. Bureau of Education No. 40.

Eriksen, A. (1985). *Playground design: Outdoor environments for learning and development.* New York: Van Norstrand Reinhold Company.

Fox, J. E., & Tipps, R. S. (1995). Young children's development of swinging behaviors. *Early Childhood Research Quarterly, 10*, 491-504.

Freidberg, P. (1970). *Play and interplay.* London: The Macmillan Company.

Frost, J. (1990). Young children and playground safety. In S. Wortham & J. Frost (Eds.), *Playgrounds for young children: National survey and perspectives* (pp. 29-48). Reston, VA: American Alliance for Health, Physical Education, Recreation and Dance.

Frost, J. (1992). *Play and playscapes.* Albany, NY: Delmar Publishing.

Frost, J. L., Brown, P., Thornton, C., & Sutterby, J. (2002). *The nature and benefits of children's climbing behaviors.* Unpublished study commissioned by GameTime, a PlayCore Inc. Company, Fort Payne, Alabama, U.S.A.

Frost, J. L., Brown, P., Thornton, C., Sutterby, J., & Therrell, J. (2001). *The developmental benefits and use patterns of overhead equipment on playgrounds.* Unpublished study commissioned by GameTime, a

PlayCore Inc. Company, Fort Payne, Alabama, U.S.A.

Frost, J., & Campbell, S. (1985). Equipment choices of primary age children on conventional and creative playgrounds. In J. Frost & S. Sunderlin (Eds.), *When children play: Proceedings of the International Conference of Play and Play Environments* (pp. 89-92). Olney, MD: Association for Childhood Education International.

Frost, J., Kim, S., Therrell, J., & Thornton, C. (2000). *Play value and safety of play equipment for crawlers, toddlers and walkers.* Unpublished industry report.

Frost, J., & Strickland, E. (1985). Equipment choices of young children during free play. In J. Frost & S. Sunderlin (Eds.), *When children play: Proceedings of the International Conference of Play and Play Environments* (pp. 93-101). Olney, MD: Association for Childhood Education International.

Frost, J., & Sweeney, T. (1996). *Cause and prevention of playground injuries: Case studies.* Olney, MD: Association for Childhood Education International.

Gentile, A. (1972). A working model of skill acquisition with application in teaching. *Quest, 17,* 3-23.

Glesne, C. (1999). *Becoming qualitative researchers* (2nd ed.). New York: Longman.

Gwyther, R. (1996). A tree and a rope sway the neighborhood. *Christian Science Monitor, 88*(160), 17.

Harrison, L. (2001). Where have all the swing sets gone? *Time Bonus Section Families, 157*(19), 11-12.

Hendricks, B. (2001). *Designing for play.* Burlington, VT: Ashgate.

Hewes, J., & Beckwith, J. (1975). *Build your own playground: A sourcebook of play sculptures.* Boston: Houghton Mifflin Company.

Hogan, P. (1982). *The nuts and bolts of playground construction. (A triology of play.)* Champagne, IL: Leisure Press.

Ihn, H. (1998). *Preschool children's play behaviors and equipment choices in an outdoor environment.* Unpublished research report, University of Texas at Austin.

Kendall, N. (1998). At the end of her rope, Mom smiles and swings. *Christian Science Monitor, 90*(127), 9.

Jambor, T. (1990). Promoting perceptual motor development in young children's play. In S. Wortham & J. Frost (Eds.), *Playgrounds for young children: National survey and perspectives.* Reston, VA: American Alliance for Health, Physical Education, Recreation and Dance.

Langendorfer, S. (1988). Rotating, spring rocking, and see-saw equipment. In L. Bruya & S. Langendorfer (Eds.), *Where our children play: Elementary school playground equipment* (pp. 107-131). Reston, VA: American Alliance for Health, Physical Education, Recreation and Dance.

Lewis, T., & Phillipsen, L. (1998). Interactions on an elementary school playground: Variations by age, gender, race, group size, and playground area. *Child Study Journal, 28*(4), 309-320.

Mero, E. (1908). *American playgrounds: Their construction, equipment, maintenance and utility.* Boston: American Gymnasia Co.

Mertens, D. (1998). *Research methods in education and psychology: Integrating diversity with quantitative and qualitative approaches.* Thousand Oaks, CA: Sage Publications.

Miles, M. B., & Huberman, A. M. (1994). *Qualitative data analysis* (2nd ed.). Newbury Park, CA: Sage Publications.

Moore, M. (1992). *An analysis of outdoor play environments and play behaviors.* Unpublished doctoral dissertation, University of Texas at Austin.

Myers, J. (1981). *Children's perceived versus actual choices of playground equipment as viewed by themselves and their teachers.* Unpublished doctoral dissertation, University of Texas at Austin.

Naylor, J. (1985). Design for outdoor play: An outdoor study. In J. Frost & S. Sunderlin (Eds.), *When children play: Proceedings of The International Conference of Play and Play Environments* (pp. 103-113). Olney, MD: Association for Childhood Education International.

Noren-Bjorn, E. (1982). *The impossible playground.* West Point, NY: Leisure Press.

Nottingham, S. (2004). *Training for proprioception and function.* Fitness Management Magazine. Retrieved June 19, 2004, from www.coachr.org/proprio.htm.

Park, Y. (1998). *Preschool children's play behaviors and equipment choices of two playgrounds.* Unpublished master's thesis, University of Texas at Austin.

Pellegrini, A., & Smith, P. (1993). School recess: Implications for education and development. *Review of Educational Research, 63,* 51-67.

Posner, D. (1982). The swinging women of Watteau and Fragonard. *Art Bulletin, 64*(1), 75-88.

Post, A. (1991). *Effects of task constraints on the relative phasing of rhythmic movements.* Unpublished doctoral dissertation, Enschede, The Netherlands: Ipskamp.

Post, A., Peper, C., & Beek, P. (2003). Effects of visual information and task constraints on intersegmental coordination in playground swinging. *Journal of Motor Behavior, 35*(1), 64-78.

Riddell, C. (1992). *The effects of contrasting playgrounds on the play behaviors of kindergarten children.* Unpublished master's thesis, University of Texas at Austin.

Shin, D. (1994). *Preschool children's symbolic play indoors and outdoors.* Unpublished doctoral dissertation, University of Texas at Austin.

Smilansky, S., & Shefatya, L. (1990). *Facilitating play: A medium for promoting cognitive, socio-emotional and academic development in young children.* Gaithersburg, MD: Psychological & Educational Publications.

Strickland, E. (1979). *Free play behaviors and equipment choices of third grade children in contrasting play environments.* Unpublished doctoral dissertation, University of Texas at Austin.

Swing Theory. (2002). *Harper's Magazine, 305*(1827), 29.

Therrell, J., Brown, P., Sutterby, J., & Thornton, C. (2002). *Age determination guidelines: Relating children's ages to toy characteristics and play behavior.* T. Smith (Ed.) Washington, DC: Consumer Product Safety Commission.

Thompson, D. (1988). Swings, slides and climbing equipment. In L. Bruya & S. Langendorfer (Eds.), *Where our children play: Elementary school playground equipment* (pp. 67-105). Reston, VA: American Alliance for Health, Physical Education, Recreation and Dance.

Thompson, D., Bruya, L., & Crawford, M. (1990). Maintaining play environments: Training, checklists and documentation. In S. Wortham & J. Frost (Eds.), *Playgrounds for young children: National survey and perspectives* (pp. 103-146). Reston, VA: American Alliance for Health, Physical Education, Recreation and Dance.

Tinsworth, D., & McDonald, J. (2001). *Special study: Injuries and deaths associated with children's playground equipment.* Washington, DC: Consumer Product Safety Commission.

Vygotsky, L. (1978). *Mind in society.* Cambridge, MA: Harvard University Press.

Welzenbach, M. (1996). My midnight swing. *Reader's Digest, 149*(893), 132-135.

Yisreal, L. (1998). *Sensory integration therapy. Fast facts on: Developmental disabilities.* Kansas City, MO: UMKC Institute for Human Development.

# CHAPTER 7
# Sand and Water Play

*If one watches children of almost any age on a sandy beach, or if one has had the opportunity to observe them at a sandbox on a playground, one knows the fascination and variation of sand play. Letting sand run through sieves, flour sifters, or fingers, making pies or building tunnels and castles all afford endless interest.* (Alschuler & Heinig, 1936, p. 111)

*Water play is where water is, regardless of what is legally permitted.* (Friedberg & Berkeley, 1970, p. 70)

While the major focus of this book is playground equipment, this chapter will address in some depth two other important elements of playgrounds—sand and water. Chapter 8 will discuss several other natural features of playgrounds. Heavy, fixed equipment on playgrounds is designed primarily for motor development, although social and cognitive development are also stimulated. Portable materials or "loose parts" and natural materials are essential to developing more broadly based, creative, developmentally sound play environments that allow and stimulate spontaneous play. Among the natural materials contributing to good playgrounds, perhaps none are more essential than simple, but profoundly malleable and creative, sand and water.

Sand and water play long have been popular among educators as effective media for children's learning and development and they are essential play materials in high-quality child development centers; yet sand and water are still absent in many public school settings. In outdoor play environments, children have access to sand and water in play tables, troughs, and sand play boxes bounded by retaining borders. Sources of water frequently are located in close proximity to allow children to explore the magic of mixing sand and water to form infinite abstractions and concrete products. Sand, or loose, resilient materials that mimic sand, are available indoors at many high-quality child development centers.

Parents and educators commonly observe that children derive great joy and learning when they play with sand and water, and many understand that such play has profound meaning for children.

## History and Context
Because children play within widely varying circumstances and in so many different, complex ways, the context and construct of play are difficult to capture empirically (Fein, 1981; Spariosu, 1989; Sutton-Smith, 1997). Regardless of such difficulty, many traditional and contemporary theorists believe that play performs an essential role in young children's learning and develop-

ment (Bretherton, 1984; Sutton-Smith, 1979; Vygotsky, 1978). Researchers generally agree that the ways in which children experience play are essential to their cognitive, social, cultural, emotional, and physical development (Bredekamp & Copple, 1997; Frost, Wortham, & Reifel, 2001; Sylva, Bruner, & Genova, 1976). Perhaps no form of play is more valuable for children's social and cognitive development than sand and water play.

Sand and water were probably the earliest play materials, and are the most common play materials today, available in nearly all parts of the planet. Sand and water are also the simplest of materials, formed from the most common of elements. Because of their unique texture and therapeutic nature, sand and water have immense appeal to children of all ages (even adults). Sand's grainy texture gives children the irresistible urge to run their fingers through it. Water encourages active play and sensory exploration, stimulating all of the senses: it is beautiful to look at, calming to listen to, refreshing to drink, energizing to smell, and wonderful to touch. The perfect combination of sand and water encourages people to sit, relax, and play. As independent materials, sand and water provide rich sensory and conceptual experiences. When brought together, they are able to create textures that can be manipulated and experienced in interesting ways.

*Sand.* Historically, sand and water were among the materials to spawn the early development of manufactured play materials for children. Manufactured sand toys can be traced back almost 200 years. In the early 19th century, for example, the Tower Guild of Massachusetts manufactured a toy that used sand as a mechanism for turning a wheel (McClary, 1997).

The focus on sand as a play material itself demands an immediate accessory: a way to contain the material. Sand, which has the basic physical properties of a flowing liquid, requires containment to keep it in place. To fit this need, Jesse Crandell invented an early sand table in 1879. It was designed to not only contain sand, but also made it feasible to bring sand into the home. Called the "sandometer," the table came with a set of forms for molding the sand. Crandell promoted the sandometer as a modern-day marvel . . . a way to bring the beach into the home. Unfortunately for Crandell, this original sand table was not a commercial success. Mothers quickly grew weary of having the beach (and all its mess) in their homes (McClary, 1997).

Although indoor play with sand may not have been smiled upon by adults, progressive park developers during the late 1800s were suggesting uses for sand in outdoor environments. Sandgardens appeared in Boston in 1895 and quickly spread to New York parks. These sandgardens, which were modeled after the sand-play areas originated in Berlin (Frost, 1992), were part of the growing recreation movement in America that already featured gymnastic-type equipment installed outdoors on the first public park playgrounds in the United States. The high play value of sand was the primary reason for providing areas for sand play, at first for very young children and later for older ones.

The high play value of sand is described in Hall's (1888) *The Story of a Sand-Pile.* In the story, a parent has a load of sand brought in for her two sons' outdoor play. The sand-pile is soon transformed into the center of attention for the boys of the neighborhood. Together, the boys create a city of sand, with roads and merchants and money. Interestingly, Hall feels like the local girls did not benefit much from this experience, claiming they got in the way of the boys' efforts to control their environment. The sand-pile was the locus of the boys' play over the entire summer. Although the sand-pile became dormant over the winter months, it quickly revived the following summer. The sand retained its appeal as the ideal neighborhood summer play spot.

Hall (1888) explained that sand play has great educational value, writing that "the sand-pile has, in the opinion of the parents, been about as much yearly educational value to the boys as the eight months of school" (p. 696). It should be noted at this point that the education of only male children was considered valuable in 1888. For that reason, Hall and the parents mentioned in his story were not concerned with any benefit sand play might offer to the girls in the neighborhood. Today, however, the education of female children is valued as highly as the education of male children and the benefits of sand play are equally applicable to both girls and boys.

Throughout the growing playground movement of the early 20th century, a growing number of writers extolled the virtues of sand as a medium for children's play. Consider:

*In all the material the child will now or later learn to use—sand, blocks, clay, cloth, beads, paper, wood, or raffia—adaptability is the main consideration. It must be plastic to his hand and mind. Not something you have shaped for him, but something he can shape for himself, is what he wants. Sand is the classic material of childhood because it is the least committed. It is the open-minded substance, to which one shape is as welcome as another, that will enter with equal geniality into any form.* (Lee, 1929, p. 97)

*No place on the playground is more popular with very young children than the sand box, and an opportunity for sand play should be provided on every playground.* (Butler, 1938, p. 19)

Shortly after the introduction of sand piles and sand boxes on American playgrounds, attention was directed to including sand in indoor and outdoor environments, ensuring that the sand area was in shade for part of the day, providing water to add substance and texture, devising a variety of containers and sand toys, and taking steps to keep the sand clean. Lids placed on outdoor sand boxes protected against trash and animals, and common recommendations called for raking and replacing the sand regularly and even using chemicals for sanitization. Chemicals, of course, should be used only by expert directive.

*Water.* Children will seek play with water because of the pleasure they gain by interacting with the substance. As they pursue this pleasure, they will not necessarily follow adult rules for water play, preferring to play first and ask questions later. Obviously, water play is as ancient as sand play, but controlled environments for water play are relatively recent. The advent of indoor, controlled water play came with the advancement of indoor plumbing, which allowed for bathing tubs and flowing water inside the home. Soon after, toy manufacturers who recognized the value of water as a play medium began producing tub toys. Since then, water toys have become common sights in toy stores, bathtubs, and swimming pools. Some of these toys have interesting histories. For example, water guns (super squirters as we know them today) were originally hand-made, using reeds and forcing water through them.

An increase in interest in water play during the 19th century can be attributed to the changing leisure patterns of Americans as they began to visit the beaches during the summer months (McClary, 1997). In time, it was recognized that swimming pools would make the pleasure of water play more accessible to American families than beaches. Pools made it possible to splash whenever the urge hit, regardless of geographical limitations.

Swimming pools have a long history. Fountains and public baths were the center of the Roman town squares and social networks. In modern times, water play is also possible in elaborately planned water parks. Water parks combine water with playground-type equipment to increase the fun and excitement. These playgrounds, due to their design and level of supervision, provide environments that are safe and accessible. Water parks also allow children to have hands-on experiences with water in a variety of ways; everything from water guns to random sprays of water are found there (Kay, 2001).

## Sand and Water Effects on Learning and Play

Sand and water long have been recognized as natural materials for play, being freely available at beaches, in rivers, puddles, and lakes. However, the inclusion of sand and water to the educational setting is comparatively recent. The importance of sand and water to children's learning lies in their suitability for active, hands-on experiences.

The connection between children's active experience and learning can be traced back to such early philosophers as Comenius, Pestalozzi, and Froebel. In the 20th century, cognitive theorists, including Piaget and Vygotsky, stressed the importance of children's active exploration of the natural world to their development of thinking skills. On the other hand, theorists Maria Montessori and Caroline Pratt expressed their view that active learning occurs best via man-made, hands-on materials and interactive environments (Morrison, 2000). More recently, active exploration of the environment has been linked to development of neural connections in the brain (Sylwester, 1995). This interaction between active engagement, learning, and materials is where sand and water demonstrate their importance.

Frost (in press) spoke of the heightened awareness and deep absorption of children who are immersed in play with natural materials, such as dirt or sand and water, as a transcendental experience, eclipsing ordinary play in magic and intrigue.

*A small stream ran out of the nearby woods and across the schoolyard, gaining vigor and intrigue following rains. Pulling off shoes and rolling up pants, we waded in and built dams of mud to capture large expanses of water. A rival group, catching the excitement, built a dam upstream and eventually let the water loose in torrents to wash out our downstream dam. This led to frantic activity and collaborative schemes to ultimately build a dam from rocks and limbs that could not be washed out by our competitors. We even selected a skillful 3rd-grader to direct the operation! Through trial and error we discovered the value of dense, heavy materials to withstand pressure and of spillways to divert water from our masterpiece of construction.*

The materials with which children interact affect both the content and type of play in which they engage. Sand and water are open-ended play materials that generally lead to divergent thinking. For younger children (2-3 years old), sand and water are associated primarily with more functional play behaviors, although more complex forms of dramatic and constructive play are being formed (Frost, Wortham, & Reifel, 2001). Abstract or non-

realistic play materials usually do not encourage dramatic play in very young children as they do with older children. Younger children may prefer more realistic looking objects with which to pretend. Older children (5-6 years old) prefer to pretend with less realistic materials. Consequently, dramatic play with sand and water is common with this age group.

Sand and water have their respective textures, and the combination of the two creates an entirely new play material. "The play value of sand is enhanced by the provision of a second fluid material, water" (Frost, 1992, p. 103). The combination, unlike sand or water alone, facilitates construction and dramatic play, leading to greater symbolic representation. Wet sand is easier to mold into shapes, which allows children to draw scientific conclusions as they make connections between the shape of the container and the shape that is produced with the wet sand (McIntyre, 1982).

## The Benefits of Sand and Water Play

Sand and water are common as play materials in classrooms and parks because of the benefits attributed to these materials. Textbooks for early childhood educators frequently mention sand and water play as being a necessary part of the play experience of children. Stone (1990), in a description of preschool programs, writes, "Sand and water are natural favorites; children seem both relaxed and intent with them. They become investigators and experimenters" (p. 20).

A number of benefits are attributed to sand and water play, which are primarily the result of children being able to actively engage with the material rather than approach it in the abstract. The potential benefits generally fit into four categories: sensory benefits, social benefits, academic benefits, and therapeutic benefits.

*Sensory Benefits.* Development of the senses is important for children's overall development. According to Carey (1999), sand play provides a "sensory experience, and meets the need that we all have for kinesthetic experiences" (p. xvii). The association of mind and body comes through the experiences of the senses. These experiences in turn contribute to brain development. Sand and water play allows physical and tactile experiences as children run their hands, fingers, and toes through the substances. Sand and water encourage experimentation with materials and, unlike solid materials such as wooden blocks or plastic toys, sand and water encourage molding and shaping, allowing children to fully control the material (Dorrell, 2000).

*Academic Benefits.* The foundation for the development of academic subjects comes through a child's early experiences with substances like sand and water. Water play promotes the development of mathematical concepts of empty/full, shallow/deep, rational counting, measure, and sets, among other skills (Crosser, 1994). Sand play helps children develop scientific concepts and skills of prediction, classification, and experimentation (McIntyre, 1982), in addition to understanding of physical properties of weight, texture, fluidity, wet/dry attributes, form/shape, and consistency.

Kieff and Casbergue (2000) explore how sand and water benefit children's development of basic concepts like wet, dry, rough, and smooth, and the skills of problem solving and making predictions. They also link sand and water play to more academic concepts, such as literacy and numeracy. They contend that including paper and writing utensils in the sand and water center will lead to literacy development, as children script, dictate, or illustrate their play experiences as stories. They suggest creating patterns in the sand and creating charts and graphs for measuring sand as activities to support children's number development.

*Social Benefits.* Sand and water environments foster social development as children engage in group play and share play materials. In order to create shared play interactions, children create frames in which they can negotiate their play (Bateson, 1972). Children explore dramatic themes during sand play. Moon's (2000) study of children's dramatic themes concludes that the materials included in sand play environments often shape children's dramatic themes. The abstract nature of sand served as a canvas as children painted a variety of themes influenced by the sand.

*Therapeutic Benefits.* Sand has a long history as a therapeutic tool. In his work on sand play therapy, Carey (1999) found that sand has especially beneficial therapeutic properties. The open-ended nature and unique texture of sand encourage positive emotional experiences in many ways. Sand play gives children a sense of control, has a calming effect and reduces anxiety, and helps create a medium of communication between children and adults (Carey, 1999).

Sand play is used in clinical therapy to explore children's feelings of anxiety, shame, and doubt associated with traumatic experiences. A number of additional materials, such as natural materials and miniature play toys, are often included in sand play therapy settings to encourage the exploration of feelings (Carey, 1999).

## Tools for Sand and Water Play

Tools are very important components of play environments, especially for sand play and water play. The two main tools for sand and water play are: 1) loose parts for manipulating the substance and 2) containers for the substances. The challenging issues for schools are how to contain sand and water and how to keep them clean. Sand and/or dirt often occur naturally on playgrounds and pools of water are available after rain storms, promoting spontaneous sand and water or mud play. In most such situations the practical need to keep school areas and children's clothing clean and dry takes precedence over the play value of these elements. Water tables, troughs, and various types of containers are common in many schools today, and they are gaining popularity as educational communities recognize the many benefits of controlled sand and water play. Plastic tubs and buckets make impromptu sand and water containers for schools that lack commercially manufactured tables (Stone, 1990).

Dinwiddle (1993) suggests the use of rain gutters as part of the outdoor curriculum. Children in her program used gutters to channel water, sand, and other materials. The differences in materials encouraged conceptual development in science as children learned about the principles of flow. Children worked with dams and combinations of gutters to create a variety of learning experiences. Working with the gutters required that the children work together toward achieving their goals, promoting social development as they moved the pieces from one area to another. The gutters also encouraged dramatic play as the children developed play themes around the movement of the liquid through the gutters.

Organizing a sand and water experience often involves the use of tools and props that can be used to manipulate the materials. Most educators recommend the inclusion of additional materials or loose parts like shovels, sieves, plastic cups, molds, animals, and other materials for scooping, shaping, and pretending with the sand and water (Frost et al., 2001). Sand tools might be sieves, strainers, and containers, while water tools might be measuring cups, funnels, and corks (Stone, 1990). The tools or materials that are available for play can encourage certain types of play, as mentioned earlier. The use of measuring materials might encourage exploratory play, while small figures or vehicles encourage dramatic play.

Tools and props, although important for sand and water play, also need to be considered carefully. Stone warns that the inclusion of too many props or having unrelated props might interfere with sand and water play (Stone, 1990). Betz (1992), on the other hand, cautions about "over-containing" children's play. He suggests that "water tables offer domesticated water, [that it is] water tamed to a civilized geometric shape" (p. 34). He suggests allowing children to play in the water and mud they find after the rain.

## Conclusion

Active play is important for children, and sand and water encourage such play. Sand and water play benefits children across the developmental domains, with important development occurring in children's sensory, academic, social, and emotional selves. Materials for sand and water help shape the children's play by encouraging the manipulation of play materials as well as the development of dramatic play themes. Because of the immense play value of sand and water, the range of educational benefits they yield, and their high level of appeal to children, adults are wise to dedicate time and effort to make sand and water play available for children's daily play. Just as the past two centuries have provided more and more advanced understandings and uses for these two natural elements as play mediums, the future promises to offer further explorations into ways to make sand and water play more available and valuable for our children.

## References

Alschuler, R. H., & Heinig, C./Association for Childhood Education (Ed.). (1936). *Childhood: The beginning years and beyond. Vol. II: Childhood play.* New York: Collier.

Bateson, G. (1972). *Steps to an ecology of mind.* New York: Ballentine.

Betz, C. (1992). The happy medium. *Young Children, 47*(3), 34-35.

Bredekamp, S., & Copple, C. (Eds.). (1997). *Developmentally appropriate practice in early childhood programs.* Washington, DC: National Association for the Education of Young Children.

Bretherton, I. (1984). Representing the social world in symbolic play: Reality and fantasy. In I. Bretherton (Ed.), *Symbolic play: The development of social understanding.* Orlando, FL: Academic Press.

Butler, G. D. (1938). *The new play areas: Their design and equipment.* New York: A. S. Barnes.

Carey, L. (1999). *Sandplay therapy with children and families.* Northvale, NJ: Jason Aronson Inc.

Crosser, S. (1994). Making the most of water play. *Young Children, 49*(5), 28-32.

Dinwiddle, S. (1993). Playing in the gutters: Enhancing children's cognitive and social play. *Young Children, 48*(6), 70-73.

Dorrell, A. (2000). Sensory experiences . . . Ooey, gooey fun. *Early Childhood News* [2001, June 28].

Fein, G. (1981). Pretend play: An integrative review. *Child Development, 52,* 1095-1118.

Friedberg, P., & Berkeley, E. (1970). *Play and interplay.* London: The Macmillan Company.

Frost, J. L. (in press). In K. G. Burriss & B. Foulks-Boyd (Eds.), *Introduction to outdoor learning and play for elementary school.* Olney, MD: Association for Childhood Education International.

Frost, J. (1992). *Play and playscapes.* Albany, NY: Delmar Publishing.

Frost, J., Wortham, S., & Reifel, S. (2001). *Play and child development.* Upper Saddle River, NJ: Merrill Prentice Hall.

Hall, G. (1888). The story of a sand-pile. *Scribners, 3*(June), 690-696.

Kay, B. (2001). Way to spray: Water playgrounds riding a wave of popularity. *Today's Playground, 1*(2), 28-33.

Kieff, J., & Casbergue, R. (2000). *Playful learning and teaching.* Boston: Allyn and Bacon.

Lee, J. (1929). *Play in education.* New York: Macmillan.

McClary, A. (1997). *Toys with nine lives: A social history of American toys.* North Haven, CT: Linnet Books.

McIntyre, M. (1982). Early childhood: Discovery through sand play. *Science and Children, 19*(6), 36-37.

Moon, K. (2000). *Dramatic themes in classroom sand play.* Austin, TX: University of Texas.

Morrison, G. (2000). *Early childhood education today* (8th ed.). Upper Saddle River, NJ: Merrill Prentice Hall.

Spariosu, M. (1989). *Dionysus reborn: Play and the aesthetic dimension in modern philosophical and scientific discourse.* Ithaca, NY: Cornell University Press.

Stone, J. (1990). *Teaching preschoolers: It looks like this in pictures.* Washington, DC: National Association for the Education of Young Children.

Sutton-Smith, B. (1979). Epilogue: Play as performance. In B. Sutton-Smith (Ed.), *Play and learning* (pp. 295-322). New York: Gardner Press.

Sutton-Smith, B. (1997). *The ambiguity of play.* Cambridge, MA: Harvard University Press.

Sylva, K., Bruner, J., & Genova, P. (1976). The role of play in the problem-solving behavior of children 3-5 years old. In J. Bruner, A. Jolly, & K. Sylva (Eds.), *Play—Its role in development and evolution* (pp. 244-261). New York: Basic Books.

Sylwester, R. (1995). *A celebration of neurons: An educators' guide to the human brain.* Alexandria, VA: Association for Supervision and Curriculum Development.

Vygotsky, L. S. (1978). *Mind in society: The development of higher mental processes.* Cambridge, MA: Harvard University Press.

# CHAPTER 8
## Playgrounds for the 21st Century

*Most people who care about child development know nothing about design, and most people who design know nothing about child development.* (Shell, 1994, p. 80)

Playgrounds come in many shapes and sizes. There are pocket parks and destination parks, school playgrounds, and playgrounds for toddlers, preschoolers, and primary school children. While playgrounds can fulfill many different needs for children, each playground cannot be all things for all people. Because playgrounds are built and designed for many users, it is important that we take into consideration the ways children grow and develop, the ways children play, and the ways that playgrounds can support both of these elements. In addition, we must look at how playground design affects interactions between children on playgrounds, as well as how adults supervise children and communicate with them while they are on the playground.

The process of playground development involves many people with expertise in numerous areas. However, the people who design play spaces for children often are not experts in children's development and play. The people who select and pay for playground equipment, such as parent-teacher organizations and service organizations like Rotary clubs or Lion's clubs, often make decisions about what to purchase based on factors like price, appearance, or their own experiences rather than on what will enhance children's play. Educating these people is an important goal of this book.

Playground equipment manufacturers also work with these organizations as they are affected by both regulations and the need to create equipment at a price that the purchaser can afford. Educating the designers of playground equipment is another goal of this book. Playground supervisors also are greatly affected by the designs of playgrounds, and they are in a unique position of being able to enhance children's play experiences through their enthusiasm, supervision, and participation. The most important element of the playground environment is people—people who care about the lives of children. We hope the following recommendations will help in the educational process for both playground builders and users.

Based on reviews of a century of playground literature, the observations, data, and findings presented in the previous chapters, and experience gained from decades of playground research, the authors of this book make the following recommendations. These recommendations are written for two different audiences, playground builders and playground users, and are focused around interrelated and sometimes overlapping areas. Playground builders include those who design and manufacture outdoor play equipment, and those who sponsor, design, install, and maintain outdoor play environments. Playground users include child care workers, teachers, and parents who supervise children in outdoor play environments. Some recommendations will apply to both of these audiences.

## RECOMMENDATIONS FOR
## PLAYGROUND DESIGNERS AND BUILDERS

*Children's access to outdoor play has evaporated like water in sunshine.* (Rivkin, 1995, p. 2)

One of the important factors affecting playground design is diminishing play space for children. Researchers have documented the decline of children's freedom to roam unsupervised. Previous generations of children generally created their own entertainment and play environments as they played in the neighborhood, found secret places, or played in natural areas (Cunningham & Jones, 1991). Although children's access to transportation such as bicycles is higher than for previous generations, fewer children are allowed to ride bicycles without supervision (with this trend being slightly more strong for girls than for boys). In addition, children's play has begun to change from an emphasis on active or investigative play to more supervised play activities, such as organized sports (Tandy, 1999).

Areas in which children once were able to play unsupervised are now often perceived to be unsafe. The urban street was often a place for play in the past; however, increases in automobile traffic reduced children's opportunities to travel independently and their opportunities to use the street as a play space (Cunningham & Jones, 1995). Since the street is no longer considered a safe place for children, adults are now required to transport children to and from play spaces (Rivkin, 1995; Tandy, 1999). Due to this diminishment of available play spaces for children, the playground becomes increasingly important as a destination for children's play.

As the playground becomes one of the few places where children are allowed to engage in spontaneous play, it is important that it is the type of environment that promotes and allows the sorts of activities and experiences that children previously were able to engage in on their own. Playground designers have to think about the experiences that children engage in on the playground rather than the type of equipment that is available (Stine, 1997). Stine suggests looking at dichotomous relationships of different cognitive, emotional, social, physical, and sensory experiences:

| | |
|---|---|
| Accessible | Inaccessible |
| Active | Passive |
| Challenge/Risk | Repetition/Security |
| Hard | Soft |
| Natural | People-Built |
| Open | Closed |
| Permanence | Change |
| Private | Public |
| Simple | Complex |

These categories help playground designers think not just in terms of what equipment can be placed in a playground, but also about the different experiences that children should have in their free time. Activity is important on playgrounds, but so is the opportunity to be a passive observer. Children need new opportunities to challenge themselves and take risks, as well as opportunities to repeat actions over and over again until they are mastered. Frost, Wortham, and Reifel (2001) also provide a list of important considerations for extending playground design beyond the usual or typical. Including these considerations makes playgrounds magical and memorable. These design elements include:

| | |
|---|---|
| Big and little | Unique and exotic |
| Story time | Loose parts |
| Real vs. artificial | Special or sacred spaces |
| Sensuality | Sense of place |
| Connection with the past | A place for doing nothing |

We have created here a sort of à la carte menu that playground designers can draw from in order to create play spaces that meet the needs of all children. In our menu of playground options, selecting more items will increase the variety of the playground meal. Continuing the meal metaphor, it is also important to select a variety of these options to avoid having too much or too little of any one item. Many of our menu options are not original; we drew from a variety of different playground designers, builders, and researchers.

For our menu we include:

| | |
|---|---|
| Sense of place/uniqueness | Variety and complexity |
| Gardening | Enhanced movement |
| Natural areas | Playground layout |
| Sand and water play | Educational resources |
| Stimulus shelters | Surfacing |
| Organized games | Accessibility |

## Sense of Place

*Most playgrounds are so tame; what we're trying to do is recapture a bit of the wild side.* (Shell, 1994, p. 79)

A consequence of the standardization of playground equipment and playground design has been the elimination of many unique elements of playgrounds. The sameness of many play spaces, such as fast food restaurant playgrounds, makes them interchangeable in the minds and emotional experiences of children. On the other hand, children form an emotional attachment to special places that are unique in some way so as to stand out—the difference between a fast food and a family-owned restaurant. The unique features of special places give children a "sense of place" (Hart, 1979). The special places that adults typically remember as most significant tend to be more natural than manicured (Francis, 1995). In addition, places where children have the opportunity to manipulate the environment through the building of forts or dens are also remembered (Sobel, 1993).

The development of a sense of place depends on the unique features that a play space contains. Unique features of a playground or a piece of playground equipment act as a "home base." The unique features then become the center of play as children leave and then return to their base. Children use unique features like grates, manhole covers, and corners as places to congregate or engage in game play. In addition, these features can be used to inspire dramatic play as, for example, children pretend a small wrought iron fence is a jail or an unusual door is an oven (Armitage, 2001; Hartle, 1996).

## Gardening

Gardening is one aspect of public parks that is difficult to implement but can have great benefits for children. Froebel, the father of the kindergarten movement, envisioned gardens as a way for children to learn unity and understand the connection between man and the universe. His gardens were combinations of individual and group plots, where children could develop responsibility and a sense of community (Brosterman, 1997). Gardens in modern parks are difficult to implement, however, as they require supervision. On preschool and elementary school playgrounds, gardens can be supervised by teachers. In addition, community gardens can be organized for public parks.

Gardens can help children learn to work together as a team, while they learn responsibility and habits of nurturance. Gardens also help children keep in touch with natural seasonal cycles. They also serve to attract birds, butterflies, and animals, providing opportunities for wildlife observation (Rivkin, 1995).

## Natural Areas

Children today are less aware of nature. Manicured suburban areas and parks typically contain fairly limited types of species of flora and fauna. Large lawns and grand trees may appear lush, but they often contain few of the flowers that birds and butterflies need to survive and they provide little cover for birds and other wildlife. Often, suburban playground spaces are developed with maintenance in mind as work crews prefer easily mowed lawns and easily maintained shrubs and trees.

Because children spend so much time indoors and have less access to natural places, they have less knowledge about the plants and animals around them; what they do know they typically have learned from either books or television rather than from personal experience. This is especially important for immigrant and Native American groups who are losing the names of plants and animals in their native language and then learning them only in English (Nabhan & St. Antoine, 1993).

All playgrounds should be planned to maintain connections with nature by reserving part of the playground for natural areas. This can be as simple as leaving an area of the playground covered in unmown grass during parts of the year. The longer grass allows for wildflowers, native grasses, and other plants that often are forced out of manicured lawns. Playground designers also should try to use native species as much as possible, as these species are adapted to the environment already and thus do not require as much maintenance. In school playgrounds, at least one teacher or parent with gardening and horticulture skills is essential to planning, preparing, and teaching children about plants, how to tend them, and about their value.

The Playground Checklist (Frost, 2004), attached as an Appendix, can aid in evaluating, designing, and using playgrounds. The rating system contains 60 items framed within three broad categories: 1) What does the playground contain?, 2) Is the playground in good repair and relatively safe?, and 3) How should the playground and the playleader function? The system is very comprehensive; few playgrounds initially achieve a score of more than 70-80 out of a possible score of 100. The system is constructed to challenge designers and sponsors to continually improve their play environments, beginning with an "optimum" plan and prioritizing over a period of time as labor, space, and financial resources become available. Good playgrounds are never finished!

## Sand and Water Play

Sand and water are time-proven, essential ingredients for children's play. We have chosen to devote Chapter 7 to this controversial topic, seeking to help dispel the wide-spread belief that sand and water play are simply messy, frivolous activities that detract from "more important" academic interests.

### Stimulus Shelters

Playgrounds also need places where children have quiet and opportunities for introspection. These places can be sacred or special for children (Frost, Wortham, & Reifel, 2001). Children have long built forts, dens, and playhouses in out-of-the-way places (Sobel, 1993). The modern playground does not lend itself to this habit of childhood, as immovable playground equipment has replaced scavenged boards and boxes. Playground designers should work to create spaces for children that offer this sense of "out of the wayness," while still complying with recommendations for safety and security. Many standardized designs for play equipment focus primarily on platforms for events like climbers and slides. By looking at all parts of the play equipment, including below the equipment, designers can go a long way toward creating the type of space that offers seclusion. Semi-enclosed spaces provide stimulus shelters where children can be away from the hustle and bustle of the playground, providing opportunities for quiet play and introspection (Goodenough, 2000; Moore, 1986).

### Organized Games

As children move from preschool into elementary school, they begin to take an interest in more organized games. An open space rather than a prepared field for games can serve many purposes. Limiting organized game fields to such traditional sports activities as baseball and soccer gives children fewer opportunities for inventing or modifying games to fit their needs. Children can use open space for chase games, parachute games, or games-with-rules; these fields also can be used as gathering places or for kite flying. Many cultures use games to help integrate members into positive ways of interacting with each other. Many cultures prefer more cooperative games, rather than the competitive ones emphasized by Western cultures (Sutton-Smith, 1999; Tudge, Lee, & Putnam, 1998). Having an open space allows all users of a playground to define how they want to engage with the play space.

### Variety and Complexity

Kritchevsky and Prescott (1977) explain that a play unit or place can be rated in terms of complexity as simple, complex, or super complex. Simple play units have obvious uses, as swings or spring rockers do. These play units define to a certain degree the way children are going to use the equipment. Complex play units involve the combination of two different types of play units, such as sand and digging equipment or materials that encourage imaginative use. Super complex units involve the combination of three or more play materials, such as sand, play materials, and water. The super complex play areas will hold children's attention longer and will accommodate more children.

Builders of outdoor play environments should ensure variety and multiple challenges. In other words, playground equipment should be flexible enough to accommodate and challenge children across a wide range of skill levels, and should be complex enough to encourage children to use many different physical and cognitive skills. It is also important to ensure that the playground includes a variety of components, such as manufactured equipment, nature and pet areas, loose parts, and such sensory materials as sand and water, to support a wide range of skill development, including upper and lower body strength, fine and gross motor skills, perceptual-motor skills, balance, flexibility, coordination, problem-solving skills, social skills, and dramatic play.

Furthermore, playgrounds for kindergarten and primary children should be designed to allow for movement from a less complex playground (for 2- to 5-year-olds) to a more complex playground (for 5- to 12-year-olds), based on skill development and age rather than age or school grade alone. According to the research presented here, skill development is more dependent upon the combination of children's play experiences and physical characteristics rather than on their age or grade level alone.

Playgrounds also should be designed to ensure that children have an abundance of opportunities for all types of social play. Equipment should be designed so that multiple children can play at the same time on the same piece of equipment or on pieces placed close to each other. Play materials should be abundant and diverse enough for pretend and dramatic play. During outdoor play, children can be observed not only playing chase, pretending, and talking, but also helping each other improve or learn skills. In education, this "scaffolding" is a highly valued action, both for the scaffolder (the one helping) and the scaffolded (the one being helped). Examples of play equipment and materials that encourage different types of social play as well as scaffolding would include wide climbing structures, dramatic play structures (such as a playhouse or a car), a superstructure that includes a wide variety of equipment and challenges, a construction area with a variety of loose parts, and a large area for organized games. Private and semi-private play areas, such as tunnels and small enclosures, also should be available where children can play independently and in small groups.

## Enhanced Movement

Some of the most popular playground equipment allows children to move faster than what they can reach under their own power. This enhanced movement can be created through swings, merry-go-rounds, slides, and track rides. The most popular equipment on playgrounds other than climbers is equipment that gives children a sense of speed and motion (Ihn, 1998; Park, 1998; Shin, 1994). As discussed in the chapter on swings, this movement is important for the development of vestibular and proprioceptive systems. Rhythmic motions also can provide a calming effect on a child, helping him to relax (Yisreal, 1998).

## Playground Layout

The layout of the playground should be tailored for the particular population it is meant to serve, and should be carefully planned to encourage development of a wide range of skills. This can be done by placing specific pieces of play equipment and materials in high traffic areas. The choice of what play equipment and materials to place in high traffic areas should depend on the need or desire for certain types of skill development. For instance, as mentioned in the chapter on overhead equipment, equipment that requires the use of upper body strength may be placed in high traffic areas of the playground to encourage children to use these pieces of equipment and thereby develop their often neglected upper bodies.

Our research demonstrates that many children in this country lack upper body strength, and that they only develop upper body strength when they are given opportunities to do so. Placing equipment that requires the use of upper body strength in high-traffic areas of the playground would increase children's opportunities for developing and using upper body strength, as well as provide challenging and varied play experiences for children. Thus, high-traffic areas on the playground can be utilized to promote specific skills as well as a wide variety of skills.

## Educational Resources

It is imperative that existing research on play, play equipment, and play materials be communicated to child care centers, schools, public parks, and other organizations sponsoring children's playgrounds. Accurate information about children's play and play environments would help those who build children's playgrounds make more educated decisions about the design, manufacture, installation, and maintenance of playgrounds. Perhaps the most comprehensive collection of books and other materials on children's play and play environments is now available in the special Joe Frost Collection at the University of the Incarnate Word in San Antonio, Texas. This material also will be available universally via Internet to all interested individuals and groups.

Manufacturers can play a crucial role in training play supervisors by making emerging research widely available in useable form. Manufacturers should carefully consider becoming familiar with current research and providing continually updated educational material appropriate for training programs designed for purchasers and users of their equipment. All the national surveys, guidelines, and standards (AAHPERD, CFA, NPPS, CPSC, and ASTM) reviewed in this book conclude that equipment designed for older groups is anthropomorphically unsuitable for younger children's play. As previously stated, preventing a mismatch between equipment and children's skills is one of the most crucial factors in preventing injuries to preschool children using outdoor playground equipment. Children quickly seek novel and more complex challenges on playgrounds, frequently extending their activities to equipment designed for older and more skillful children. Adults commonly support and encourage this, not realizing that doing so puts children in potentially hazardous situations. Educational materials would help adults understand why certain play structures are designed for certain age and skill ranges. These materials should focus on safety and child development, and should include information presented through multiple types of media such as PowerPoint presentations, pictures, videos, and printed materials.

Playground sponsors should ensure that these and other educational materials are made available to help adults make wise decisions about selecting and supervising playgrounds for children. Providing workshops on playground safety for teachers and parents is one way to do this. Posting signs in prominent areas around the playground regarding the age or developmental ranges for which playgrounds are designed is another. Generally, better efforts are needed to help adults and children make educated choices about using play equipment designed for specified skill levels.

## Proper Surfacing

Proper playground surfacing under and around equipment, and its maintenance (per CPSC and ASTM), are very important for the protection of children and the maximization of children's play experiences. Appropriate surfacing should be provided based on the type of equipment present. Poured-in-place surfacing or resilient mats should be placed under and around equipment such as swings and at the ends of slides. Loose surfacing, such as sand and wood chips, in these areas tends to dissipate quickly with use. Poured-in-place surfacing and resilient mats are ideal for maintaining a constant level of resilient surfacing. At least 12 inches of loose, non-compacted surfacing is best under tall equipment, such as climbing and overhead equipment. This type of equipment is placed at 5 to 7 feet above ground level, depending upon age of users. To prevent injuries from falls, the areas beneath should be covered in soft, absorbent, and resilient surfacing that is consistently filled to an appropriate depth. Our observations indicate that building a retaining wall around loose-fill, resilient surfacing is one of the best ways to diminish the rate of surfacing erosion.

Additionally, play equipment designers, manufacturers, and installers should take into consideration the reality that many playground equipment purchasers, installers, and even manufacturer's representatives do not always insist on appropriate surfacing under newly installed play structures. All of these parties should be educated in and encouraged to pay close attention to safety issues in relation to children's play and development.

## Accessibility

*Yes, I can drive through the playground, but I can't play with the different things that are there.* (Prellwitz & Tamm, 1999, p. 170)

Accessibility is one of the critical issues of playground design for the future. The United States Access Board has issued a Final Rule (36 CFR Part 1191) regulating the accessibility of playgrounds. Currently, the Final Rule recommends three primary elements for making playgrounds accessible: approach, enter, and use. This means that playgrounds should be designed with the following considerations in mind:

- A route to the playground (approach)
- A route to the play equipment inside the playground (enter)
- Accessible play elements (use).

The route or approach to the playground typically refers to a way of getting to the playground from a parking lot, usually a concrete walking path. Entering the playground can be a trickier element in that it requires having a path from the sidewalk up to the playground equipment. This design issue is trickier because of raised curbs to keep surfacing in place. The play area thus needs a curb cut or ramp in order to get past the containment curbs. In addition, many surfacing options are not accessible, including pea gravel, sand, and wood mulch. Currently, the preferred accessible surface is poured rubber surfacing or engineered wood fibers (Hendy, 2001; Spencer, 2003; Sutterby, 2004; Thompson, Hudson, & Bowers, 2002).

Use of the equipment is a complicated formula, as designers must find ways for children to actually engage with the playground equipment. While the law does not require that every play event be usable by every child, designers should consider ground level components that are more easily accessible and use of ramps or transfer stations to make upper level components accessible (Hendy, 2001; Spencer, 2003; Sutterby, 2004; Thompson, Hudson, & Bowers, 2002).

## Play in the Real World for Playground Builders

It is very important to consider the ways children use equipment. Playground builders should assume that children will access unintended parts of the play structure and play environment. They should take into consideration how children might place themselves at risk, even on equipment designed to be "safe" according to manufacturers' and adults' definitions of use. Children's play is defined partly by their need to experiment and change. Children will attempt to modify their environment; for example, they might use boxes and sand to make sliding more challenging.

In addition, children's play on play structures often is not supervised or supervised by adults who assume that playgrounds are completely safe. Responsible parties should assume that the play structure will not be supervised, and that unsupervised children are likely to misuse equipment in ways that increase their risk of falling from tall equipment. Thus, providing proper and consistently adequate surfacing is currently the best way of preventing injuries on the playground.

Manufacturers also must continue to improve playground equipment design so that safety can be manufactured into the products without sterilizing the play space. Creating play spaces that can compete with video games and television will be a challenge, but one that we can work together to overcome. Including as many of the elements described above, like sand and water play, enhanced motion, and gardening, as well as incorporating natural elements, variety, complexity, and, above all, a sense of place, will give children lasting and pleasant memories of their time spent playing in these unique places.

## RECOMMENDATIONS FOR PLAYGROUND USERS

### Understanding Skill Development

Playground supervisors, including teachers and parents, must develop skills in observing children at play in order to assess their levels of skill development. Given the wide variation of skill levels within chronological age groups, adults should observe children carefully to match abilities of children with complexity of equipment. For example, some beginning school-age children should continue to use equipment designed for preschoolers until they gain appropriate skill levels. By being able to locate children in the developmental spectrum, play supervisors will be more prepared to make quick decisions about productive versus hazardous play activities. This knowledge also would help play supervisors introduce increasingly challenging equipment and activities as children's skills improve. This keeps children engaged and interested, and prevents them from using equipment, especially tall equipment, in ways not intended by designers and manufacturers.

Supervisors also should be aware that during the initial period of skill development, children are at a higher risk for injury when using manufactured play equipment. This provides yet another reason for responsible adults to ensure that children not use equipment designed for skill levels far beyond their current development.

### Playground Rules

It is also recommended that schools and teachers allow children to experiment safely with different forms of play. Rules should not be arbitrary, nor should they be made without the proper information about children's play and development. In many of the studies presented in this book, teachers were required to ask children to desist from playing in certain ways. For example, children were prohibited by school rules from swinging on their stomachs. The researchers could not see a hazard in allowing children to swing on their stomachs, and many children did so illicitly. In fact, children liked exploring the swings in novel ways, and may have derived some benefits from swinging on their stomachs. This seemingly arbitrary rule stifled not only some children's swing play, but perhaps also some creative thinking and problem-solving skill development.

Wien (2004) described a thoughtful process of reflection about the meanings and uses of rules. Many rules have proliferated based on the safety imperative or on licensing regulations, and may not have been based on a real assessment of a hazard. Such rules often turn adults into police, spending so much time looking for activities to regulate that they do not engage with the children during play. One center found they had 26 rules just for outdoor play activities. Teachers at the center collaborated to examine the rules and determine which ones were necessary and which ones were not. Removing many of the rules eventually led to less stress for staff and more interaction with the children. Teachers who work supervising children's play should consider the rules they have for outdoor play and how they are being used. Rules should make play safe, but not overly limit the child's natural desire to explore.

## Participating in Maintenance

Playground users are more likely to notice playground maintenance needs than those who do not access the playground daily. Thus, it is important that play supervisors pay attention to the condition of the play equipment, materials, and environment on a daily basis. Play supervisors should understand the basic CPSC guidelines so that they can spot such hazards as open s-hooks, exposed concrete footings, and the wearing away of loose fill surfacing. They should be trained to take the time to replenish the loose fill surfacing that has worn away under such heavy traffic areas as under swings, climbers, and overhead equipment, and at slide exits. They should be aware of possible entrapment and entanglement hazards in the play environment, as well as any equipment deterioration (rusted metal, termite-infested wood, broken equipment). If problems are noticed, they should alert the people who do the majority of the playground maintenance and seek correction in a timely fashion. In these simple ways, playground supervisors can play a large part in daily playground maintenance.

Play supervisors also can help children understand the importance of surfacing and the possibility of hazards on the playground so that the children themselves can perform the same types of daily maintenance observations as the play supervisor. Children can take responsibility for pushing loose fill surfacing under a piece of equipment before they access the equipment, picking up loose parts and putting them away at the end of recess, and reporting any signs of exposed concrete footers or equipment deterioration to the teacher. By sharing the responsibility of maintaining the play environment with children, play supervisors teach children to respect and care for their play environment.

## RECOMMENDATIONS FOR ALL GROUPS

## Skill and Age

The wide range of individual differences in development among children of like chronological age leads to the conclusion that levels of skill development, as well as chronological age, should be carefully considered when matching children to appropriate playground equipment sizes and types. The current age designations adopted by CPSC and ASTM restrict children to two broad chronological age designations (2-5 years and 5-12 years). This categorization has limited authenticity in practice and is inconsistent with the National Association for the Education of Young Children's emphasis on developmental appropriateness of materials, curriculum, and instruction for young children (Bredekamp & Copple, 1997). Researchers observed that even the degrees of risky behaviors exhibited on the playground differ widely among children of the same age. Chronological age, experience, physical characteristics, and skill development all should be considered when making decisions about the appropriateness of playground equipment and the type of play being accommodated.

## Physical Activity

One overarching concern of the researchers during all of these studies was children's physical activity during play and its relationship to children's perceived health. As obesity is a growing concern for parents and pediatricians here in the United States, the researchers considered whether or not physical activity and obesity were the actual topic of study. One of the principal reasons for encouraging children to play actively outdoors is to promote the lifelong healthful habit of physical activity. However, as we see playgrounds and recess decreasing across the United States, and as we see added emphasis on testing and cognitive development partnered with a striking de-emphasis on physical education and outdoor free play, we as early childhood educators and researchers feel the need to defend outdoor free play and encourage playground builders and users to do the same.

As members of communities, we need to insist on healthful habits and balance for children. We must demand healthful options for our children in schools. We must be adamant about the fact that physical activity is good for children, and we must encourage schools and play supervisors to make the most of outdoor play times by learning about children's play and development. We must train them to promote physical activity and a variety of play during recess and physical education classes.

We must promote a culture of physical activity. Appropriate play environments, including properly installed and maintained equipment and surfacing, as well as other play materials, play structures, and play areas, are only part of the equation. The human factor is a very important part of encouraging a culture of lifelong physical activity. Adults and children alike can encourage or discourage children's play. Promoting physical activity for all children should be a large part of teacher training, since many children receive their best opportunities for outdoor free play under the supervision of their teachers. Schools should hold workshops for parents on the appropriateness of certain types of play for situations in which the parents are the main play supervisors on the playground. Educating the public about physical activity and the benefits of appropriate outdoor play is one of the best investments playground builders and users can make with regard to children's current and future well-being.

## Responsibility

Playground injury data sometimes can be misleading, in that it promotes the view that outdoor play is dangerous. Many playground injuries are a result of poorly designed equipment and play areas, improperly installed and poorly maintained equipment, insufficient resilient surfacing, and inadequate or absent supervision. The writers also see growing evidence that lack of opportunities to engage in active outdoor play, coupled with increasing participation in sedentary activities and poor eating habits, is contributing to a decline in fitness levels of children. We believe that children lacking such fitness qualities as strength, coordination, flexibility, and perceptual-motor skills are at greater risk of injury on playgrounds.

Outdoor play is extremely beneficial for all children, and a well-designed, well-maintained, and well-supervised playground can be one of the most exciting and interesting play areas available to children. Outdoor play for children should not be unreasonably limited or excluded because adults fail to provide the proper outdoor play environments for children. It is the responsibility of playground builders and users, as well as schools, parks, and other entities that sponsor outdoor environments for children, to provide children with play environments that strive to meet all of the recommendations presented in this book.

## PLAY IN THE REAL WORLD FOR PLAYGROUND USERS

Playground users also must be aware that children have decreasing opportunities for outdoor play. The accountability movement in schools has created an environment in which play is considered a waste of time. Without strong advocates for play, this trend will continue into the future and children raised without experiences of outdoor play themselves will not encourage their own children to play outdoors. If people continue to see outdoor play as frivolous and inconsequential, the need to maintain parks and playgrounds in safe and enjoyable condition also will be diminished.

## References

Armitage, M. (2001). The ins and outs of school playground play: Children's use of "play places." In J. Bishop & M. Curtis (Eds.), *Play today in the primary school playground* (pp. 37-58). London: Open University Press.

Bredekamp, S., & Copple, C. (1997). *Developmentally appropriate practice in early childhood programs.* Washington, DC: National Association for the Education of Young Children.

Brosterman, N. (1997). *Inventing kindergarten.* New York: Harry N. Abrams.

Cunningham C., & Jones, M. (1991). Girls and boys come out to play. *Landscape Australia, 4,* 305-311.

Cunningham C., & Jones, M. (1995). The child in the suburb: Erosion of the play environment. *Child friendly environments* (pp. 16-21). Sydney: NSW Play Alliance.

Francis, M. (1995). Childhood's garden: Memory and meaning of gardens. *Children's Environments, 12*(2), 183-191.

Frost, J. (1992). *Play and playscapes.* Albany, NY: Delmar.

Frost, J., Wortham, S., & Reifel, S. (2001). *Play and child development.* Upper Saddle River, NJ: Merrill, Prentice Hall.

Goodenough, E. (Ed.). (2000). Special issue: Secret spaces of childhood, Part 2. *Michigan Quarterly Review, 39*(3), 678.

Hart, R. (1979). *Children's sense of place.* New York: Irvington.

Hartle, L. (1996). Effects of additional materials on preschool children's outdoor play behaviors. *Journal of Research in Childhood Education, 11*(1), 68-81.

Hendy, T. (2001). The Americans With Disabilities Act insures the right of every child to play. *Parks & Recreation, 36,* 4, 108-118.

Ihn, H. (1998). *Preschool children's play behaviors and equipment choices in an outdoor environment.* Unpublished research report, University of Texas at Austin.

Kritchevsky, S., & Prescott, E. (1977). *Planning environments for young children: Physical space* (2nd ed.). Washington, DC: National Association for the Education of Young Children.

Moore, R. (1986). *Childhood's domain: Play and place in child development.* London: Croom Helm.

Nabhan, G., & St. Antoine, S. (1993). The loss of floral and fauna story: The extinction of experience. In S. Kellert & E. Wilson (Eds.), *The biophilia hypothesis.* Washington, DC: Island Press/ Shearwater.

Park, Y. (1998). *Preschool children's play behaviors and equipment choices of two playgrounds.* Unpublished master's thesis, University of Texas at Austin.

Prellwitz, M., & Tamm, M. (1999). Attitudes of key persons to accessibility problems in playgrounds for children with restricted mobility: A study in a medium-sized municipality in northern Sweden. *Scandinavian Journal of Occupational Therapy, 6,* 166-173.

Rivkin, M. S. (1995). *The great outdoors: Restoring children's right to play outside.* Washington, DC: National Association for the Education of Young Children.

Shell, E. (1994). Kids don't need equipment, they need opportunity. *Smithsonian, 25*(4), 78-86.

Shin, D. (1994). *Preschool children's symbolic play indoors and outdoors.* Unpublished doctoral dissertation, University of Texas at Austin.

Sobel, D. (1993). *Children's special places: Exploring the role of forts, dens, and bush houses in middle childhood.* Tucson, AZ: Zephyr.

Spencer, A. (2003). Accessibility and your playground: A profile of facilities taking action. *Parks & Recreation, 4,* 40-49.

Stine, S. (1997). *Landscapes for learning: Creating outdoor environments for children and youth.* New York: John Wiley and Sons.

Sutterby, J. (2004, January). Texas accessibility guidelines for playgrounds. *The Texas Council for Exceptional Children Newsletter,* 5-8.

Sutton-Smith, B. (1999). Evolving a consilience of play definitions: Playfully. In S. Reifel (Ed.), *Play and culture studies, 2* (pp. 239-256). Stamford, CT: Ablex Publishing Company.

Tandy, C. (1999). Children's diminishing play space: A study of intergenerational change in children's use of their neighborhoods. *Australian Geographical Studies, 37*(2), 154-164.

Thompson, D., Hudson, S., & Bowers, L. (2002). Play areas and the ADA: Providing access and opportunities for all children. *The Journal of Physical Education, Recreation & Dance, 73*(2), 37-42.

Tudge, J., Lee., S., & Putnam, S. (1998). Children's play in sociocultural context: South Korea and the United States. In M. Duncan, G. Chick, & A. Aycock (Eds.), *Play and culture studies: Explorations in the fields of play* (pp. 77-90). Greenwich, CT: Ablex.

Wien, C. (2004). From policing to participation: Overturning the rules and creating amiable classrooms. *Young Children, 59*(1), 34-40.

Yisreal, L. (1998). *Sensory integration therapy. Fast facts on: Developmental disabilities.* Kansas City, MO: UMKC Institute for Human Development.

# Playground Checklist

© Joe L. Frost

**NOTE:** This checklist is not intended as a research tool but rather as an aid to planning and evaluating playgrounds.

| CHECK | SECTION I. What does the playground contain? Consider age and skill levels of children. |
|---|---|
| | 1. A hard-surfaced area with space for games and a network of paths for wheeled toys. Goals for such activities as basketball and soccer strategically placed. |
| | 2. Sand and sand play equipment, including a variety of toys, blocks, scoops, and containers. |
| | 3. Water play areas with fountains, pools and sprinklers, and water play equipment. |
| | 4. Dramatic play structures (playhouses, car, or boat with complementary equipment, such as adjacent sand and water, and housekeeping equipment). |
| | 5. A superstructure with room for many children at a time and with a variety of challenges and exercise options (entries, exits, and levels). |
| | 6. Mound(s) of earth for climbing and digging. |
| | 7. Trees, shrubs, and natural areas for shade, nature study, and play. |
| | 8. Continuous challenge, linkage of areas, functional physical boundaries, and vertical and horizontal treatment (hills and valleys). |
| | 9. Construction area with such materials as tires, crates, planks, boards, bricks, and nails; tools should be provided and demolition and construction allowed. |
| | 10. A purchased or built vehicle, airplane, boat, or car that has been made safe, but not stripped of its play value (should be changed or relocated after a period of time to renew interest). |
| | 11. Equipment for active motor play: a variety of overhead apparatus, climbers, slides, balancing devices, swings, etc. |
| | 12. A large soft area (grass, bark mulch, etc.) for organized games. A concrete or asphalt area for organized games. |
| | 13. Small, semi-private spaces at the child's own scale: tunnels, niches, playhouses, private or special places partially enclosed by trellises, plants, berms. |

|  | 14. | Fences, gates, walls, and windows that provide security for young children and are adaptable for learning/play. |
|---|---|---|
|  | 15. | A garden for flowers and vegetables located so that they are protected from play, but with easy access for children to tend them. Special nature areas such as butterfly gardens. Gardening tools are available. A greenhouse for plants greatly enhances nature study. |
|  | 16. | Provisions for housing of pets. Pets and supplies available. Special areas to attract birds and insects. Storage for supplies. |
|  | 17. | A transitional space from outdoors to indoors. This can be a covered play area immediately adjoining the playroom, which will protect the children from the sun and rain and extend indoor activities to the outdoors. |
|  | 18. | Storage for outdoor play equipment, tools for construction and garden areas, and maintenance tools. Storage can be separate: wheeled toys stored near the wheeled vehicle track; sand play equipment near the sand enclosure; tools near the construction area. Storage can be next to the building or fence. Storage should aid in children's picking up and putting away equipment at the end of each play period. |
|  | 19. | Easy access from outdoor play areas to coats, toilets, and drinking fountains. Shaded areas, benches, tables, and support materials for group activities (art, reading, etc.). |
|  | 20. | Accessibility, materials, and equipment for children of all abilities/disabilities. |

| CHECK | SECTION II. Is the playground in good repair and relatively safe? |
|---|---|
|  | 1. A protective fence (with lockable gates) next to hazardous areas (streets, deep ditches, water, etc.). |
|  | 2. Ten to twelve inches of non-compacted sand, wood mulch, or equivalent manufactured surfacing under all climbing and moving equipment, extending through fall zones and secured by retaining wall as needed. |
|  | 3. Size of equipment appropriate to age and skill levels served. Climbing heights limited to six to seven feet, or just above standing/reaching height of children. Special attention to reduced heights for preschool children. |
|  | 4. Area free of litter (e.g., broken glass), electrical hazards, high voltage power lines, toxic hazards. See CPSC for toxic hazards in wood products. |

|  | 5. | Moving parts free of defects (e.g., no pinch and crush points, bearings not excessively worn). |
|  | 6. | Equipment free of sharp edges and broken, loose, or missing parts. |
|  | 7. | Swing seats constructed of soft or lightweight material (e.g., rubber, plastic).  Basketball goal posts padded.  Soccer goals secure in ground. |
|  | 8. | All safety equipment in good repair (e.g., guard rails, padded areas, protective covers). |
|  | 9. | No openings that can entrap a child's head (approximately 3.5" x 9", see CPSC/ASTM for measurements and tests). |
|  | 10. | Equipment structurally sound.  No bending, warping, breaking, sinking, etc.  Heavy fixed and moving equipment secured in ground and concrete footings recessed under ground at least four inches. |
|  | 11. | Adequate space between equipment—typically six feet, depending upon type and location of equipment (see CPSC/ASTM). |
|  | 12. | No signs of underground rotting, rusting, or termites in support members (probe under ground). |
|  | 13. | No metal slides or decks exposed to sun.  Use plastic components or place in permanent shade. |
|  | 14. | Guardrail and protective barriers in place that meet CPSC/ASTM height and other requirements. |
|  | 15. | No loose ropes, suspended ropes, or cables in movement area. |
|  | 16. | All balance beams, cables, and chains at low heights—prescribed by CPSC/ASTM. |
|  | 17. | Signs at entry alerting to appropriate ages of users, need for adult supervision, and any hazards. |
|  | 18. | No protrusion or entanglement hazards. |
|  | 19. | No tripping or fall hazards in equipment use areas (e.g., exposed concrete footings). |
|  | 20. | No water hazards—access to pools, creeks.  No traffic hazards — streets, parking lots, delivery areas. |

*This is an overview of relevant safety items.  For details, refer to current issues of the United States Consumer Product Safety Commission's *Handbook for Public Playground Safety* and the American Society for Testing Materials' *Standard Consumer Safety Performance Specification for Playground Equipment for Public Use.*

| CHECK | SECTION III.  How should the playground and/or the playleader function? |
|---|---|
| | 1.   Encourages play:<br>• Inviting, easy access<br>• Open, flowing, and relaxed space<br>• Clear movement from indoors to outdoors<br>• Appropriate equipment for the age group(s) |
| | 2.   Stimulates the child's senses:<br>• Changes and contrasts in scale, light, texture, and color<br>• Flexible equipment<br>• Diverse experiences |
| | 3.   Nurtures the child's curiosity:<br>• Equipment that the child can change<br>• Materials for experiments and construction<br>• Plants and animals |
| | 4.   Supports the child's social and physical needs:<br>• Comfortable to the child<br>• Scaled to the child<br>• Physically challenging |
| | 5.   Allows interaction between the child and the resources:<br>• Systematic storage that defines routines<br>• Semi-enclosed spaces to read, work a puzzle, or be alone |
| | 6.   Allows interaction between children:<br>• Variety of spaces<br>• Adequate space to avoid conflicts<br>• Equipment that invites socialization |
| | 7.   Allows interaction between the child and adults:<br>• Organization of spaces to allow general supervision<br>• Rest areas for adults and children |
| | 8.   Supports functional, exercise, gross motor, active play.  Children are not denied a range of challenging swings, overhead equipment, and climbing equipment scaled to their ages and skill levels. |
| | 9.   Supports constructive, building, creating play.  Children are taught safe ways of using tools and materials for construction. |
| | 10.   Supports dramatic, pretend, make-believe play.  Sufficient time is given during recess or play time for children to generate and engage fully in pretend play. |
| | 11.   Supports organized games and games with rules.  Adults and older children teach traditional games, then step out of the way, and provide equipment for sports activities. |

| | |
|---|---|
| | 12. Supports special play forms (e.g., chase games, rough and tumble, sand and water play). Chase and rough and tumble are carefully but unobtrusively supervised. |
| | 13. Promotes solitary, private, meditative play. Children assist in preparing nature areas and small built spaces (e.g., gazebos) for semi-privacy. |
| | 14. Promotes group, cooperative, sharing play. Children are encouraged to include new and reticent peers in their play groups. |
| | 15. Involves children in care and maintenance of playground. Adults model and teach maintenance skills—tool use, hazard identification, etc. |
| | 16. Involves adults in children's play—regular adult/child planning and evaluation. Adults help children learn to solve playground problems through cooperative planning and analysis of problems. |
| | 17. Integrates indoor/outdoor play and work/play activities—art, music, science, etc. |
| | 18. Promotes interaction between children and nature—plants, animals, etc. Knowledgeable adults are identified to lead field trips, provide direct instruction, and interact with children. |
| | 19. Adults are trained in play values, playground maintenance and safety, emergency procedures. Playleaders receive annual workshops to maintain skills. |
| | 20. The play environment is constantly changing—growing in appeal, challenge and complexity. Good playgrounds are never finished. |

# INDEX

# AUTHORS

Joe L. Frost, Ed.D, is Consultant and Parker Centennial Professor Emeritus, University of Texas, Austin, Texas.

Pei-San Brown is an Early Education and Playground consultant. Director of Community Outreach and Education at Ballet Austin. She has a Master's degree in Education from the University of Texas at Austin.

Candra D. Thornton is Assistant Professor, Curriculum and Teaching, Auburn University, Auburn, Alabama.

John A. Sutterby is Instructor, Curriculum & Instruction Department, The University of Texas at Brownsville and Texas Southmost College, Brownsville, Texas.

Jim Therrell is Assistant Professor, Education, Northwestern Oklahoma State University, Alva, Oklahoma.

Debora Wisneski is Assistant Professor, University of Wisconsin-Milwaukee.